Anyone who fails to recognize that he or she has much to learn from the great thinkers of the past—including the distant past—is a fool. But it's not enough merely to acknowledge that we can learn from these thinkers. We have to actually read their writings. That's why I warmly welcome—and commend—this new collection of "great books" published by Zondervan. Those who take advantage of this opportunity to learn from the true teachers of humanity will enrich themselves intellectually, morally, and spiritually.

—ROBERT P. GEORGE, McCormick Professor
of Jurisprudence, Princeton University

Learning the Good Life is a magnificent compilation of the timeless principles of human flourishing. Strolling through it, the reader cannot help but appreciate how often wise thinkers independently have come to similar ideas about living well. Across time and place, certain principles—such as detachment from earthly things, being honest, kind, and virtuous for their own sake, and leading a life aligned with one's internal principles—have stood the test of time, earning endorsements from teachers interested in helping us pursue good living together. This book pulls together works from different thinkers and traditions that might at first seem desperate—from Confucius to Plato to Frederick Douglass—but the texts and the introduction help the reader see how they contribute to a harmonious whole.

Each text and author in this book contributes to the Great Conversation, the iterative dialogue on questions of origin, purpose and destiny that thoughtful people have been engaging in across human history. This anthology is essential reading for the Christian student of any age; it serves as a powerful reminder that all truth is God's truth, and that people of all backgrounds can, and have, come to appreciate his wisdom, even independent of his revelation.

—ALEXANDRA HUDSON, writer, speaker,
and founder of Civic Renaissance

Learning the Good Life is like an encyclopedia of the humanities that should be on the shelf of every classical school educator and every Christian educator. Starting in 450 BC, renowned scholars and teachers offer concise yet deep reflections on the wisdom of the greatest books and most important ideas that have shaped human civilization. Every chapter is food for the soul, and readers will undoubtedly come away with new knowledge and new habits that make learning fun. Particularly moving are the prayers written by scholars at the end of the book—a wellspring of faith and inspiration for anyone who cares about integrating the head and the heart.

—MARGARITA MOONEY SUAREZ, associate professor of practical
theology at Princeton Theological Seminary, founder of the Scala Foundation,
and author of *The Love of Learning: Seven Dialogues on the Liberal Arts*

There's nothing I love more than timeless literature, and this collection has it in spades. So many books today are enslaved to the pressure of the here and now; *Learning the Good Life* is a welcome breath of fresh air, gathering wisdom from all across the world that has proven its worth for thousands of years. Magnificent!

—JEREMY WAYNE TATE, chief executive officer, Classic Learning Test

The terrors of the past threaten to tear apart the future. And perhaps that is as it should be, for none of us deserve a better future than the one we've made. But hope springs eternal from this hothouse of past and future, especially as we follow those who thought their way out of terrifying pasts toward viable and even flourishing futures. At least this is what the authors of this splendid volume would have us believe. And why not believe them? If they are right, it will be the past that saves us and books like this that get us there.

—JONATHAN TRAN, George W. Baines Chair of Religion, Baylor University

LEARNING
THE
GOOD LIFE

Wisdom from the Great Hearts
and Minds That Came Before

Jessica Hooten Wilson
and Jacob Stratman

ZONDERVAN
ACADEMIC

ZONDERVAN ACADEMIC

Requests for information should be addressed to:
Zondervan, *3900 Sparks Dr. SE, Grand Rapids, Michigan 49546*

Zondervan titles may be purchased in bulk for educational, business, fundraising, or sales promotional use. For information, please email SpecialMarkets@Zondervan.com.

Library of Congress Cataloging-in-Publication Data

Names: Wilson, Jessica Hooten, editor. | Stratman, Jacob, editor.
Title: Learning the good life : wisdom from the great hearts and minds that came before / Jessica Hooten
    Wilsonv and Jacob Stratman.
Description: Grand Rapids : Zondervan, 2022. | Includes index.
Identifiers: LCCN 2021036632 (print) | LCCN 2021036633 (ebook) | ISBN 9780310127963 (hardcover)
    | ISBN 9780310127970 (ebook)
Subjects: LCSH: Wisdom in literature. | Wisdom--History. | Christians--Books and reading.
Classification: LCC PN56.W54 L43 2022 (print) | LCC PN56.W54 (ebook) | DDC 801--dc23/
    eng/20211020
LC record available at https://lccn.loc.gov/2021036632
LC ebook record available at https://lccn.loc.gov/2021036633

Published in association with the literary agency of WordServe Literary Group, Ltd., www.wordserveliterary.com.

Cover design: Derek Thornton / Notch Design
Cover art: © Fabio Marangoni
Interior design: Kait Lamphere

Printed in the United States of America

22 23 24 25 26 27 28 29 30 31 32 /TRM/ 15 14 13 12 11 10 9 8 7 6 5 4 3 2 1

To my teachers: David Lyle Jeffrey, Ralph Wood, Stephen Prickett, Paul Contino, and Louise Cowan

—JESSICA HOOTEN WILSON

———

To my students

—JACOB STRATMAN

Contents

Part 1: 450 BC to AD 600

Part 2: AD 600 to AD 1700

Part 4: AD 1900 to Present Day

Acknowledgments

We began composing this book to fill a gap. As we served on a committee together at John Brown University (JBU) for addressing first-year seminars, Jake and I could not find a text that showed students what it meant to be a Christian learner. We especially sought one that drew from the Great Tradition rather than speaking didactically and only within present concerns. This book grew from that need and those conversations, so thank you, JBU, for that service opportunity. Thanks to all of our contributors for giving their time, talent, and energy to make this book what it is. Also, thank you to our student worker Eden Hinton, who diligently submitted permissions requests, kept track of contributions, and corresponded on our behalf. She is the secret to the successful compilation of this book. Finally, we need to acknowledge our families for supporting us in this extracurricular work. This book was not made as part of our jobs, but it was made as a gift to future generations.

Excerpts from *A Room of One's Own* by Virginia Woolf. Copyright ©1929 by Houghton Mifflin Harcourt Publishing Company, renewed 1957 by Leonard Woolf. Reprinted by permission of Mariner Books, an imprint of HarperCollins Publishers LLC. All rights reserved.

"The Enduring Chill" © 1956, 1957, 1958, 1960, 1961, 1962, Flannery O'Connor. Copyright renewed 1993 by Regina Cline O'Connor. Reprinted by permission of the Mary Flannery O'Connor Charitable Trust via Harold Matson Ben Camardi, Inc. All rights reserved. © 2013 by the Mary Flannery O'Connor Charitable Trust via Harold Matson Company, Inc. All rights reserved.

"Reflections on the Right Use of School Studies with a View to the Love of God" from *Waiting for God* by Simone Weil, translated by Emma Craufurd, translation copyright 1951, renewed © 1979 by G. P. Putnam's Sons. Used by permission of G. P. Putnam's Sons, an imprint of Penguin Publishing Group, a division of Penguin Random House LLC. All rights reserved.

Foreword
Sawdust and Dishwater

DAVID I. SMITH

A little over fifty years before John Bunyan's *Pilgrim's Progress*, a Moravian bishop named John Amos Comenius wrote another great allegorical tale called *The Labyrinth of the World and the Paradise of the Heart*. In this story, Comenius had his pilgrim tour the various vocations that made up society. The pilgrim had a pair of glasses foisted upon him, designed to make him see only in safe and conventional ways, but he managed to peep out around the edges, and what he saw was a world built on foolishness and violence.

In a wicked satire of the academics of his day, Comenius portrayed his pilgrim entering a hall of scholars, an argumentative crowd of folk preparing potions (theories) that they poured into little boxes (books).[1] One or two scholars carefully gathered ingredients to make medicines that gave life. Most were more concerned with making their boxes beautiful and impressive. They tossed in dust and dirty dishwater and stole from their nearest neighbor if it helped them cram more ingredients in faster. They gobbled down whatever came to hand, only to expel it from both ends of their anatomy. "Then I understood," Comenius's pilgrim remarked, "why it is that so few of them attained inner freshness of mind. For the more of these medicines a person gulped down, the more he vomited, turned pale, faded, and wasted away." He continued, "I pitied some who could have had complete peace, yet needlessly and uselessly gave themselves to this quackery."[2]

Comenius was highly invested in education (he devoted much of a long and active life to attempting to reform schools), yet he also recognized that studying can affect a person's health in more than one way, and that it is not automatically a good thing. Some ways of going about it give life while others make a person sick, even if they seem convenient at first. Cramming for a test, competing for status, putting others down by pretending to be smart, swallowing nonsense whole because it's in a book, going through the motions—there are plenty of

---

1. John Comenius, *The Labyrinth of the World and the Paradise of the Heart*, trans. Howard Louthan and Andrea Sterk (Mahwah, NJ: Paulist Press, 1998), 98–100.
2. Comenius, 99.

strategies for getting through a course of study in a way that might have some degree of pragmatic effectiveness in the short term and yet leave a person's soul sick and mind malnourished, as well as cause bystanders to wrinkle their noses at what comes out of the person. Along with the question of what to study comes the question of *how* to study, and that question is about more than tips for exam preparation.

It turns out that the question of how to study is connected to even more elusive and contentious questions about what we should believe, what our beliefs have to do with our actions, and how the things we are taught—in and out of school—relate to the basic meaning and purpose of life. The kind of learner you become has something to do with the kind of person you become, and your basic beliefs shape how you learn. Where do you go, then, to get a sense of how learning might leave you whole instead of causing you to waste away?

If you want to understand what is making you physically sick, you typically look to someone with medical training, placing implicit trust in the science behind their advice. It might not be perfect, but it is probably better than that thing you heard from a friend's cousin. But what if you want to figure out how your faith in God (or that of the person down the street) relates to what you learn and how study might shape your spirit? Modern culture tempts us to think of our bodies as complex and mysterious machines but of our faith as mostly personal opinion and private preference. Is this an area where we are better off making do with what Aunt Ethel said, or those few Bible verses we noticed, or that thing we read on a blog that time?

Connecting faith and learning is not a new idea. For millennia, Christians have been among those who have thought carefully and rigorously (and, like Comenius, imaginatively and satirically) about what we know, how we know it, and what counts as a wholesome path through the complexity, joy, and suffering of life. None of them were right about everything. Few of them were right about most things. But they have been part of a careful, evolving, deepening conversation in which ideas have been tested and refined. If you want to understand how Christian faith, a faith that seeks to lay us bare to "the depth of the riches of the wisdom and knowledge of God" (Rom. 11:33), relates to a complicated, changing, challenging world, it seems smart to take at least a little time to see what wise voices from years past have suggested.

This book invites you not so much into a list of past conclusions as into the guild of those who have struggled, and who still struggle today, to be wise learners. It does not claim that every past idea is better. It does not suggest that it is somehow good for your soul simply to know the names of as many dead authors as possible. Rather, it invites you to consider whether some who managed to articulate insights that lasted long beyond their lifetime might be able to improve our homemade recipe for relating faith and learning. You don't have to assume they are right. You just need to assume that learning to study well is not simple, and that wise conversation partners would be good for your health as a student, as a Christian, as a human being.

This book invites you not just to expand your reading, take some notes, pass some tests, and gain some academic credit, but to use what you read to reflect on your approach to being a student. Connecting faith and learning is not just about ideas; it is about *practices* too. It is about how we treat the world and the thoughts of others. It is about the personal disciplines and habits we develop or bypass. It is about the gratitude and wonder we cultivate or neglect. Whatever future callings you might have, if you are enrolled in education, one of your present callings is to be a student. How will your faith shape the choices you make as a student? How will those choices shape you? Will they prove to be medicine or poison, nourishment or dust and dishwater? Such questions are more than academic. Enjoy the company as you look for answers.

Introduction

JESSICA HOOTEN WILSON

Why do you learn? You may never have considered the question. If you're an American, school has been mandatory since you were a child. You didn't really have a choice in the matter, and perhaps no one explained to you what exactly you were doing and why you were doing it. Do you know where the word *school* comes from? The ancients (like Socrates and Virgil) used the Greek word *scholé* and the Latin word *scola*, from which our word *school* is derived, and it means "leisure." When you think of leisure, you may envision lazing in a hammock under a tree or floating on a tube on a sunny day down a flowing river. But Greeks and Romans meant something much larger than that. They thought of leisure as "contemplation," as attention toward the highest goods in life, such as truth and beauty. The great Greek philosopher Aristotle said, "We are unleisurely in order to have leisure."[1] He meant, *We work diligently so we can go to school*. Or put another way, we work actively so we can dedicate time to contemplation. School should be the space or place that provides you the time to learn higher things; you may learn more about what it means to live well, love what's worth loving, and become wise.

If you are entering college, you may have assumed this four-year stint was a box to be checked before getting to the real task of being an adult. The coursework was preliminary for the job you hope to hold and the money you plan to make. Yet life is about so much more than servile work and consumable goods. At the end of each workday, there are hours to be filled with loving, thinking, and enjoying this world. As Christians, we should learn how to love this world without assuming it is the end for which we were made. We have been called to more than checking boxes or filling our calendars. Our work itself should draw us out of ourselves toward loving others and glorifying him who crafted talents within us. When entering college, imagine that each day is an opportunity to become more or less like Christ, which includes how you learn, study, read, think, and live. These next four years are not preliminary; they are not limbo. They are gifts—grace to contemplate and direct your talents and knowledge for serving the world's needs.

---

1. Aristotle, *Nicomachean Ethics*, 1177b5–6.

If you are not on your way to college or those days are behind you, this book should serve to remind you of your highest end. While much of the day is filled with to-do lists, work, laundry, or the mundane activities of the practical life, we were made to be contemplatives. We have received the gifts of philosophy, history, poetry, song, letter writing—all these things in which animals and computers feel no desire to participate. But, for human beings, what is life apart from the *humanities*? Apart from those gifts that remind us what it means to be human? In this book, other human beings from across time and space invite you to participate in a shared human end—contemplation.

This book looks like a textbook because of the various authors and professors who introduce these passages to you, but I invite you to reimagine what you hold in your hands. Imagine the world is in ruins. The apocalypse has occurred and only a remnant of believers are left, of which you are one. You stumble upon this book. Inside it are hundreds of pages from some of the greatest minds and hearts who have ever lived, a treasured manuscript of wisdom. And all the writers have a message for you. All of them are calling you to die to yourself, to your habits of indulgence, to your pride and ambition, and instead, to dedicate your time to learning, thinking, and loving.

What does it mean to learn as a Christian? Is it different from how one learns if one does not believe that Christ is God incarnate, who lived, died, and was resurrected? How might our ways of thinking, imagining, reading, and conversing look if we did not believe in this triune God and his scriptural revelations to us? The writers and contributors in this book—even those who weren't themselves Christian—show you how learning should be different for the Christian. First, you do not seek to glorify yourself, which means all your efforts should be selfless, not aimed at grades, performance, or reputation, which are secondary blessings from the prioritizing of God's glory. Second, people become the heart of the learning experience as you form relationships with teachers and fellow students and even with the texts you read, which were written by real people with hearts and minds like you.

Third, the Christian faith is founded upon a book of wisdom that is being lived out in the church; the Scriptures are stories, poems, history, law, and sermons. The Bible reveals to us so much about what it means to learn as Christians. If we believe in a God who *spoke* the world into being, then we should highly praise the art of rhetoric and the practice of conversation. If we believe in a God who calls himself "the Word," then we should be eager to read words, love language, and create habits that place reading before viewing or consuming. And if we believe in a God who laid down his life for others, then we should humble ourselves before the texts we study, the teachers who delight in educating us, and the needs of our community. We should learn as a calling to worship the One who made us and is sending us out daily.

The famous hymn, "They'll Know We Are Christians by Our Love," written in the mid-1960s, prescribes more than niceness or tolerance of sin or acceptance of every identity. Love requires sacrifice; it asks us to become more than our lowest desires, weaknesses, inexperience, or opinions. When we learn as Christians, with humility and grace, seeking the wisdom and glorification of God, others will know us by our example, and the world will be hard-pressed not to say, "Do you see how they love?"

Part 1

450 BC to AD 600

CHAPTER 1

Lao Tzu

Introduction to *Tao Te Ching*

PAUL J. PASTOR

The *Tao Te Ching* is an influential classic of Chinese philosophy and one of the most translated books of world literature. Although the book is traditionally attributed to a sixth-century BC sage called Lao Tzu ("Old Master"), scholars debate the its exact date of writing and its authorship. What is beyond argument, however, is the originality and insight of the work. Besides forming a significant expression of Taoist philosophy, the book has inspired generations of artists, writers, and thinkers worldwide.

As presented in the *Tao Te Ching*, the *Tao* (pronounced dow and usually translated "Way") is the plain but ultimately indescribable essential process of the universe—observable in nature, human life, and society. A person who lives in harmony with this Way enters a paradoxical flow state of both simplicity and sagacity, something like swimming with the current of a strong river rather than against it. To find this harmony, a state of intentional surrender allows the wise to return to an immediacy and purity similar to that of children.

Qualities such as unreflective hurry, grasping for power, arrogance, or the thoughtless use of force all run contrary to the Tao and tend to carry their own exhaustion and undoing within them. Composed of eighty-one brief poem-chapters observing principles of this Tao from nature, human behavior, and social life, the *Tao Te Ching* is a literary embodiment of the simple/complex principles it describes. Though short enough to be read in a quick sitting, it can reveal fresh insights for many years.

Embracing that sense of unifying paradox is essential to appreciating the *Tao Te Ching*. Though the *Tao Te Ching* may initially seem foreign to many Westerners, Christians have a head start here—one of the key virtues of Christian learning is the mature ability to hold diverging ideas in tension. After all, our tradition is steeped in the wisdom tradition of the Hebrews, including the biblical books of Proverbs, Job, Ecclesiastes, and James, which contain enigmatic contemplations that would have delighted Lao Tzu. Likewise, while Taoist and Christian teachings are different in many important ways, the subversive parables of Jesus are complemented beautifully by many of Lao Tzu's observations, and with essential discernment they are profoundly enriching.

In reflecting on Lao Tzu's Tao and Christ's Way, we are challenged to consider that our world may not be ordered quite as it first appears. Up is sometimes down. Becoming like a child is the spiritual ideal. Waiting can be action. The defeated is the one who wins. You can gain the world but lose your own soul. The poor in spirit might be the true owners of everything. We need to lose our lives to find them. In these radical statements we hear a resonance with the good news that in Christ this world's "very good" order is being restored and even magnified.

The *Tao Te Ching* provides an important counterbalance to many strictly analytical modes of learning or knowledge. It is a deep reminder that becoming "sage" is the true goal of human understanding and that education and learning might not always be the same thing. The reflections of Lao Tzu should prompt us to ask not only what we are learning but what kind of humanity our learning is cultivating in us. It is the way of lowly love that the Sage recommends to us—a kind of knowledge that releases a need to control and finds in that surrender an immense, counterintuitive power to cultivate virtue and the common good.

Excerpts from the *Tao Te Ching*[1]
TRANSLATED BY LIN YUTANG
From Chapter 1

The Tao that can be told of
Is not the Absolute Tao;
The Names that can be given
Are not Absolute Names. . . .
Therefore:
Oftentimes, one strips oneself of passion
In order to see the Secret of Life;
Oftentimes, one regards life with passion,
In order to see its manifest forms.
These two (the Secret and its manifestations)
Are (in their nature) the same;
They are given different names
When they become manifest.
They may both be called the Cosmic Mystery:
Reaching from the Mystery into the Deeper Mystery
Is the Gate to the Secret of All Life.

---

1. Lao Tzu, *Tao Te Ching*, trans. Lin Yutang, LIGO Lab, Caltech, https://labcit.ligo.caltech.edu/~mevans/docs/DDJ-LinYutang.html#1.

From Chapter 2

... Being and non-being interdepend in growth;
Difficult and easy interdepend in completion;
Long and short interdepend in contrast;
High and low interdepend in position;
Tones and voice interdepend in harmony;
Front and behind interdepend in company.
Therefore the Sage:
Manages affairs without action;
Preaches the doctrine without words;
All things take their rise, but he does not turn away from them;
He gives them life, but does not take possession of them;
He acts, but does not appropriate;
Accomplishes, but claims no credit.
It is because he lays claim to no credit
That the credit cannot be taken away from him.

From Chapter 5

... How the universe is like a bellows!
Empty, yet it gives a supply that never fails;
The more it is worked, the more it brings forth.
By many words is wit exhausted.
Rather, therefore, hold to the core.

From Chapter 7

... the Sage puts himself last,
And finds himself in the foremost place;
Regards his body as accidental,
And his body is thereby preserved.
Is it not because he does not live for Self
That his Self is realized?

From Chapter 8

The best of men is like water;
Water benefits all things
And does not compete with them.
It dwells in (the lowly) places that all disdain—
Wherein it comes near to the Tao.

From Chapter 9

Stretch (a bow) to the very full,
And you will wish you had stopped in time.
Temper a (sword-edge) to its very sharpest,
And the edge will not last long.
When gold and jade fill your hall,
You will not be able to keep them safe.
To be proud with wealth and honor
Is to sow seeds of one's own downfall.
Retire when your work is done,
Such is Heaven's way.

From Chapter 13

. . . he who values the world as his self
May then be entrusted with the government of the world;
And he who loves the world as his self—
The world may then be entrusted to his care.

From Chapter 15

. . . Who can find repose in a muddy world?
By lying still, it becomes clear.
Who can maintain his calm for long?
By activity, it comes back to life.
He who embraces this Tao
Guards against being over-full.
Because he guards against being over-full,
He is beyond wearing out and renewal.

From Chapter 19

. . . Reveal thy simple self,
Embrace thy original nature,
Check thy selfishness,
Curtail thy desires.

From Chapter 22

To yield is to be preserved whole.
To be bent is to become straight.
To be hollow is to be filled.

To be tattered is to be renewed.
To be in want is to possess.
To have plenty is to be confused.
Therefore the Sage embraces the One,
And becomes the model of the world.
He does not reveal himself,
And is therefore luminous.
He does not justify himself,
And is therefore far-famed.
He does not boast of himself,
And therefore people give him credit.
He does not pride himself,
And is therefore the chief among men. . . .

Chapter 24

He who stands on tiptoe does not stand (firm);
He who strains his strides does not walk (well);
He who reveals himself is not luminous;
He who justifies himself is not far-famed;
He who boasts of himself is not given credit;
He who prides himself is not chief among men.
These in the eyes of Tao
Are called "the dregs and tumors of Virtue";
Which are things of disgust.
Therefore the man of Tao spurns them.

From Chapter 27

A good runner leaves no track.
A good speech leaves no flaws for attack.
A good reckoner makes use of no counters.
A well-shut door makes use of no bolts,
And yet cannot be opened.
A well-tied knot makes use of no rope,
And yet cannot be untied. . . .

. . . the good man is the Teacher of the bad.
And the bad man is the lesson of the good.
He who neither values his teacher

Nor loves the lesson
Is one gone far astray,
Though he be learned.
—Such is the subtle secret.

From Chapter 28

He who is familiar with honor and glory
But keeps to obscurity
Becomes the valley of the world.
Being the valley of the world,
He has an eternal power which always suffices,
And returns again to the natural integrity of uncarved wood. . . .

Chapter 29

There are those who will conquer the world
And make of it (what they conceive or desire).
I see that they will not succeed.
(For) the world is God's own Vessel
It cannot be made (by human interference).
He who makes it spoils it.
He who holds it loses it.
For: Some things go forward,
Some things follow behind;
Some blow hot,
And some blow cold;
Some are strong,
And some are weak;
Some may break,
And some may fall.
Hence the Sage eschews excess, eschews extravagance,
Eschews pride.

Chapter 33

He who knows others is learned;
He who knows himself is wide.
He who conquers others has power of muscles;
He who conquers himself is strong.
He who is contented is rich.

He who is determined has strength of will.
He who does not lose his center endures.
He who dies yet (his power) remains has long life.

From Chapter 36

He who is to be made to dwindle (in power)
Must first be caused to expand.
He who is to be weakened
Must first be made strong.
He who is to be laid low
Must first be exalted to power.
He who is to be taken away from
Must first be given,
—This is the Subtle Light.

Chapter 45

The highest perfection is like imperfection,
And its use is never impaired.
The greatest abundance seems meager,
And its use will never fail.
What is most straight appears devious,
The greatest skill appears clumsiness;
The greatest eloquence seems like stuttering.
Movement overcomes cold,
(But) keeping still overcomes heat.
Who is calm and quiet becomes the guide for the universe.

From Chapter 46

. . . he who is contented with contentment
Shall be always content.

Chapter 47

Without stepping outside one's doors,
One can know what is happening in the world,
Without looking out of one's windows,
One can see the Tao of heaven.
The farther one pursues knowledge,
The less one knows.

Therefore the Sage knows without running about,
Understands without seeing,
Accomplishes without doing.

From Chapter 52

. . . He who can see the small is clear-sighted;
He who stays by gentility is strong.
Use the light,
And return to clear-sightedness—
Thus cause not yourself later distress.
—This is to rest in the Absolute.

From Chapter 54

. . . Cultivated in the individual, character will become genuine;
Cultivated in the family, character will become abundant;
Cultivated in the village, character will multiply;
Cultivated in the state, character will prosper;
Cultivated in the world, character will become universal.
Therefore:
According to (the character of) the individual,
judge the individual;
According to (the character of) the family,
judge the family;
According to (the character of) the village,
judge the village;
According to (the character of) the state,
judge the state;
According to (the character of) the world,
judge the world.

From Chapter 55

Who is rich in character
Is like a child.

From Chapter 63

Whether it is big or small, many or few,
Requite hatred with virtue.
Deal with the difficult while yet it is easy;
Deal with the big while yet it is small.

The difficult (problems) of the world
Must be dealt with while they are yet easy;
The great (problems) of the world
Must be dealt with while they are yet small.
Therefore the Sage by never dealing with great (problems)
Accomplishes greatness.
He who lightly makes a promise
Will find it often hard to keep his faith.
He who makes light of many things
Will encounter many difficulties.
Hence even the Sage regards things as difficult,
And for that reason never meets with difficulties.

From Chapter 64

... the Sage desires to have no desire,
And values not objects difficult to obtain.
Learns that which is unlearned,
And restores what the multitude have lost.
That he may assist in the course of Nature
And not presume to interfere.

From Chapter 66

How did the great rivers and seas become the Lords
of the ravines?
By being good at keeping low.

Chapter 67

All the world says: my teaching (Tao) greatly resembles folly.
Because it is great; therefore it resembles folly.
If it did not resemble folly,
It would have long ago become petty indeed!
I have Three Treasures;
Guard them and keep them safe:
the first is Love.
The second is, Never too much.
The third is, Never be the first in the world.
Through Love, one has no fear;
Through not doing too much, one has amplitude
(of reserve power);

Through not presuming to be the first in the world,
One can develop one's talent and let it mature.
If one forsakes love and fearlessness,
forsakes restraint and reserve power,
forsakes following behind and rushes in front,
He is doomed!
For love is victorious in attack,
And invulnerable in defense.
Heaven arms with love
Those it would not see destroyed.

Chapter 70

My teachings are very easy to understand
And very easy to practice,
But no one can understand them and
No one can practice them.
In my words there is a principle.
In the affairs of men there is a system.
Because they know not these,
They also know me not.
Since there are few that know me,
Therefore I am distinguished.
Therefore the Sage wears a coarse cloth on top
And carries jade within his bosom.

From Chapter 71

Who knows that he does not know is the highest;
Who (pretends to) know what he does not know is sick-minded.
And who recognizes sick-mindedness as sick-mindedness
Is not sick-minded.

From Chapter 76

When man is born, he is tender and weak;
At death, he is hard and stiff.
When the things and plants are alive, they are soft and supple;
When they are dead, they are brittle and dry.
Therefore hardness and stiffness are the companions of death,
And softness and gentleness are the companions of life.

Chapter 77

The Tao (way) of Heaven,
Is it not like the bending of a bow?
The top comes down and the bottom-end goes up,
The extra (length) is shortened, the insufficient (width) is expanded.
It is the way of Heaven to take away from those that have too much
And give to those that have not enough.
Not so with man's way:
He takes from those that have not
And gives it as tribute to those that have too much.
Who can have enough and to spare to give to the entire world?
Only the man of Tao.
Therefore the Sage acts, but does not possess,
Accomplishes but lays claim to no credit,
Because he has no wish to seem superior.

Chapter 81

True words are not fine-sounding;
Fine-sounding words are not true.
A good man does not argue;
He who argues is not a good man.
The wise one does not know many things;
He who knows many things is not wise.
The Sage does not accumulate (for himself).
He lives for other people,
And grows richer himself;
He gives to other people,
And has greater abundance.
The Tao of Heaven
Blesses, but does not harm.
The Way of the Sage
Accomplishes, but does not contend.

Discussion Questions

1. What is the relationship of certainty to uncertainty in the Christian life?
2. How do Lao Tzu's insights relate to the original human mandate to be stewards of creation?
3. Often modern Christian study prioritizes analytical knowing at the expense

of "softer" ways of knowing, such as through intuition, emotion, art, or natural observation. How do we strike a healthy balance?

4. What was the role of the riddle or paradox for the writers of biblical wisdom literature and for Jesus? How do we carry forward this tradition of reflective truth telling today?

5. What is one insight from Lao Tzu that you would like to carry with you for further contemplation?

CHAPTER 2

Confucius

Introduction to *The Analects*

RAVI JAIN

A key element of all virtue traditions, such as the Confucian, Greco-Roman, and Judeo-Christian traditions, is that virtue (Gk., *arete*; Chi., 德 *de*) is its own reward. Right living and right thinking lead to happiness. Christians believe that true virtue and thus true happiness are found only through union with Christ, living in him by the power of the Holy Spirit, and ultimately beholding him face-to-face. But even Plato, Aristotle, and the Stoics thought true happiness could be gained not merely through the possession of wealth, power, and glory but through wisdom and a virtuous life. Confucius (Kongfuzi), born in China around 550 BC, was in agreement. His thought paralleled the classical tradition with its emphasis on the formative power of music for soul craft. "To [Confucius], as to the ancient Greeks, [music] was important above all as an instrument of education. It promotes virtue; it is an intrinsic part of the Way."[1]

For Confucius, the *Way* was the eternal moral wisdom, which leads to human flourishing. A person advanced in this *Way* was a *junzi* (君子), a gentleman. The second chapter of C. S. Lewis's book *The Abolition of Man*, titled "The Way," explored this concept known in Chinese as the *Tao* (道 *dao*). *Tao* is a multilayered word that holds a meaning overlapping with that of the Greek word *logos*. Thus, the first chapter of the Gospel of John in Chinese reads, "In the beginning was the *Tao*."

Like the ancient Greeks, Romans, and Hebrews, Confucius emphasized piety toward parents, rulers, and unto Heaven with proper ceremonies. And as the prophet Isaiah had preached, so Confucius focused on the heart attitudes of people as they conducted rituals and not merely on outward formalities. Jesus had a similar emphasis, and he quoted Isaiah, "These people honor me with their lips, but their hearts are far from me" (Matt. 15:8). To understand Confucius's concept of ritual (禮 *li*) better, consider the English word *manners*, which often refers to one's general moral conduct.[2] While there may or may not be any direct influence between the East and West regarding these themes, these parallels shed

---

1. Confucius, *The Analects of Confucius*, trans. Arthur Waley (London: Allen and Unwin, 1938), 69. The following version of the *Analects* is the Waley translation.

2. In William Wilberforce's campaign for a "Reformation of Manners," the word *manners* referred to

light on Confucius's thought. His emphasis on ritual and propriety, according to Lewis, sought to participate in the timeless moral order (*Tao*) of the cosmos.

Sometimes, especially in academic settings, piety and philosophy are pitted against each other, as in faith versus reason. But Confucius did not do that. While Confucius seldom spoke of the gods, he held heaven in high regard. Confucius, with mysterious reverence, upheld an ancient sacrificial system in which a goat was killed even though many did not understand why he upheld this tradition. The Chinese character for righteousness (義 *yi*), one of the chief Confucian virtues, is a pictogram of a lamb over the personal pronoun for "me" or "I." The parallel between this character, "lamb over me," and the Jewish Passover lamb foreshadowing Jesus, the Lamb of God, is poignant. How did this notion of another's sacrifice for us leading to our righteousness arise in ancient Chinese thought? Perhaps people made in the image of God have a sense of their distance from God and their need to bridge it by a sacrifice they cannot pay.

Scholastic studies can support one's faith and need not corrode it. Furthermore, surprising wisdom lies in studying other cultural traditions. For understanding the East Asian tradition, Confucius is a great place to start.

From *The Analects*
Book 1

1. The Master said, To learn and at due times to repeat what one has learnt, is that not after all a pleasure? That friends should come to one from afar, is this not after all delightful? To remain unsoured even though one's merits are unrecognized by others, is that not after all what is expected of a gentleman?

2. Master Yu said, Those who in private life behave well towards their parents and elder brothers, in public life seldom show a disposition to resist the authority of their superiors. And as for such men starting a revolution, no instance of it has ever occurred. It is upon the trunk that a gentleman works. When that is firmly set up, the Way grows. And surely proper behavior towards parents and elder brothers is the trunk of Goodness?[3]

4. Master Tseng said, Every day I examine myself on these three points: In acting on behalf of others, have I always been loyal to their interests?

---

the entirety of English moral conduct. Also, the concept of "custom" played an essential role for Edmund Burke in transmitting the "rights of an Englishman."

3. This analect, quoted by C. S. Lewis, offers an interesting parallel to Cicero, who says, "Piety is the foundation of all other virtues," according to Russell Kirk in *The Roots of American Order* (Wilmington, DE: Intercollegiate Studies Institute, 2003), 103. Scott Barnwell describes the importance of piety in the Confucian tradition: "Xiao 孝, 'filial piety,' was also a highly admired virtue and was considered by some the 'root of De' (德之本), or perhaps, 'the basis of all virtues.'" Barnwell cites Xiaojing 1 孝經 (c. mid-third century BCE). Scott A. Barnwell, "The Evolution of the Concept of De 德 in Early China," Sino-Platonic Papers 235, March 2013, www.sino-platonic.org/complete/spp235_de_character_early_China.pdf.

In intercourse with my friends, have I always been true to my work? Have I failed to repeat the precepts that have been handed down to me?

9. Master Tseng said, When proper respect towards the dead is shown at the End and continued after they are far away the moral force (*de*) of a people has reached its highest point.

Book 2

1. The Master said, He who rules by moral force (*de*) is like the pole-star, which remains in its place while all the lesser stars do homage to it.

2. The Master said, If out of the three hundred Songs I had to take one phrase to cover all my teaching, I would say "Let there be no evil in your thoughts."

3. The Master said, Govern the people by regulations, keep order among them by chastisements, and they will flee from you, and lose all self-respect. Govern them by moral force (*de*), keep order among them by ritual and they will keep their self-respect and come to you of their own accord.

4. The Master said, At fifteen I set my heart upon learning. At thirty, I had planted my feet firm upon the ground. At forty, I no longer suffered from perplexities. At fifty, I knew what were the biddings of Heaven. At sixty, I heard them with docile ear. At seventy, I could follow the dictates of my own heart; for what I desired no longer overstepped the boundaries of right.

7. Tzu-yu asked about the treatment of parents. The Master said, "Filial sons" nowadays are people who see to it that their parents get enough to eat. But even dogs and horses are cared for to that extent. If there is no feeling of respect, wherein lies the difference?

11. The Master said, He who by reanimating the Old can gain knowledge of the New is fit to be a teacher.

12. The Master said, A gentleman is not an implement.

13. Tzu-kung asked about the true gentleman. The Master said, He does not preach what he practices till he has practiced what he preaches.

14. The Master said, A gentleman can see a question from all sides without bias. The small man is biased and can see a question only from one side.

15. The Master said, "He who learns but does not think, is lost." He who thinks but does not learn is in great danger.

16. The Master said, He who sets to work upon a different strand destroys the whole fabric.

17. The Master said, Yu, shall I teach you what knowledge is? When you know a thing, to recognize that you know it, and when you do not know a thing, to recognize that you do not know it. That is knowledge.

21. Someone, when talking to Master K'ung, said, How is it that you are not in the public service? The Master said, The Book says: "Be filial, only be filial and friendly towards your brothers, and you will be contributing to government." There are other sorts of service quite different from what you mean by "service."

22. The Master said, I do not see what use a man can be put to, whose word cannot be trusted. How can a wagon be made to go if it has no yoke-bar or a carriage, if it has no collar-bar?

Book 3

3. The Master said, A man who is not Good, what can he have to do with ritual? A man who is not Good, what can he have to do with music?

4. Lin Fang asked for some main principles in connexion with ritual. The Master said,

> A very big question.
> In ritual at large it is a safe rule always to be too sparing rather than too lavish; and in the particular case of mourning-rites, they should be dictated by grief rather than by fear.

12. Of the saying, "The word 'sacrifice' is like the word 'present'; one should sacrifice to a spirit as though that spirit was present," the Master said, If I am not present at the sacrifice, it is as though there were no sacrifice.

13. Wang-sun Chia asked about the meaning of the saying,

> Better pay court to the stove
> Than pay court to the Shrine.

The Master said, It is not true. He who has put himself in the wrong with Heaven has no means of expiation left.

17. Tzu-kung wanted to do away with the presentation of a sacrificial sheep at the announcements of each new moon. The Master said, Ssu! You grudge [care about] sheep, but I grudge [care about] ritual.

Book 4

1. The Master said, It is Goodness[4] that gives to a neighborhood its beauty. One who is free to choose, yet does not prefer to dwell among the Good—how can he be accorded the name of wise?

---

4. "Goodness" here and elsewhere is translated from the Chinese 仁 (ren, "benevolence" or "humaneness"). Related to the Chinese word for "man" (人 ren). Compare with the Latin *humanitas*.

2. The Master said, Without Goodness a man cannot for long endure adversity, cannot for long enjoy prosperity. The Good man rests content with Goodness; he that is merely wise pursues Goodness in the belief that it pays to do so.

13. The Master said, If it is really possible to govern countries by ritual and yielding, there is no more to be said. But if it is not really possible, of what use is ritual?

14. The Master said, He does not mind not being in office; all he minds about is whether he has qualities that entitle him to office. He does not mind failing to get recognition; he is too busy doing the things that entitle him to recognition.

15. The Master said, Shen! My Way has one (thread) that runs right through it. Master Tseng said, Yes. When the Master had gone out, the disciples asked, saying What did he mean? Master Tseng said, Our Master's Way is simply this: Loyalty, consideration.

16. The Master said, A gentleman takes as much trouble to discover what is right as lesser men take to discover what will pay.

25. The Master said, Moral force (de) never dwells in solitude; it will always bring neighbors.

Book 5

12. Tzu-kung said, Our Master's views concerning culture and the outward insignias of goodness, we are permitted to hear; but about Man's natures and the ways of Heaven he will not tell us anything at all.

14. Tzu-kung asked saying, Why was K'ung Wen Tzu called Wen ("The Cultured")? The Master said, Because he was diligent and so fond of learning that he was not ashamed to pick up knowledge even from his inferiors.

Book 6

25. The Master said, A gentleman who is widely versed in letters and at the same time knows how to submit his learning to the restraints of ritual is not likely, I think, to go far wrong.

Book 7

6. The Master said, Set your heart upon the Way (dao), support yourself by its power, lean upon Goodness, seek distraction in the arts.

19. The Master said, I for my part am not one of those who have innate knowledge. I am simply one who loves the past and who is diligent in investigating it.

21. The Master said, Even when walking in a party of no more than three I can always be certain of learning from those I am with. There will be good qualities that I can select for imitation and bad ones that will teach me what requires correction in myself.

22. The Master said, Heaven begat the power (*de*) that is in me. What have I to fear from such a one as Huan T'ui?

24. The Master took four subjects for his teaching: culture, conduct of affairs, loyalty to superiors and the keeping of promises.

26. The Master fished with a line but not with a net; when fowling he did not aim at a roosting bird.

Book 8

8. The Master said, Let a man be first incited by the Songs then given a firm footing by the study of ritual, and finally perfected by music.

11. The Master said, If a man has gifts as wonderful as those of the Duke of Chou, yet is arrogant and mean, all the rest is of no account.

12. The Master said:

One who will study for three years
Without thought of reward
Would be hard indeed to find.

13. The Master said, Be of unwavering good faith, love learning, if attacked be ready to die for the good Way. Do not enter a State that pursues dangerous courses, nor stay in one where the people have rebelled. When the Way prevails under Heaven, then show yourself; when it does not prevail, then hide. When the Way prevails in your own land, count it a disgrace to be needy and obscure; when the Way does not prevail in your land, then count it a disgrace to be rich and honored.

17. The Master said, Learn as if you were following someone whom you could not catch up, as though it were someone you were frightened of losing.

Book 9

7. The Master said, Do I regard myself as a possessor of wisdom? Far from it. But if even a simple peasant comes in all sincerity and asks me a question, I am ready to thrash the matter out, with all its pros and cons, to the very end.

17. The Master said, I have never yet seen anyone whose desire to build up his moral power was as strong as sexual desire.

28. The Master said, he that is really Good can never be unhappy. He that is really wise can never be perplexed. He that is really brave is never afraid.

Book 11

6. K'ang-tzu of the Chi Family asked which of the disciples had a love of learning. Master K'ung replied, There was Yen Hui. He was fond of learning, but unfortunately his allotted span was a short one, and he died. Now there is none.

19. Tzu-chang asked about the Way of the good people. The Master said, He who does not tread in the tracks cannot expect to find his way into the Inner Room.

25. Once when Tzu-lu, Tseng Hsi, Jan Ch'iu and Kung-hsi Hua were seated in attendance upon the Master, he said, you consider me as a somewhat older man than yourselves. Forget for a moment that I am so. At present you are out of office and feel that your merits are not recognized. Now supposing someone were to recognize your merits, what employment would you choose? Tzu-lu promptly and confidently replied, Give me a country of a thousand war-chariots, hemmed in by powerful enemies, or even invaded by hostile armies, with drought and famine to boot; in the space of three years I could endow the people with courage and teach them in what direction right conduct lies.

Our Master smiled at him. What about you, Ch'iu? he said. Ch'iu replied saying, Give me a domain of sixty to seventy or say fifty to sixty (leagues), and in the space of three years I could bring it about that the common people should lack for nothing. But as to rites and music, I should have to leave them to a real gentleman.

What about you, Ch'ih?

(Kung-hsi Hua) answered saying, I do not say I could do this; but I should like at any rate to be trained for it. In ceremonies at the Ancestral Temple or at a conference or general gathering of the feudal princes I should like, clad in the Straight Gown and Emblematic Cap, to play the part of junior assistant.

Tien, what about you?

The notes of the zither he was softly fingering died away; he put it down, rose and replied saying, I fear my words will not be so well chosen as those of the other three. The Master said, What harm is there in that? All that matters is that each should name his desire.

Tseng Hsi said, At the end of spring, when the making of the Spring Clothes has been completed, to go with five times six newly-capped youths and six times seven uncapped boys, perform the lustration in the river I, take the air at the Rain Dance altars, and then go home singing. The Master heaved a deep sigh and said, I am with Tien.

When the three others went away, Tseng Hsi remained behind and said, What about the sayings of those three people? The Master said, After all, it was agreed that each should tell his wish; and that is just what they did.

Tseng said, Why did you smile at Yu?

The Master said, "Because it is upon observance of ritual that the governance of a State depends; and his words were lacking in the virtue of cession. That is why I smiled at him."

"I suppose you were contrasting him with Ch'iu, who (by domain) certainly did not mean kingdom?

"Where have you ever seen 'a domain of sixty to seventy or fifty to sixty leagues' that was not a kingdom?"

"I suppose, then, you were contrasting him with Ch'ih, who was certainly not asking for a kingdom."

The business of the Ancestral Temple and such things as conferences and general gatherings can only be undertaken by feudal princes. But if Ch'ih were taking a minor part, what prince is there who is capable of playing a major one?[5]

Book 12

24. Master Tseng said, The gentleman by his culture collects friends about him, and through these friends promotes Goodness.

Book 13

3. Tzu-lu said, If the prince of Wei were waiting for you to come and administer his country for him, what would be your first measure? The Master said, It would certainly be to correct language. Tzu-lu said, Can I have heard you aright? Surely what you say has nothing to do with the matter. Why should language be corrected? The Master said, Yu! How boorish you are! A gentleman, when things he does not understand are mentioned, should maintain an attitude of reserve. If language is incorrect, then what is said does not concord with what was meant; and if what is said does not concord with what was meant what is to be done cannot be effected. If what is to be done cannot be effected, then rites and music do not flourish, then mutilations and lesser punishments will go astray. And if mutilations and lesser punishments go astray, then the people have nowhere to put hand or foot. Therefore the gentleman uses only such language as is proper for speech, and only speaks of what it would be proper to carry into effect. The gentleman, in what he says, leaves nothing to mere chance.

---

5. This unique analect was much admired by Zhu Xi, the twelfth-century neo-Confucian scholar who tried to reemphasize that the right attitude must accompany right action in the Confucian tradition. The main character in this analect, Tseng Hsi (*Zeng Xi*), was also the father of Confucius's famous disciple Zengzi, a key transmitter of Confucianism.

Book 14

3. The Master said, The knight of the Way who thinks only of sitting quietly at home is not worthy to be called a knight.

4. The Master said, When the Way prevails in the land, be bold in speech and bold in action. When the Way does not prevail, be bold in action but conciliatory in speech.

5. The Master said, One who has accumulated moral power (*de*) will certainly also possess eloquence; but he who has eloquence does not necessarily possess moral power. A Good man will certainly also possess courage; but a brave man is not necessarily Good.

7. The Master said, It is possible to be a true gentleman and yet lack Goodness. But there has never yet existed a Good man who was not a gentleman.

8. The Master said, How can he be said truly to love, who exacts no effort from the objects of his love? How can he be said to be truly loyal, who refrains from admonishing the object of his loyalty?

25. The Master said, In old days men studied for the sake of self-improvement; nowadays men study in order to impress other people.

Book 15

3. The Master said, Yu, Those who understand moral force (*de*) are few.

17. The Master said, The gentleman who takes the right as his material to work upon and ritual as the guide in putting what is right into practice, who is modest in setting out his projects and faithful in carrying them to their conclusion, he indeed is a true gentleman.

18. The Master said, A gentleman is distressed by his own lack of capacity; he is never distressed at the failure of others to recognize his merits.

20. The Master said, "The demands that a gentleman makes are upon himself; those that a small man makes are upon others."

23. Tzu-kung asked saying, Is there any single saying that one can act upon all day and every day? The Master said, Perhaps the saying about consideration: "Never do to others what you would not like them to do to you."

Book 16

9. Master K'ung said, Highest are those who are born wise. Next are those who become wise by learning. After them come those who have to toil painfully in order to acquire learning. Finally, to the lowest class of the common people belong those who toil painfully without ever managing to learn.

Book 17

8. The Master said, Yu, have you ever been told of the Six Sayings about the Six Degenerations? Tzu-lu replied, No, never. (The Master said,) Come, then; I will tell you. Love of Goodness without love of learning degenerates into silliness. Love of wisdom without love of learning degenerates into utter lack of principle. Love of keeping promises without love of learning degenerates into villainy. Love of uprightness without love of learning degenerates into harshness. Love of courage without love of learning degenerates into turbulence. Love of courage without love of learning degenerates into mere recklessness.

9. The Master said, Little ones, Why is it that none of you study the Songs? For the Songs will help you to incite people's emotions, to observe their feelings, to keep company, to express your grievances. They may be used at home in the service of one's father; abroad, in the service of one's prince. Moreover, they will widen your acquaintance with the names of birds, beasts, plants and trees.

11. The Master said, Ritual, ritual! Does it mean no more than presents of jade and silk? Music, music! Does it mean no more than bells and drums?

Book 18

4 . The people of Ch'i sent to Lu a present of female musicians and Chi Huan-tzu accepted them. For three days no Court was held, whereupon Master K'ung left Lu.

Book 19

6. Tzu-hsia said,

One who studies widely and with set purpose,
Who questions earnestly, then thinks for himself about what he has
   heard—such a one will incidentally achieve Goodness.

7. Tzu-hsia said, Just as the hundred apprentices must live in workshops to perfect themselves in their craft, so the gentleman studies, that he may improve himself in the Way.

Book 20

3. The Master said, He who does not understand the will of Heaven cannot be regarded as a gentleman. He who does not know the rites cannot take his stand. He who does not understand words, cannot understand.

Discussion Questions

1. Does Confucius feel familiar to you or more foreign? Does he seem similar or different to other ancient cultures you have studied, such as the Greeks, Hebrews, and Romans?
2. How would you explain Confucius's concept of *The Way* to another person?
3. Are there any rituals or customs in your life that you find meaningful? Are there any that you feel are just meaningless? What makes the difference?
4. The greatest neo-Confucian interpreter, Zhu Xi, who lived in the twelfth century, was fond of Analect 11.25. By that time, Confucianism had become dry and legalistic, and Zhu Xi wanted to revive its true spirit. How does that analect symbolize true Confucianism?
5. Confucianism has sometimes been used by tyrants to defend their oppressive rule because it emphasizes respect of authority. Others believe that Confucianism actually gives its followers permission to oppose tyrants. Based on the readings above, which do you think best represents the authentic spirit of Confucianism, and why?

Plato

Introduction to "The Allegory of the Cave"

JASON BAEHR

"The Allegory of the Cave" is perhaps the most famous passage of one of the most influential works in the history of philosophy: Plato's *Republic*. The allegory tells the story of a man who has spent his entire life as a prisoner in an underground cave. Once the man is released, his understanding of what is ultimately real and good gets completely upended.

One point of the allegory is to illustrate Plato's intriguing and enduring "theory of forms," according to which the world we perceive with our senses (the world inside the cave) is an imperfect and transitory reflection of another world—a realm of perfect, immaterial, unchanging, and eternal "ideas" or essences (*eidos*). As Plato himself makes clear toward the end of the selection, the allegory is also supposed to show something important about the ultimate aim or purpose of education.

The character of Socrates, who speaks for Plato and narrates the story, observes that some people think of education as a strictly intellectual or cognitive affair, like depositing knowledge into students' heads or "putting sight into blind eyes" (518c). For Plato, this is a badly mistaken view of the psychology of learning. To see why, imagine hearing an unfamiliar noise coming from immediately behind you. What would you do to identify the source of the noise? One thing you *wouldn't* do is simply rotate your eyeballs. Instead, because the sound came from directly behind you, you'd likely turn your entire body around and then look to see what caused the noise.

Plato thought something similar applied to learning in general. Commenting on "the power to learn that is present in everyone's soul, and the instrument with which each of us learns," Socrates says, "Just as an eye cannot be turned around from darkness to light except by turning the whole body, so this instrument must be turned around . . . with the whole soul until it is able to bear to look at what is and at the brightest thing that is" (518c). In other words, to learn what is truly real and good, our entire selves or souls must be oriented in the right direction. Knowledge worth having isn't simply deposited into our minds by our teachers. We must desire it, care about it, fight for it, and delight in it.

This picture of learning is worth keeping in mind as you enter into the remaining years of your formal education. If Plato is right, your job as a student is not just to absorb and regurgitate information. Nor is it merely to develop skills that will serve you well in the job market. Instead, it is to *reorient* your entire self—your values, cares, and desires—so that you are deeply and personally open to what is ultimately real and good. In doing so, you will begin, as Socrates puts it, "to ascend the ascent" (519c). You will begin your own journey out of the cave.

"The Allegory of the Cave" from *The Republic*, Book 7

Socrates: Next, I said, compare the effect of education and the lack of it on our nature to an experience like this: Imagine human beings living in an underground, cave-like dwelling, with an entrance a long way up, which is both open to the light and as wide as the cave itself. They've been there since childhood, fixed in the same place, with their necks and legs fettered, able to see only in front of them, because their bonds prevent them from turning their heads around. Light is provided by a fire burning far above and behind them. Also behind them, but on higher ground, there's a path stretching between them and the fire. Imagine that along this path a low wall has been built, like the screen in front of puppeteers above which they show their puppets.

Glaucon: I'm imagining it.

Socrates: Then also imagine that there are people along the wall, carrying all kinds of artifacts that project above it—statues of people and other animals, made out of stone, wood, and every material. And, as you'd expect, some of the carriers are talking, and some are silent.

Glaucon: It's a strange image you're describing, and strange prisoners.

Socrates: They're like us. Do you suppose, first of all, that these prisoners see anything of themselves and one another besides the shadows that the fire casts on the wall in front of them?

Glaucon: How could they, if they have to keep their heads motionless throughout life?

Socrates: What about the things being carried along the wall? Isn't the same true of them?

Glaucon: Of course.

Socrates: And if they could talk to one another, don't you think they'd suppose that the names they used applied to the things they see passing before them?

Glaucon: They'd have to.

Socrates: And what if their prison also had an echo from the wall facing them? Don't you think they'd believe that the shadows passing in front of them were talking whenever one of the carriers passing along the wall was doing so?

Glaucon: I certainly do.

Socrates: Then the prisoners would in every way believe that the truth is nothing other than the shadows of those artifacts.

Glaucon: They must surely believe that.

Socrates: Consider, then, what being released from their bonds and cured of their ignorance would naturally be like. When one of them was freed and suddenly compelled to stand up, turn his head, walk, and look up toward the light, he'd be pained and dazzled and unable to see the things whose shadows he'd seen before. What do you think he'd say, if we told him that what he'd seen before was inconsequential, but that now—because he is a bit closer to the things that are and is turned toward things that are more—he sees more correctly? Or, to put it another way, if we pointed to each of the things passing by, asked him what each of them is, and compelled him to answer, don't you think he'd be at a loss and that he'd believe that the things he saw earlier were truer than the ones he was now being shown?

Glaucon: Much truer.

Socrates: And if someone compelled him to look at the light itself, wouldn't his eyes hurt, and wouldn't he turn around and flee towards the things he's able to see, believing that they're really clearer than the ones he's being shown?

Glaucon: He would.

Socrates: And if someone dragged him away from there by force, up the rough, steep path, and didn't let him go until he dragged him into the sunlight, wouldn't he be pained and irritated at being treated that way? And when he came into the light, with the sun filling his eyes, wouldn't he be unable to see a single one of the things now said to be true?

Glaucon: He would be unable to see them, at least at first.

Socrates: I suppose, then, that he'd need time to get adjusted before he could see things in the world above. At first, he'd see shadows most easily, then images of men and other things in water, then the things themselves. Of these, he'd be able to study the things in the sky and the sky itself more easily at night, looking at the light of the stars and the moon, than during the day, looking at the sun and the light of the sun.

Glaucon: Of course.

Socrates: Finally, I suppose, he'd be able to see the sun, not images of it in water or some alien place, but the sun itself, in its own place, and be able to study it.

Glaucon: Necessarily so.

Socrates: And at this point he would infer and conclude that the sun provides the seasons and the years, governs everything in the visible world, and is in some way the cause of all the things that he used to see.

Glaucon: It's clear that would be his next step.

Socrates: What about when he reminds himself of his first dwelling place, his fellow prisoners, and what passed for wisdom there? Don't you think that he'd count himself happy for the change and pity the others?

Glaucon: Certainly.

Socrates: And if there had been any honors, praises, or prizes among them for the one who was sharpest at identifying the shadows as they passed by and who best remembered which usually came earlier, which later, and which simultaneously, and who could thus best divine the future, do you think that our man would desire these rewards or envy those among the prisoners who were honored and held power? Instead, wouldn't he feel, with Homer, that he'd much prefer to "work the earth as a serf to another, one without possessions," and go through any sufferings, rather than share their opinions and live as they do?

Glaucon: I suppose he would rather suffer anything than live like that.

Socrates: Consider this too. If this man went down into the cave again and sat down in his same seat, wouldn't his eyes—coming suddenly out of the sun like that—be filled with darkness?

Glaucon: They certainly would.

Socrates: And before his eyes had recovered—and the adjustment would not be quick—while his vision was still dim, if he had to compete again with the perpetual prisoners in recognizing the shadows, wouldn't he invite ridicule? Wouldn't it be said of him that he'd returned from his upward journey with his eyesight ruined and that it isn't worthwhile even to try to travel upward? And, as for anyone who tried to free them and lead them upward, if they could somehow get their hands on him, wouldn't they kill him?

Glaucon: They certainly would.

Socrates: This whole image, Glaucon, must be fitted together with what we said before. The visible realm should be likened to the prison dwelling, and the light of the fire inside it to the power of the sun. And if you interpret the upward journey and the study of things above as the upward journey of the soul to the intelligible realm, you'll grasp what I hope to convey, since that is what you wanted to hear about. Whether it's true or not, only the god knows. But this is how I see it: In the knowable realm, the form of the good is the last thing to be seen, and it is reached only with difficulty. Once one has seen it, however, one must conclude that it is the cause of all that is correct and beautiful in anything, that it produces both light and its source in the visible realm, and that in the intelligible realm it controls and provides truth and understanding, so that anyone who is to act sensibly in private or public must see it.

Glaucon: I have the same thoughts, at least as far as I'm able.

Socrates: Come, then, share with me this thought also: It isn't surprising that the ones who get to this point are unwilling to occupy themselves with human affairs and that their souls are always pressing upwards, eager to spend their time above, for, after all, this is surely what we'd expect, if indeed things fit the image I described before.

Glaucon: It is.

Socrates: What about what happens when someone turns from divine study to the evils of human life? Do you think it surprising, since his sight is still dim, and he hasn't yet become accustomed to the darkness around him, that he behaves awkwardly and appears completely ridiculous if he's compelled, either in the courts or elsewhere, to contend about the shadows of justice or the statues of which they are the shadows and to dispute about the way these things are understood by people who have never seen justice itself?

Glaucon: That's not surprising at all.

Socrates: No, it isn't. But anyone with any understanding would remember that the eyes may be confused in two ways and from two causes, namely, when they've come from the light into the darkness and when they've come from the darkness into the light. Realizing that the same applies to the soul, when someone sees a soul disturbed and unable to see something, he won't laugh mindlessly, but he'll take into consideration whether it has come from a brighter life and is dimmed through not yet having become accustomed to the dark or whether it has come from greater ignorance into greater light and is dazzled by the increased brilliance. Then he'll declare the first soul happy in its experience in life, and he'll pity the latter—but even if he chose to make fun of it, at least he'd be less ridiculous than if he laughed at a soul that has come from the light above.

Glaucon: What you say is very reasonable.

Socrates: If that's true, then here's what we must think about these matters: Education isn't what some people declare to be, namely, putting knowledge into souls that lack it, like putting sight into blind eyes.

Glaucon: They do say that.

Socrates: But our present discussion, on the other hand, shows that the power to learn is present in everyone's soul and that the instrument with which each learns is like an eye that cannot be turned around from darkness to light without turning the whole body. This instrument cannot be turned around from that which is coming into being without turning the whole soul until it is able to study that which is and the brightest thing that is, namely, the one we call the good. Isn't that right?

Glaucon: Yes.

Socrates: Then education is the craft concerned with doing this very thing, this turning around, and with how the soul can most easily and effectively be made to do it. It isn't the craft of putting sight into the soul. Education takes for granted that sight is there but that it isn't turned the right way or looking where it ought to look, and it tries to redirect it appropriately.

Glaucon: So it seems.

Discussion Questions

1. For Plato, the most real thing is goodness itself or the form of the Good. For Christians, God is the ultimate basis of reality and goodness. What would it look like to adapt Plato's allegory to a distinctively Christian worldview? What details might you add or subtract?

2. How do you tend to think about the ultimate aim or purpose of education? That is, what is education *for*?

3. Does Plato's allegory challenge you to think differently about the purpose of your education? If so, how?

4. How would your life as a student look different if you were to take this allegory to heart?

CHAPTER 4

Seneca the Younger

Introduction to "On the Shortness of Life"

MATTHEW D. WRIGHT

Do you ever get the sense that life slips away faster than we can really live it? We may be tempted to think that social media and the frenetic pace of our globally interconnected modern life leave us more susceptible than ever to the constant preoccupation that stifles reflection. Yet the reflections of first-century AD Roman philosopher and politician Seneca the Younger demonstrate that the transience of time is a perennial human problem. Then, as now, people struggled to overcome time-wasting vices, found themselves pulled in a million different directions with too many "good" things to do, and were, in the words of T. S. Eliot, "distracted from distraction by distraction.[1]" Thus, Seneca argues, the real difficulty is not that life is so short, but that we don't make the time we have count.

He knew of what he spoke. The son of a famous Roman teacher of rhetoric, Seneca was educated in Rome and later pursued a career there in politics and law. He was soon caught up in the machinations of imperial Roman politics and found himself banished to Corsica by the emperor Claudius. After several years of quiet study and writing, the emperor's wife had Seneca recalled to Rome, where he built a powerful group of allies and became tutor to the emperor's adopted son, Nero. Then, upon the sudden death of Claudius, Seneca became a top adviser to the teenage emperor Nero and enjoyed years of political prominence before withdrawing from public life to return to his philosophical and dramatic writing. He was not beyond Nero's reach, however, and was forced to commit suicide in AD 65 after being accused by his political enemies of plotting to murder the emperor.

Despite his colorful political career, Seneca is best known as a Stoic philosopher. Our popular usage of the word *stoic*, meaning to be unmoved by passions or feelings, derives from the weight Stoics placed on composure of character that results from subordinating the passions to reason. To cultivate virtue along with reason, Stoics argued, is to bring one's soul into alignment with the deep structure of the universe. Because reason pervades the cosmic order, we can face the

---

1. T. S. Eliot, "Burnt Norton," line 101, in *Four Quartets* (New York: Harcourt, Brace, 1943).

trials and uncertainties of life with confident resolve. Because that rational order connects all things and all people, we have a duty to pursue a just common good for the universal human community. "On the Shortness of Life" demonstrates these Stoic commitments by challenging the reader to face one of life's central difficulties—the fleetingness of time—with thoughtfulness and virtue. The problem is not with nature. The problem is with souls disordered by unruly passions and misplaced ambition. The solution Seneca offered directs us not only to the careful stewardship of our time, but just as importantly, to deep conversation with thinkers of the past who light the way in our own pursuit of wisdom. If we heed his advice, we may just find ourselves with all the time in the world.

From "On the Shortness of Life"
TRANSLATED BY AUBREY STEWART

The greater part of mankind, my Paulinus, complains of the unkindness of Nature, because we are born only for a short space of time, and that this allotted period of life runs away so swiftly, nay so hurriedly, that with but few exceptions men's life comes to an end just as they are preparing to enjoy it. Nor is it only the common herd and the ignorant vulgar who mourn over this universal misfortune, as they consider it to be. This reflection has wrung complaints even from great men. Hence comes that well-known saying of physicians, that art is long but life is short. Hence arose that quarrel, so unbefitting a sage, which Aristotle picked with Nature, because she had indulged animals with such length of days that some of them lived for ten or fifteen centuries, while man, although born for many and such great exploits, had the term of his existence cut so much shorter.

We do not have a very short time assigned to us, but we lose a great deal of it. Life is long enough to carry out the most important projects. We have an ample portion, if we do but arrange the whole of it aright. But when it all runs to waste through luxury and carelessness, when it is not devoted to any good purpose, then at the last we are forced to feel that it is all over, although we never noticed how it glided away. Thus it is: we do not receive a short life, but we make it a short one, and we are not poor in days, but wasteful of them. When great and kinglike riches fall into the hands of a bad master, they are dispersed straightway, but even a moderate fortune, when bestowed upon a wise guardian, increases by use. In like manner, our life has great opportunities for one who knows how to dispose of it to the best advantage.

Why do we complain of Nature? She has dealt kindly with us. Life is long enough, if you know how to use it. One man is possessed by an avarice which nothing can satisfy, another by a laborious diligence in doing what is totally useless. Another is sodden by wine; another is benumbed by sloth. One man is exhausted by an ambition which makes him court the good will of others. Another, through his eagerness as a merchant, is led to visit every land and every sea by the hope of gain. Some are plagued by the love of soldiering, and are always either endangering other men's lives or in trembling for their own. Some wear away their lives in that voluntary slavery, the unrequited service of great men. Many are occupied either in laying claim to other men's fortune or in complaining of their own. A great number have no settled purpose, and are tossed from one new scheme to another by a rambling, inconsistent, dissatisfied, fickle habit of mind. Some care for no object sufficiently to try to attain it, but lie lazily yawning until their fate comes upon them, so that I cannot doubt the truth of that verse which the greatest of poets has dressed in the guise of an oracular response: "We live a small part only of our lives." But all duration is time, not life.

Vices press upon us and surround us on every side, and do not permit us to regain our feet, or to raise our eyes and gaze upon truth, but when we are down keep us prostrate and chained to low desires. Men who are in this condition are never allowed to come to themselves. If ever by chance they obtain any rest, they roll to and fro like the deep sea, which heaves and tosses after a gale, and they never have any respite from their lusts. Do you suppose that I speak of those whose ills are notorious? Nay, look at those whose prosperity all men run to see: they are choked by their own good things. To how many men do riches prove a heavy burden? How many men's eloquence and continual desire to display their own cleverness has cost them their lives? How many are sallow with constant sensual indulgence? How many have no freedom left them by the tribe of clients that surges around them? Look through all these, from the lowest to the highest: this man calls his friends to support him, this one is present in court, this one is the defendant, this one pleads for him, this one is on the jury. But no one lays claim to his own self; every one wastes his time over someone else. Investigate those men whose names are in everyone's mouth. You will find that they bear just the same marks: A is devoted to B, and B to C. No one belongs to himself. Moreover some men are full of most irrational anger. They complain of the insolence of their chiefs because they have not granted them an audience when they wished for it—as if a man had any right to complain of being so haughtily shut out by another, when he never has leisure to give his own conscience a hearing. This chief of yours, whoever he is, though he may look at you in an offensive manner, still will someday look at you, open his ears to your words, and give you a seat by his side. But you never design to look upon yourself, to listen to your own grievances. You ought not, then, to claim these services from another, especially since while you yourself were doing so, you did not wish for an interview with another man, but were not able to obtain one with yourself.

Were all the brightest intellects of all time to employ themselves on this one subject, they never could sufficiently express their wonder at this blindness of men's minds: men will not allow anyone to establish himself upon their estates, and upon the most trifling dispute about the measuring of boundaries, they betake themselves to stones and cudgels. Yet they allow others to encroach upon their lives, nay, they themselves actually lead others in to take possession of them. You cannot find anyone who wants to distribute his money; yet among how many people does everyone distribute his life? Men covetously guard their property from waste, but when it comes to waste of time, they are most prodigal of that of which it would become them to be sparing.

Let us take one of the elders, and say to him, "We perceive that you have arrived at the extreme limits of human life. You are in your hundredth year, or even older. Come now, reckon up your whole life in black and white. Tell us how much of your time has been spent upon your creditors, how much on your mistress, how much on your king, how much on your clients, how much in quarrelling with your wife, how much in keeping your slaves in order, how much in running up and down the city on business. Add to this the diseases which we bring upon us with our own hands, and the time which has laid idle without any use having been made of it. You will see that you have not lived as many years as you count. Look back in your memory and see how often you have been consistent in your projects, how many days passed as you intended them to do when you were at your own disposal, how often you did not change color and your spirit did not quail, how much work you have done in so long a time, how many people have without your knowledge stolen parts of your life from you, how much you have lost, how large a part has been taken up by useless grief, foolish gladness, greedy desire, or polite conversation, how little of yourself is left to you. You will then perceive that you will die prematurely."

What, then, is the reason of this? It is that people live as though they would live forever. You never remember your human frailty; you never notice how much of your time has already gone by. You spend it as though you had an abundant and overflowing store of it, though all the while that day which you devote to some man or to some thing is perhaps your last. You fear everything, like mortals as you are, and yet you desire everything as if you were immortals. You will hear many men say, "After my fiftieth year I will give myself up to leisure; my sixtieth shall be my last year of public office." And what guarantee have you that your life will last any longer? Who will let all this go on just as you have arranged it? Are you not ashamed to reserve only the leavings of your life for yourself, and appoint for the enjoyment of your own right mind only that time which you cannot devote to any business? How late it is to begin life just when we have to be leaving it! What a foolish forgetfulness of our mortality, to put off wholesome counsels until our fiftieth or sixtieth year, and to choose that our lives shall begin at a point which few of us ever reach.

. . .

Finally, all are agreed that nothing, neither eloquence nor literature, can be done properly by one who is occupied with something else; for nothing can take deep root in a mind which is directed to some other subject, and which rejects whatever you try to stuff into it. No man knows less about living than a business man: there is nothing about which it is more difficult to gain knowledge. Other arts have many folk everywhere who profess to teach them. Some of them can be so thoroughly learned by mere boys, that they are able to teach them to others. But one's whole life must be spent in learning how to live, and, which may perhaps surprise you more, one's whole life must be spent in learning how to die. Many excellent men have freed themselves from all hindrances, have given up riches, business, and pleasure, and have made it their duty to the very end of their lives to learn how to live. And yet the larger portion of them leave this life confessing that they do not yet know how to live, and still less know how to live as wise men. Believe me, it requires a great man and one who is superior to human frailties not to allow any of his time to be filched from him. And therefore it follows that his life is a very long one, because he devotes every possible part of it to himself; no portion lies idle or uncultivated or in another man's power, for he finds nothing worthy of being exchanged for his time, which he husbands most grudgingly. He, therefore, had time enough, whereas those who gave up a great part of their lives to the people of necessity had not enough.

. . .

Life is divided into three parts: that which has been, that which is, and that which is to come. Of these three stages, that which we are passing through is brief, that which we are about to pass is uncertain, and that which we have passed is certain. This it is over which Fortune has lost her rights, and which can fall into no other man's power. And this is what busy men lose, for they have no leisure to look back upon the past, and even if they had, they take no pleasure in remembering what they regret. They are, therefore, unwilling to turn their minds to the contemplation of ill-spent time, and they shrink from reviewing a course of action whose faults become glaringly apparent when handled a second time, although they were snatched at when we were under the spell of immediate gratification. No one, unless all his acts have been submitted to the infallible censorship of his own conscience, willingly turns his thoughts back upon the past. He who has ambitiously desired, haughtily scorned, passionately vanquished, treacherously deceived, greedily snatched, or prodigally wasted much, must needs fear his own memory. Yet this is a holy and consecrated part of our time, beyond the reach of all human accidents, removed from the dominion of Fortune, and which cannot be disquieted by want, fear, or attacks of sickness. This can neither be troubled nor taken away from one: we possess it forever undisturbed. Our present consists only of single days, and those, too, taken one hour at a time, but all the days of past times appear before us when bidden, and allow themselves to be examined and lingered over, albeit busy men cannot find time for so doing. It is the privilege of a tranquil and peaceful mind to review all the parts of its life, but the minds of busy men are like animals under the yoke, and cannot bend aside or look back. Consequently, their life passes away into vacancy, and as you do no good however much you may pour into a vessel which cannot keep or hold what you put there, so also it matters not how much time you give men if it can find no place to settle in, but leaks away through the chinks and holes of their minds. Present time is very short, so much so that to some it seems to be no time at all; for it is always in motion, and runs swiftly away. It ceases to exist before it comes, and can no more brook delay than can the universe or the host of heaven, whose unresting movement never lets them pause on their way. Busy men, therefore, possess present time, alone, that being so short that they cannot grasp it, and when they are occupied with many things they lose even this.

. . .

The only persons who are really at leisure are those who devote themselves to philosophy. They alone really live, for they do not merely enjoy their own lifetime, but they annex every century to their own. All the years which have passed before them belong to them. Unless we are the most ungrateful creatures in the world, we shall regard these noblest of men, the founders of divine schools of thought, as having been born for us, and having prepared life for us. We are led by the labor of others to behold most beautiful things which have been brought out of darkness into light. We are not shut out from any period. We can make our way into every subject, and, if only we can summon up sufficient strength of mind to overstep the narrow limit of human weakness, we have a vast extent of time wherein to disport ourselves. We may argue with Socrates, doubt with Carneades, repose with Epicurus, overcome human nature with the Stoics, outherod [outdo or surpass] it with the Cynics. Since Nature allows us to commune with every age, why do we not abstract ourselves from our own petty fleeting span of time, and give ourselves up with our whole mind to what is vast, what is eternal, what we share with better men than ourselves? Those who gad about in a round of calls, who worry themselves and others, after they have indulged their madness to the full, and crossed every patron's threshold daily, leaving no open door unentered, after they have hawked about their interested greetings in houses of the most various character: after all, how few people are they able to see out of so vast a city, divided among so many different ruling passions? How many will be moved by sloth, self-indulgence, or rudeness to deny them admittance? How many, after they have long plagued them, will run past them with feigned hurry? How many will avoid coming out through their entrance hall with its crowds of clients, and will escape by some concealed backdoor? As though it were not ruder to deceive their visitor than to deny him admittance! How many, half asleep and stupid with yesterday's debauch, can hardly be brought to return the greeting of the wretched man who has broken his own rest in order to wait on that of another, even after his name has been whispered to them for the thousandth time, save by a most offensive yawn of his half-opened lips? We may truly say that those men are pursuing the true path of duty, who wish every day to consort on the most familiar terms with Zeno, Pythagoras, Democritus, and the rest of those high priests of virtue, with Aristotle and with Theophrastus. None of these men will be "engaged"; none of these will fail to send you away after visiting him in a happier frame of mind and on better terms with yourself; none of them will let you leave him empty-handed. Yet their society may be enjoyed by all men, and by night as well as by day.

None of these men will force you to die, but all of them will teach you how to die. None of these will waste your time, but will add his own to it. The talk of these men is not dangerous, their friendship will not lead you to the scaffold; their society will not ruin you in expenses. You may take from them whatsoever you will; they will not prevent your taking the deepest draughts of their wisdom that you please. What blessedness, what a fair old age awaits the man who takes these for his patrons! He will have friends with whom he may discuss all matters, great and small, whose advice he may ask daily about himself, from whom he will hear truth without insult, praise without flattery, and according to whose likeness he may model his own character.

Discussion Questions

1. Seneca points out that not only vices but also good things, like positions of leadership and influence, steal away our time. What are some of the greatest distractions of our age?
2. Do you see yourself in Seneca's descriptions?
3. Seneca admonishes Paulinus to be stingy with his time. Is that consistent with the Christian ethic of love, which gives to others sacrificially?
4. Seneca thinks that some of the problems of time are overcome—or at least ameliorated—by reflection on the past. What implications, if any, does this have for learning?

5. Seneca calls these thinkers of the past our "betters." Is that a helpful way to think about engaging the past?

6. If Seneca is right, a grave danger facing college students is that they skitter through four years trying to pour knowledge into a leaky sieve of a mind. What habits and practices might help you absorb knowledge and be truly transformed in the pursuit of wisdom?

CHAPTER 5

Athanasius

Introduction to *On the Incarnation*

ADAM J. JOHNSON

While the title of Athanasius's little book is *On the Incarnation*, the question he was asking was "Why the incarnation?" Why did God become human? As you read this excerpt from his book, much will seem familiar to you. But the angels are in the details, for Athanasius invited readers to think about the incarnation and work of Jesus in terms that are refreshingly different from what we hear in contemporary theology.

The differences begin with how we understand sin. While Athanasius was quite comfortable talking about our guilt and the punishment we deserve, in this passage he described our plight as being utterly destitute in our ignorance. Sin doesn't just make us guilty—it reverses the creative project of God, pulling us back down among the ignorant beasts, only worse.

But the problem isn't just ours. In fact, Athanasius made the surprising move of describing human sin as God's problem! While a castle might not want to fall into ruin, the one who is truly dismayed by this, of course, is the king who built the castle. Athanasius thought that it would be unworthy of God to stand by, letting human beings be deceived by the demons and becoming increasingly ignorant of God. There would be no profit or glory to God corresponding to his effort and purpose in creating. To be sure, Athanasius wasn't excusing us from sin, but he was inviting us to think about it in terms of a bigger picture. Creation isn't just about creatures; it is about the Creator. And it would be supremely unworthy of the goodness of God to make creatures that know and love him, only to have those creatures fail and collapse into ignorance and the death it brings.

And this takes us to the dilemma: How can God be supremely consistent to himself while relating to a fallen creation? Athanasius's answer, in short, was that God became man in order that man might become divine and participate in God. God took upon himself the corruption of fallen creation in the death of Jesus so we might be remade in the image of God. We are remade in the Son of God—remade by knowing him.

This line of thought bears profound implications for learning. We were meant to know God, to walk with him—and by knowing God to know all things in relation to him. Yet we, in our pride and folly, turned away toward ignorance and blindness. What was God to do with these blind and foolish creatures? How was he to be supremely consistent with his goal of inviting us into his life to know and love him? God became man that he might suffer the folly of our ignorance and that we might know him. All education, all learning, and all the power of knowledge are but a glimpse into the purpose for which we were created: to know and love God and all things in him. And it was for this that God became man.

From *On the Incarnation*

(11) When God the Almighty was making mankind through His own Word, He perceived that they, owing to the limitation of their nature, could not of themselves have any knowledge of their Artificer, the Incorporeal and Uncreated. He took pity on them, therefore, and did not leave them destitute of the knowledge of Himself, lest their very existence should prove purposeless. For of what use is existence to the creature if it cannot know its Maker? How could men be reasonable beings if they had no knowledge of the Word and Reason of the Father, through Whom they had received their being? They would be no better than the beasts, had they no knowledge save of earthly things; and why should God have made them at all, if He had not intended them to know Him? But, in fact, the good God has given them a share in His own Image, that is, in our Lord Jesus Christ, and has made even themselves after the same Image and Likeness. Why? Simply in order that through this gift of Godlikeness in themselves they may be able to perceive the Image Absolute, that is the Word Himself, and through Him to apprehend the Father; which knowledge of their Maker is for men the only really happy and blessed life.

But, as we have already seen, men, foolish as they are, thought little of the grace they had received, and turned away from God. They defiled their own soul so completely that they not only lost their apprehension of God, but invented for themselves other gods of various kinds. They fashioned idols for themselves in place of the truth and reverenced things that are not, rather than God Who is, as St. Paul says, "worshipping the creature rather than the Creator." Moreover, and much worse, they transferred the honor which is due to God to material objects such as wood and stone, and also to man; and further even than that they went, as we said in our former book. Indeed, so impious were they that they worshipped evil spirits as gods in satisfaction of their lusts. They sacrificed brute beasts and immolated men, as the just due of these deities, thereby bringing themselves more and more under their insane control. Magic arts also were taught among them, oracles in sundry places led men astray, and the cause of everything in human life was traced to the stars as though nothing existed but that which could be seen. In a word, impiety and lawlessness were everywhere, and neither God nor His Word was known. Yet He had not hidden Himself from the sight of men nor given the knowledge of Himself in one way only; but rather He had unfolded it in many forms and by many ways.

(12) God knew the limitation of mankind, you see; and though the grace of being made in His Image was sufficient to give them knowledge of the Word and through Him of the Father, as a safeguard against their neglect of this grace, He provided the works of creation also as means by which the Maker might be known. Nor was this all. Man's neglect of the indwelling grace tends ever to increase; and against this further frailty also God made provision by giving them a law, and by sending prophets, men whom they knew. Thus, if they were tardy in looking up to heaven, they might still gain knowledge of their Maker from those close at hand; for men can learn directly about higher things from other men. Three ways thus lay open to them, by which they might obtain the knowledge of God. They could look up into the immensity of heaven, and by pondering the harmony of creation come to know its Ruler, the Word of the Father, Whose all-ruling providence makes known the Father to all. Or, if this was beyond them, they could converse with holy men, and through them learn to know God, the Artificer of all things, the Father of Christ, and to recognize the worship of idols as the negation of the truth and full of all impiety. Or else, in the third place, they could cease from lukewarmness and lead a good life merely by knowing the law. For the law was not given only for the Jews, nor was it solely for their sake that God sent the prophets, though it was to the Jews that they were sent and by the Jews that they were persecuted. The law and the prophets were a sacred school of the knowledge of God and the conduct of the spiritual life for the whole world.

So great, indeed, were the goodness and the love of God. Yet men, bowed down by the pleasures of the moment and by the frauds and illusions of the evil spirits, did not lift up their heads towards the truth. So burdened were they with their wickednesses that they seemed rather to be brute beasts than reasonable men, reflecting the very Likeness of the Word.

(13) What was God to do in face of this dehumanising of mankind, this universal hiding of the knowledge of Himself by the wiles of evil spirits? Was He to keep silence before so great a wrong and let men go on being thus deceived and kept in ignorance of Himself? If so, what was the use of having made them in His own Image originally? It would surely have been better for them always to have been brutes, rather than to revert to that condition when once they had

shared the nature of the Word. Again, things being as they were, what was the use of their ever having had the knowledge of God? Surely it would have been better for God never to have bestowed it, than that men should subsequently be found unworthy to receive it. Similarly, what possible profit could it be to God Himself, Who made men, if when made they did not worship Him, but regarded others as their makers? This would be tantamount to His having made them for others and not for Himself. Even an earthly king, though he is only a man, does not allow lands that he has colonized to pass into other hands or to desert to other rulers, but sends letters and friends and even visits them himself to recall them to their allegiance, rather than allow his work to be undone. How much more, then, will God be patient and painstaking with His creatures, that they be not led astray from Him to the service of those that are not, and that all the more because such error means for them sheer ruin, and because it is not right that those who had once shared His Image should be destroyed.

What, then, was God to do? What else could He possibly do, being God, but renew His Image in mankind, so that through it men might once more come to know Him? And how could this be done save by the coming of the very Image Himself, our Savior Jesus Christ? Men could not have done it, for they are only made after the Image; nor could angels have done it, for they are not the images of God. The Word of God came in His own Person, because it was He alone, the Image of the Father Who could recreate man made after the Image.

In order to effect this re-creation, however, He had first to do away with death and corruption. Therefore He assumed a human body, in order that in it death might once for all be destroyed, and that men might be renewed according to the Image. The Image of the Father only was sufficient for this need. Here is an illustration to prove it.

(14) You know what happens when a portrait that has been painted on a panel becomes obliterated through external stains. The artist does not throw away the panel, but the subject of the portrait has to come and sit for it again, and then the likeness is re-drawn on the same material. Even so was it with the All-holy Son of God. He, the Image of the Father, came and dwelt in our midst, in order that He might renew mankind made after Himself, and seek out His lost sheep, even as He says in the Gospel: "I came to seek and to save that which was lost." This also explains His saying to the Jews: *"Except a man be born anew . . ."* He was not referring to a man's natural birth from his mother, as they thought, but to the re-birth and re-creation of the soul in the Image of God.

Nor was this the only thing which only the Word could do. When the madness of idolatry and irreligion filled the world and the knowledge of God was hidden, whose part was it to teach the world about the Father? Man's, would you say? But men cannot run everywhere over the world, nor would their words carry sufficient weight if they did, nor would they be, unaided, a match for the evil spirits. Moreover, since even the best of men were confused and blinded by evil, how could they convert the souls and minds of others? You cannot put straight in others what is warped in yourself. Perhaps you will say, then, that creation was enough to teach men about the Father. But if that had been so, such great evils would never have occurred. Creation was there all the time, but it did not prevent men from wallowing in error. Once more, then, it was the Word of God, Who sees all that is in man and moves all things in creation, Who alone could meet the needs of the situation. It was His part and His alone, Whose ordering of the universe reveals the Father, to renew the same teaching. But how was He to do it? By the same means as before, perhaps you will say, that is, through the works of creation. But this was proven insufficient. Men had neglected to consider the heavens before, and now they were looking in the opposite direction. Wherefore, in all naturalness and fitness, desiring to do good to men, as Man He dwells, taking to Himself a body like the rest; and through His actions done in that body, as it were on their own level, He teaches those who would not learn by other means to know Himself, the Word of God, and through Him the Father.

(15) He deals with them as a good teacher with his pupils, coming down to their level and using simple means. St. Paul says as much: "Because in the wisdom of God the world in its wisdom knew not God, God thought fit through the simplicity of the News proclaimed to save those who believe." Men had turned from the contemplation of God above, and were looking for Him in the opposite direction, down among created things and things of sense. The Savior of us all, the Word of God, in His great love took to Himself a body and moved as Man among men, meeting their senses, so to speak, half way. He became Himself an object for the senses, so that those who were seeking God in sensible things might apprehend the Father through the works which He, the Word of God, did in the body. Human and human minded as men were, therefore, to whichever side they looked in the sensible world they found themselves taught the truth. Were they awe-stricken by creation? They beheld it confessing Christ as Lord. Did their minds tend to regard men as Gods? The uniqueness of the Savior's works marked Him, alone of men, as Son of God. Were they drawn to evil spirits? They saw them driven out by the Lord and learned that the Word of God alone was God and that the evil spirits were not gods at all. Were they inclined to hero-worship and the cult of the dead? Then the fact that the Savior

had risen from the dead showed them how false these other deities were, and that the Word of the Father is the one true Lord, the Lord even of death. For this reason was He both born and manifested as Man, for this He died and rose, in order that, eclipsing by His works all other human deeds, He might recall men from all the paths of error to know the Father. As He says Himself, "I came to seek and to save that which was lost."

(16) When, then, the minds of men had fallen finally to the level of sensible things, the Word submitted to appear in a body, in order that He, as Man, might center their senses on Himself, and convince them through His human acts that He Himself is not man only but also God, the Word and Wisdom of the true God. This is what Paul wants to tell us when he says: "That ye, being rooted and grounded in love, may be strong to apprehend with all the saints what is the length and breadth and height and depth, and to know the love of God that surpasses knowledge, so that ye may be filled unto all the fullness of God." The Self-revealing of the Word is in every dimension—above, in creation; below, in the Incarnation; in the depth, in Hades; in the breadth, throughout the world. All things have been filled with the knowledge of God.

For this reason He did not offer the sacrifice on behalf of all immediately He came, for if He had surrendered His body to death and then raised it again at once He would have ceased to be an object of our senses. Instead of that, He stayed in His body and let Himself be seen in it, doing acts and giving signs which showed Him to be not only man, but also God the Word. There were thus two things which the Savior did for us by becoming Man. He banished death from us and made us anew; and, invisible and imperceptible as in Himself He is, He became visible through His works and revealed Himself as the Word of the Father, the Ruler and King of the whole creation.

Discussion Questions

1. Athanasius's insight revolves around God's unparalleled consistency to both himself and to creation. What are some of the factors Athanasius mentions (and others that you can come up with) with which God is consistent—in both his character and the nature of creation?

2. Sin is certainly a matter of our disobedience and guilt before a just God. But it is more than that. What are some of the other ways Athanasius invites us to think about our sin, and how do they change our view of ourselves and of God?

3. What changes when we think about the atonement not merely in terms of our sin and guilt but in terms of God as a craftsman bringing his project to completion?

4. Central for Athanasius is a vision of God as incorruptible. What would it mean for us to share in God's incorruptibility? What would life be like, physically, emotionally, mentally, and spiritually?

5. Based on this passage, what are some insights or questions that emerge for a Christian understanding of creation care? (Remember that it is key for Athanasius not merely that God loves his creation but that he must also be consistent with himself.)

CHAPTER 6

Gregory of Nazianzus

Introduction to *On My Own Verses*

PHILIP IRVING MITCHELL

Both a theologian and a literary artist, Gregory of Nazianzus (c. 329–389/90) is remembered today as one of the Cappadocian fathers, the three great theological writers who helped defend and clarify the doctrines of the Trinity and of Christ's divinity and humanity. Gregory was also an elegant Greek stylist and a riveting orator. His public sermons and speeches, as well as his poetry, reveal someone who carefully crafted his words, and he is justly remembered as one of the most talented writers of his time. Gregory's commitment to literature made him part of the Theodosian revival, a fourth-century movement among Christian educators, writers, and intellectuals that sought to develop an authentic and classically sensitive alternative curriculum for Christian students.

Gregory was part of the first generation to grow up in a Roman Empire in which Christianity was legal and even encouraged, but that position was still far from assured. When the emperor Julian "the Apostate" rejected a Christian upbringing and turned to Neoplatonic philosophy, he made a number of moves to force Christians back out of the public square. Julian posed a particular threat to Christians in education. In an edict of 362, the emperor made it impossible for them to teach in the classic academies or to employ traditional non-Christian texts, claiming such works should only be taught by those who believed them. Though Julian died in battle shortly after issuing this edict, it was a wake-up call for educated Christians. They committed themselves to expanding Greek and Latin texts along Christian themes, as well as showing their facility with classical allusions and style.

Written in the last few years of Gregory's life after his official retirement, *On My Own Verses* was one of a number of poems he wrote to defend his legacy as an intellectual, as a rhetorician, and as a bishop. It was also his way of modeling serious Christian literature. Throughout the poem, he assumes the ideal of the Christian philosopher, one who gives himself to study and contemplation with the goal of the wise life. Such an existence is calm, ordered, and focused on the higher truths of God, as well as on the true, the good, and the beautiful. Gregory's defense of poetry, then, was also a defense of education as Christian formation.

47

On My Own Verses confronts us with important questions: What makes our art and literature Christian? And what role does Christian truth play in engaging books written by those outside the faith? Gregory asks us to examine our motives to see whether, in our speaking and writing, we are concerned with delighting in the truth. He holds that we have a responsibility to set for ourselves a high standard because well-written poetry or prose can reach people at the level of their imaginations. It can also shape us as students who love the goodness and beauty of classic texts. As you read the poem, note for yourself how Gregory keeps in view the noble purposes of his verse—contemplation of truth, joy in goodness, and skill in language.

An Apologetic for Poetry (*On My Own Verses*)
TRANSLATED BY PHILIP IRVING MITCHELL

Beholding many in the modern age who write
Unmetrical words that gush forth without effort,
Yet who, time after time, are constantly worn down,
From which there is no gain except empty gossip;
Yes, they are writing on like a great despot   5
Things that happen to be stuffed with all kinds of nonsense,
Mostly sand of the seas or Egypt's gnawing swarms—
Indeed, to you I offer this most pleasant proverb:
Hurl away every single word; deliver these up;
We should only hold to God's inspirited ones,   10
As those who flee the swell seek out calm anchor.
For if the Scriptures grant such a wealth of firm places,
Spirit, this course is from you—the wisest poetic,
That which is a stimulating defense for all
Against empty words from evil intended deeds.   15

When you write, against your dark-nether perceptions,
Do you set out fully reasons beyond dispute?
Yet since this is by far easier said than done,
The world has shattered into scores of divorcing schools,
Each one with support for its own private escape;   20
In my writing I have led down this other path—
(Another which I've searched; I reckon, at any rate,
A good one, or at least for me, one beloved)
To offer up some part of my hardships in verse.
Not as many of the living might suppose suspecting   25

All too easily that I'm cultivating fame—
A void, as they suggest. No, it's just the reverse;
I know only too well those who hunt down my words
For their own public approval, since most line out
By their own plumb-line and by those nearby at hand;   30
It's not because I worship my works above God's.
Could God's word ever be less than any such prizing?
Perhaps I've yet to suit your curiosity:
First off, strongly I willed through other hard jobs
To keep control of my own ill-measured excess;   35
So that in writing, I might not write out too much,
Laboring with my measure. Second, for the young
(Above all to those who delight in well-planned words)
To provide a lovely remedy for the ear,
Persuasion leading them on to useful matters,   40
Skill sweetening the sharp-piercing injunctions.
Consider, the lyre-string enjoys being loosened some,
As you might wish to do, if for nothing more than
As an alternative to songs and lyre-strumming.
I serve this up for you to play, if you care to play   45
In a way that never stops your way to good-beauty.
Third, I own up—though this reason may seem rather
Shabby of me—to my motive that I cannot
Concede that those alien should best us in words;
I speak of these, their strained-showy-defiling words,   50
Since for us, the good is seen in contemplation.
So for you, wise ones, we have brought forth this pastime.
Admit to me the grace of the lion-hearted.
Fourth, I have found when burdened under sickness,
These to be a fit portent, as an ancient swan,   55
My vocalise for myself upon whispering wings,
Not in threnody, but as a hymn of departure.

Finally, you wise ones, you may now apprehend
What lies in myself. Yet if you yield bested, reason
Was your superlative need, for words are just playthings   60
For champions. Still, nothing here's lengthy or too filling,
Nor unprofitable, as I myself am convinced.
The words can disciple if you cooperate.

Some of them are mine and some are others';
Some commend nobility, others condemn faults;   65
Some dogma, some instruction, some sharpened speech;
They encourage memory by tightly bound word-choice.
If they seem ineffective, create something better.

You critique the meter? No wonder, unmetered man,
Iambic-hack writer, you abortive scribbler.   70
What blinded person can make out the one with sight?
What novice runner can pace with a thoroughbred?
Hold on. You can't pocket what you pay to hush up,
And then critique, what you black-market by yourself—
Scribbled verse, and that wholly disjointed doggerel.   75
Whatever piece he disdains, trust demands an encore,
Yet we see, the prosaic sweetie has sunk our show.
You wise ones, go cunningly craft such stuff yourself;
Is it not clearly deception, a confidence trick?
He displays for us an ape; now, it's a lion.   80
Thus, we are taken in and fall for desired fame.

Learn this above all, that Scripture has many poems,
which the wise sages of Hebrew descent do speak;
If the sounds from their strings don't strike us as metered,
As the ancients' tradition tuned concordant words,   85
Bringing forth, I hold, by a well-crafted support
The noble, and by melodic impress a right course,
Then Saul may persuade you, since from the spirit he
Was freed by the manner of the plectored kinnor.

Do you really think there is danger for the young   90
To be brought to fellowship with God by grand things?
Since they cannot bear up under demanding change,
For now, they'll require a more high-class mixture.
It's fitting that in time they have a hold on the good,
Then we'll take down their vaulting supports so that like   95
An arch they may retain their sound construction.
What could produce a more serviceable result?
Do you not yourself put some sweet tastes in your food,
You solemn sourpuss with furrowed meeting eyebrows?

Why then critique my metrical ability,   100
Others' meters measured out by your foundations?
Far separate are the Mysian and Phrygian borders.
Far separate in height the nests of eagles and crows.

Discussion Questions

1. How does Gregory defend his own motives for writing beautiful verse, as well as the writing and study of poetry for Christians?
2. Does Gregory's use of insults fit the overall message of the poem? Why does he include them?
3. How can Scripture, especially the Psalms, be an example for good writing?
4. What are some ways you can make your own writing less like a crow and more like an eagle?

CHAPTER 7

Augustine of Hippo

Introduction to *On the Teacher*

J. L. AIJIAN

What's the difference between believing something you've been told and knowing something because you've come to understand it yourself? This is the question Augustine is investigating in *On the Teacher*, a dialogue with his son, Adeodatus. They begin by talking about the nature of words. How do we come to understand the meaning of words? This actually turns out to be a thorny problem. If I want to teach you the meaning of the word *flumph*, how do I do it? Let's say *flumph* is another word for a cup. If you knew the word *cup* already, this would be easy; I would simply tell you *flumph* meant "cup." But that doesn't solve the problem, because to learn one sign by another sign, we already have to know some signs. How did we learn those? Augustine and Adeodatus conclude that we must begin by knowing *things* before we can know the meaning of words. If I want to teach you what a flumph is, I should point to a cup and say "flumph." Your experience of the thing will teach you the meaning of the word.

This process of learning signs by way of things works pretty well with physical objects we can point to, although problems still remain. What if you thought I was pointing to the coffee in the cup? Or the color of the cup? What if you decided that *flumph* meant "cylinder" or "ceramic"? But the problems get worse as we think about signs of things to which we can't point and of which we may not have any direct experience. How do you explain a word like *justice*, for instance? Not only is justice an idea rather than a physical object, but it's arguably an idea we have never seen perfectly enacted on earth. How can I even come up with an idea for justice if I've never seen it? How can I learn the meaning of the word *justice* if no one can point to it and teach me its name?

If Plato were answering this question, he would say that the way we learn about these perfect, nonmaterial ideas is that our preexistent souls *did* see them before we were given bodies. When we think about ideal realities like justice (or a perfect circle), we're not learning these ideas in the present; we're remembering what we already knew. This is why good questions help us to come to the answers ourselves, instead of just telling us what to think, and when an idea is explained to us well, it rings true for us. We're not just believing on someone else's authority; true understanding comes with a sense that, "Of course, I've always known that."

Augustine thought Plato was on the right track here. There is a problem that needs explaining: How do I just seem to know what true justice, true love, or even a perfect circle ought to be like, even though I've never seen them? However, as a Christian, he couldn't argue that we get this knowledge from our preexistent souls' experiences in the land of ideas. Instead, Augustine thought of John 1. In the beginning was Christ, the Word (*logos*), the eternal truth of God. Because each of us has a rational soul (another meaning for the same Greek word, *logos*), we literally have Christ within us as our Teacher. If we come to a question with genuine willingness to be wrong and to discover the Truth, we will find that it (He) is within us, ready to guide us aright.

From *On the Teacher*
TRANSLATED BY FRANCIS E. TOURSCHER, OSA
VILLANOVA COLLEGE, VILLANOVA, PENNSYLVANIA, 1924
Chapters 11–14 (excerpted)

So far words have value (to give them their very most): they remind us only to look for realities, they do not so exhibit the realities that we know them. But that one teaches me something, who holds out to my eyes, or to any one of the senses of the body, or even to the mind the things which I desire to know. By means of words, therefore, we learn only words: more still, only the sound and noise of words. For if those things which are not signs cannot be words; though a word may be heard, I yet do not know that it is a word until I know its signification. By means, therefore, of realities known, the knowledge of words also is made perfect: but by means of words heard, words are not learned; for we do not learn words that we know; nor can we say that we have learned words, which we did not know, except by getting their meaning, which is, not by the hearing of sounds sent forth, but by the knowledge of realities signified. For it is the truest reason, and most truly said, that when words are uttered, we either know their meaning, or we do not: if we know, then we are said to be recalling rather than learning; but if we know not the meaning, then we are said not even to be recalling, but possibly we are moved to inquire. . . .

But, referring now to all things that we understand, we consult, not the one speaking, whose words sound without, but truth within, presiding over the mind, reminded perhaps by words to take note (to mark evidence). But he teaches who is consulted, Christ, who is said to "dwell in the interior man": that is, the changeless power of God, and the everlasting wisdom, which truly every rational soul consults: but so far is it opened out to each one, as each one is capable to grasp by reason of a good or a bad habit of life. And, if sometimes errors are made, that is not by reason of fault in the objective evidence consulted; just as it is also not the fault of this light, which is bright without, that the eyes of the body are frequently deceived: This light (external) we acknowledge is sought in reference to things visible in order that it may show us visible objects so far as we have the power to discern.

But, if we consult the light in reference to colors and the other properties which we perceive through the body; if we consult the elements of this world, the same also corporeal, the objects of our senses; if we consult the organic senses themselves, which the mind uses as interpreters to know such things; and, if in reference to those things that we understand, we consult interior evidence, what can be said to have it made clear that by means of words we learn nothing but the sound that strikes the ear? And indeed everything that we perceive, we perceive either by a corporeal organ of sense, or by the power of the mind. These former are the object of the senses, the latter of understanding: or, to speak after the manner of our own (Christian) authors, We give the name carnal to the former, spiritual to the latter.

When we are questioned concerning these former, we answer what we perceive if they are present: as when we are questioned looking at the new moon as to its size and position. Here he who asks, if he does not see the moon, believes our words, and often he believes not: but he does not learn at all, unless he himself sees what is described. Here now he learns, not by means of the words which are sounded, but by means of objective reality and his own senses. For the same words sound to one seeing, as they also sounded to him not seeing. But when there is question, not about things which we perceive present, but about what we have formerly perceived, we speak then, not of things themselves, but of images impressed by them and stored in the memory. As to these, how we can utter them truly, if we do not behold them as true, I do not know, except that we tell or recount, not what we see or perceive, but what we have seen or have perceived. Thus do we carry in the inner courts of memory those images, documents of things perceived before. Contemplating these in mind we utter no falsehood when we speak in good conscience. But these documents are for us; for he who hears us (telling of past experience), if he has perceived the facts that I tell, and if he was present, does not learn by my words; but he recalls by means of the impressions which he has taken away of the same facts; but if he did not himself experience what I tell, who does not see that such a one learns not but rather believes my words?

But when there is question of those things which we view in the mind, that is, by means of understanding and reason, we speak truly the things which we behold as present in interior light of truth, by which he who is called the interior man is enlightened, whence also comes his joy. But then also our hearer, if he himself sees those things with the simple and unseen eye, knows what I say, not by means of my words, but by his own judgment—the vision of his own mind. Therefore I, speaking what is true, do not teach even this one viewing the same true things in his own mind; for he is taught, not by means of my words, but by means of the same mental realities which God, by the natural light of intelligence opens out within the soul: whence, if questioned, he might have answered the very same.

But what is more unreasonable than to think that he is taught by my speech, who, if he were questioned before I spoke, could have answered the very same? For, it frequently happens, being questioned, someone answers in the negative, and then when he is urged by other questions, replies affirmatively. That is done by reason of the weakness of the one who seeing cannot consult this light on the entire problem. He is reminded to do this in particular points, when he is questioned upon them one by one. The very same which he cannot do in the entire problem, he can discern in the parts of which the whole is made up, whereto, he is directed by the words of the one who questions, not yet by teaching words, but by words inquiring in that measure in which he who is questioned is within, in the inner powers of the soul, fit to learn. Just as, when I was asking this very question on which we are now engaged: whether or not nothing can be taught by means of words, and first it seemed to you unreasonable, because you were unable to see clearly the whole problem. So, therefore, should I have placed my questions as to make them correspond to the powers of your mind to hear that master teaching within. Thus I would express what you acknowledge to be true while I am talking: and you are sure, and you affirm that you know these things. Whence did you learn them? You might say, perhaps, that I taught them. Then I would reply: What if I were to say that I had seen a man flying? Would my words so then make you secure as if you were to hear it said that men of understanding are better than fools? You would answer in the negative surely; and you might reply that you do not believe the former; or, even though you were to believe, that you know nothing about it; but this latter, you would say you know most surely. From this now, by way of example, you would understand that you have not learned anything by means of my words: not in that, about which, after my stating it, you remained in ignorance (the flying exploit), and not in that which you knew very well (the relative worth of reasoning men and fools). And indeed, even though you were to be questioned about each one of these points, you could take an oath that that is unknown, that this is well known to you.

Then, in truth, would you acknowledge all that you had formerly denied, when you knew, as points clear and certain, the elements of which all that is made up: namely that all things that we speak stand in one of three relations to our hearers: either the hearer knows not whether or not they are true, or he knows that they are untrue, or he knows that they are true. In the first case of these three he will either believe (take on trust) or he will form an opinion, or he will hesitate. In the second case he will either take a stand against what is said, or he will reject it. In the third he simply witnesses to what has been said (confirming its truth). In no case of these three, therefore, does he learn. For he who, after hearing our words, still remains ignorant as to their objective meaning; as he also, who knows that what he has heard is untrue; and he again who could have expressed the very same thought, if he had been asked, is proved surely to have learned nothing by means of my words.

From the foregoing it follows, therefore, that in the things which are discerned by the mind, one who cannot grasp that which the mind of the speaker discerns, hears his words to no purpose, excepting the case where it is practicable to take a thing on trust so long as it cannot be known. But he (in this division of realities of the mind) who sees clearly what words mean, is, in the court of the mind, a disciple of the truth; in the world of external things, he is the judge of the one who speaks, or more properly of his speech. Not unfrequently indeed the hearer knows what has been said, while the speaker may perhaps not know the force of his own words. As where someone who follows the Epicurean school of philosophy, and who believes that the human soul is mortal, may express those very reasons by which more far-seeing thinkers have proved its immortality. He hearing, who can judge things spiritual, thinks that such a one has uttered valid arguments: but he who speaks them knows not that they are true; even though he thinks that they are quite untrue. Is he, therefore, to be thought of as teaching what he does not know? But he uses the very same words, which one who knows could also use. Wherefore now not even this is left to words, that by them the mind of the speaker at least is made manifest, since it is not certain whether he knows what he is talking about. . . . But now I go back and I grant that when words are perceived by the hearing of one who knows their meaning, he may be assured that the speaker has been thinking of those realities which the words signify: does it follow from this the point which we are studying here that he learns also whether or not the speaker has uttered the truth?

Do teachers make the claim that their own thoughts, and not rather the branches of learning which they think they deliver by talking, are perceived and retained by pupils? Who, indeed, is so unreasonably careful as to send his child to school to learn what the teacher thinks? But all these branches of learning, which teachers profess to teach, the doctrine of virtue even and of wisdom itself, when they have explained them by means of words; then they who are called pupils, consider in the inner court of the mind whether what has been said is true, that is, in the measure of their own mental power they see the agreement that is within. Then, therefore, they learn; and when they find within that true things have been spoken, they applaud, not knowing that their applause belongs rather to those who are taught than to their teachers: if, indeed, the teachers know what they are talking about. But men are deceived, so that they call those teachers, who are not teachers at all, just because generally no pause intervenes between the time of speaking and the time of thinking: and because after the suggestion of the one who speaks they learn instantaneously within, they think that they have learned from him who spoke from without.

But what the full advantage is of words, not a small advantage indeed, if it is rightly viewed, we shall study, if God so grants, elsewhere. For the present I have brought to your notice that we must not give to words more than belongs to them. So that now we may not only believe, but we may begin to understand also how truly the word is written on divine authority that we claim no one as our master on earth, because one is the Master of all in heaven. But what the meaning is of this "in heaven," He will teach us, by whom we are reminded through the instrumentality of men, by means of word symbols, and from without, so that turned to Him within, we may become learned in the inner life of the soul. He will teach us, to love whom and to know whom is itself the happiness of life; that happiness which all men declare that they seek; but few have rejoiced in finding it. But now I want you to tell me what you think of this whole explanation of mine. For if you have approved all that has been said as true, then you might have answered on every sentence, one by one, that you know it, if you had been questioned. You see, therefore, from whom you have learned these points. Surely not from me, to whom you could have given the correct answer in every point, if I had asked. But if you have not known these things to be true, then neither do I teach you, nor he (the inner man, the judgment of reason from within): but I do not teach, because I never can teach; he does not teach, because you as yet are incapable of learning.

But I have learned by the admonition of your words that by the means of words a man can do no more than be admonished to learn; and that it is very little, indeed, some little fraction only of the thought of the one who speaks that is made apparent by the means of his language. But whether the things that are spoken are true or not, I have learned that he alone can teach who dwells within, who reminds us that he is dwelling within, when words are spoken without. This same dweller within I shall now, by his own favor, love the more ardently as I advance in knowing him better.

Discussion Questions

1. Think back to a moment when you came to understand a new concept. How would you describe the change between hearing someone talk about an idea before you understood it and hearing them talk about it after you understood?
2. What's the difference between learning and remembering? Which of these two words do you think best describes coming to understand a new idea?
3. If humans are made by the same person who created the world, how might we expect that to impact how we can learn and make discoveries about the world?
4. Does it take faith to learn? Why or why not?

CHAPTER 8

Augustine of Hippo

Introduction to *On Christian Doctrine*, Book 1

HELEN RHEE

Augustine (354–430 CE), a doctor of the church in the West, is considered by many to be the most extraordinary Latin theologian in early Christianity and beyond. He was born in Thagaste in North Africa; his father was a town councilor of modest means, and his mother, Monica, was a Christian. His father managed to obtain a first-class education for Augustine in the hope that the family would rise on the social and economic ladder through the successful career of the gifted son. Indeed, as a result of this elite education, Augustine taught rhetoric in Carthage, Rome, and Milan. Though he had been a member of the Manichaean religion for ten years, he converted to Christianity and received baptism by Ambrose, the bishop of Milan, in 387. Ambrose taught Augustine a form of Christianity interpreted in Neoplatonic terms. Although Augustine had lived an unchaste life for a long time—typical of a Roman of his social standing—after his conversion and baptism, he embraced a life of chastity and cenobitic monasticism and gave up his personal property for the poor (in stages). On a visit to the city of Hippo Regius, Augustine was unexpectedly ordained a priest against his will in 391. He served as the bishop of the city from 395/396 until his death in 430, while Hippo was under siege by the Vandals.

Augustine synthesized Christian, Platonic, and Latin Roman traditions, and his legacy has had an enormous influence on the Western church and theology. The following excerpt comes from *On Christian Doctrine* (*De Doctrina Christiana*), which is divided into four books and was written over a thirty-year span (c. 395/396 to 425/426). Our reading starts with Augustine's basic distinction between "use" (*uti*) and "enjoyment" (*frui*). While he believed some things are meant to be enjoyed for their own sake, other things are to be used to attain something else. According to Augustine, we are pilgrims on earth, and to return to our spiritual homeland, we must *use* this world and *enjoy* God, who exists in Trinity as the Father, Son, and the Holy Spirit. To enjoy God as the Trinity, the human eye must be purged, and we must journey to God along his chosen way.

What is God's chosen way? Augustine here stated the essentials of Christian belief in God with an important preamble that God is ineffable; in other words, we can say nothing truly meaningful about one who transcends the categories of human language. Then Augustine talked about the unchangeable wisdom of God and God's plan for human redemption and healing, as expressed in the incarnation, death, and resurrection of Christ. All of this brings us back to the matter of enjoyment and use of things. Every part of our being should be occupied with the effort to enjoy the eternal and unchangeable, which are the only things worth enjoying. If we enjoy God, the unchangeable and eternal, true enjoyment will occur.

From *On Christian Doctrine,* Book 1
Chapter 3

3. There are some things, then, which are to be enjoyed, others which are to be used, others still which are to be enjoyed and used. Those things which are objects of enjoyment make us happy. Those things which are objects of use assist, and (so to speak) support us in our efforts after happiness, so that we can attain the things that make us happy and rest in them. We ourselves, again, who enjoy and use these things, being placed among both kinds of objects, if we set ourselves to enjoy those which we ought to use, are hindered in our course, and sometimes even led away from it; so that, getting entangled in the love of lower gratifications, we lag behind in, or even altogether turn back from, the pursuit of the real and proper objects of enjoyment.

Chapter 4

4. For to enjoy a thing is to rest with satisfaction in it for its own sake. To use, on the other hand, is to employ whatever means are at one's disposal to obtain what one desires, if it is a proper object of desire; for an unlawful use ought rather to be called an abuse. Suppose, then, we were wanderers in a strange country, and could not live happily away from our fatherland, and that we felt wretched in our wandering, and wishing to put an end to our misery, determined to return home. We find, however, that we must make use of some mode of conveyance, either by land or water, in order to reach that fatherland where our enjoyment is to commence. But the beauty of the country through which we pass, and the very pleasure of the motion, charm our hearts, and turning these things which we ought to use into objects of enjoyment, we become unwilling to hasten the end of our journey; and becoming engrossed in a factitious delight, our thoughts are diverted from that home whose delights would make us truly happy. Such is a picture of our condition in this life of mortality. We have wandered far from God; and if we wish to return to our Father's home, this world

must be used, not enjoyed, that so the invisible things of God may be clearly seen, being understood by the things that are made, Romans 1:20—that is, that by means of what is material and temporary we may lay hold upon that which is spiritual and eternal.

Chapter 5

5. The true objects of enjoyment, then, are the Father and the Son and the Holy Spirit, who are at the same time the Trinity, one Being, supreme above all, and common to all who enjoy Him, if He is an object, and not rather the cause of all objects, or indeed even if He is the cause of all. For it is not easy to find a name that will suitably express so great excellence, unless it is better to speak in this way: The Trinity, one God, of whom are all things, through whom are all things, in whom are all things (Romans 11:36). Thus the Father and the Son and the Holy Spirit, and each of these by Himself, is God, and at the same time they are all one God; and each of them by Himself is a complete substance, and yet they are all one substance. The Father is not the Son nor the Holy Spirit; the Son is not the Father nor the Holy Spirit; the Holy Spirit is not the Father nor the Son: but the Father is only Father, the Son is only Son, and the Holy Spirit is only Holy Spirit. To all three belong the same eternity, the same unchangeableness, the same majesty, the same power. In the Father is unity, in the Son equality, in the Holy Spirit the harmony of unity and equality; and these three attributes are all one because of the Father, all equal because of the Son, and all harmonious because of the Holy Spirit.

Chapter 6

6. Have I spoken of God, or uttered His praise, in any worthy way? Nay, I feel that I have done nothing more than desire to speak; and if I have said anything, it is not what I desired to say. How do I know this, except from the fact that God is unspeakable? But what I have said, if it had been unspeakable, could not have been spoken. And so God is not even to be called unspeakable, because to say even this is to speak of Him. Thus there arises a curious contradiction of words, because if the unspeakable is what cannot be spoken of, it is not unspeakable if it can be called unspeakable. And this opposition of words is rather to be avoided by silence than to be explained away by speech. And yet God, although nothing worthy of His greatness can be said of Him, has condescended to accept the worship of men's mouths, and has desired us through the medium of our own words to rejoice in His praise. For on this principle it is that He is called *Deus* (God). For the sound of those two syllables in itself conveys no true knowledge of His nature; but yet all who know the Latin tongue are led,

when that sound reaches their ears, to think of a nature supreme in excellence and eternal in existence.

Chapter 7

7. For when the one supreme God of gods is thought of, even by those who believe that there are other gods, and who call them by that name, and worship them as gods, their thought takes the form of an endeavor to reach the conception of a nature, than which nothing more excellent or more exalted exists. And since men are moved by different kinds of pleasures, partly by those which pertain to the bodily senses, partly by those which pertain to the intellect and soul, those of them who are in bondage to sense think that either the heavens, or what appears to be most brilliant in the heavens, or the universe itself, is God of gods: or if they try to get beyond the universe, they picture to themselves something of dazzling brightness, and think of it vaguely as infinite, or of the most beautiful form conceivable; or they represent it in the form of the human body, if they think that superior to all others. Or if they think that there is no one God supreme above the rest, but that there are many or even innumerable gods of equal rank, still these too they conceive as possessed of shape and form, according to what each man thinks the pattern of excellence. Those, on the other hand, who endeavor by an effort of the intelligence to reach a conception of God, place Him above all visible and bodily natures, and even above all intelligent and spiritual natures that are subject to change. All, however, strive emulously to exalt the excellence of God: nor could any one be found to believe that any being to whom there exists a superior is God. And so all concur in believing that God is that which excels in dignity all other objects.

Chapter 8

8. And since all who think about God think of Him as living, they only can form any conception of Him that is not absurd and unworthy who think of Him as life itself; and, whatever may be the bodily form that has suggested itself to them, recognize that it is by life it lives or does not live, and prefer what is living to what is dead; who understand that the living bodily form itself, however it may outshine all others in splendor, overtop them in size, and excel them in beauty, is quite a distinct thing from the life by which it is quickened; and who look upon the life as incomparably superior in dignity and worth to the mass which is quickened and animated by it. Then, when they go on to look into the nature of the life itself, if they find it mere nutritive life, without sensibility, such as that of plants, they consider it inferior to sentient life, such as that of

cattle; and above this, again, they place intelligent life, such as that of men. And, perceiving that even this is subject to change, they are compelled to place above it, again, that unchangeable life which is not at one time foolish, at another time wise, but on the contrary is wisdom itself. For a wise intelligence, that is, one that has attained to wisdom, was, previous to its attaining wisdom, unwise. But wisdom itself never was unwise, and never can become so. And if men never caught sight of this wisdom, they could never with entire confidence prefer a life which is unchangeably wise to one that is subject to change. This will be evident, if we consider that the very rule of truth by which they affirm the unchangeable life to be the more excellent, is itself unchangeable: and they cannot find such a rule, except by going beyond their own nature; for they find nothing in themselves that is not subject to change.

Chapter 9

9. Now, no one is so egregiously silly as to ask, "How do you know that a life of unchangeable wisdom is preferable to one of change?" For that very truth about which he asks, how I know it? is unchangeably fixed in the minds of all men, and presented to their common contemplation. And the man who does not see it is like a blind man in the sun, whom it profits nothing that the splendor of its light, so clear and so near, is poured into his very eye-balls. The man, on the other hand, who sees, but shrinks from this truth, is weak in his mental vision from dwelling long among the shadows of the flesh. And thus men are driven back from their native land by the contrary blasts of evil habits, and pursue lower and less valuable objects in preference to that which they own to be more excellent and more worthy.

Chapter 10

10. Wherefore, since it is our duty fully to enjoy the truth which lives unchangeably, and since the triune God takes counsel in this truth for the things which He has made, the soul must be purified that it may have power to perceive that light, and to rest in it when it is perceived. And let us look upon this purification as a kind of journey or voyage to our native land. For it is not by change of place that we can come nearer to Him who is in every place, but by the cultivation of pure desires and virtuous habits.

Chapter 11

11. But of this we should have been wholly incapable, had not Wisdom condescended to adapt Himself to our weakness, and to show us a pattern of holy life in the form of our own humanity. Yet, since we when we come to Him

do wisely, He when He came to us was considered by proud men to have done very foolishly. And since we when we come to Him become strong, He when He came to us was looked upon as weak. But the foolishness of God is wiser than men; and the weakness of God is stronger than men (1 Corinthians 1:25). And thus, though Wisdom was Himself our home, He made Himself also the way by which we should reach our home.

Chapter 12

And though He is everywhere present to the inner eye when it is sound and clear, He condescended to make Himself manifest to the outward eye of those whose inward sight is weak and dim. For after that, in the wisdom of God, the world by wisdom knew not God, it pleased God by the foolishness of preaching to save them that believe (1 Corinthians 1:21).

12. Not then in the sense of traversing space, but because He appeared to mortal men in the form of mortal flesh, He is said to have come to us. For He came to a place where He had always been, seeing that He was in the world, and the world was made by Him. But, because men, who in their eagerness to enjoy the creature instead of the Creator had grown into the likeness of this world, and are therefore most appropriately named the world, did not recognize Him, therefore the evangelist says, and the world knew Him not (John 1:10). Thus, in the wisdom of God, the world by wisdom knew not God. Why then did He come, seeing that He was already here, except that it pleased God through the foolishness of preaching to save them that believe?

Chapter 13

In what way did He come but this, The Word was made flesh, and dwelt among us? (John 1:14). Just as when we speak, in order that what we have in our minds may enter through the ear into the mind of the hearer, the word which we have in our hearts becomes an outward sound and is called speech; and yet our thought does not lose itself in the sound, but remains complete in itself, and takes the form of speech without being modified in its own nature by the change: so the Divine Word, though suffering no change of nature, yet became flesh, that He might dwell among us.

Chapter 14

13. Moreover, as the use of remedies is the way to health, so this remedy took up sinners to heal and restore them. And just as surgeons, when they bind up wounds, do it not in a slovenly way, but carefully, that there may be a certain degree of neatness in the binding, in addition to its mere usefulness,

so our medicine, Wisdom, was by His assumption of humanity adapted to our wounds, curing some of them by their opposites, some of them by their likes. And just as he who ministers to a bodily hurt in some cases applies contraries, as cold to hot, moist to dry, etc., and in other cases applies likes, as a round cloth to a round wound, or an oblong cloth to an oblong wound, and does not fit the same bandage to all limbs, but puts like to like; in the same way the Wisdom of God in healing man has applied Himself to his cure, being Himself healer and medicine both in one. Seeing, then, that man fell through pride, He restored him through humility. We were ensnared by the wisdom of the serpent: we are set free by the foolishness of God. Moreover, just as the former was called wisdom, but was in reality the folly of those who despised God, so the latter is called foolishness, but is true wisdom in those who overcome the devil. We used our immortality so badly as to incur the penalty of death: Christ used His mortality so well as to restore us to life. The disease was brought in through a woman's corrupted soul: the remedy came through a woman's virgin body. To the same class of opposite remedies it belongs, that our vices are cured by the example of His virtues. On the other hand, the following are, as it were, bandages made in the same shape as the limbs and wounds to which they are applied: He was born of a woman to deliver us who fell through a woman: He came as a man to save us who are men, as a mortal to save us who are mortals, by death to save us who were dead. And those who can follow out the matter more fully, who are not hurried on by the necessity of carrying out a set undertaking, will find many other points of instruction in considering the remedies, whether opposites or likes, employed in the medicine of Christianity.

Chapter 15

14. The belief of the resurrection of our Lord from the dead, and of His ascension into heaven, has strengthened our faith by adding a great buttress of hope. For it clearly shows how freely He laid down His life for us when He had it in His power thus to take it up again. With what assurance, then, is the hope of believers animated, when they reflect how great He was who suffered so great things for them while they were still in unbelief! And when men look for Him to come from heaven as the judge of quick and dead, it strikes great terror into the careless, so that they betake themselves to diligent preparation, and learn by holy living to long for His approach, instead of quaking at it on account of their evil deeds. And what tongue can tell, or what imagination can conceive, the reward He will bestow at the last, when we consider that for our comfort in this earthly journey He has given us so freely of His Spirit, that in the adversities

of this life we may retain our confidence in, and love for, Him whom as yet we see not; and that He has also given to each gifts suitable for the building up of His Church, that we may do what He points out as right to be done, not only without a murmur, but even with delight?

Chapter 16

15. For the Church is His body, as the apostle's teaching shows us; and it is even called His spouse. His body, then, which has many members, and all performing different functions, He holds together in the bond of unity and love, which is its true health. Moreover He exercises it in the present time, and purges it with many wholesome afflictions, that when He has transplanted it from this world to the eternal world, He may take it to Himself as His bride, without spot or wrinkle, or any such thing.

Chapter 17

16. Further, when we are on the way, and that not a way that lies through space, but through a change of affections, and one which the guilt of our past sins like a hedge of thorns barred against us, what could He, who was willing to lay Himself down as the way by which we should return, do that would be still gracious and more merciful, except to forgive us all our sins, and by being cruci-fied for us to remove the stern decrees that barred the door against our return?

Chapter 18

17. He has given, therefore, the keys to His Church, that whatsoever it should bind on earth might be bound in heaven, and whatsoever it should loose on earth might be loosed in heaven; that is to say, that whosoever in the Church should not believe that his sins are remitted, they should not be remitted to him; but that whosoever should believe and should repent, and turn from his sins, should be saved by the same faith and repentance on the ground of which he is received into the bosom of the Church. For he who does not believe that his sins can be pardoned, falls into despair, and becomes worse as if no greater good remained for him than to be evil, when he has ceased to have faith in the results of his own repentance. . . .

Chapter 22

20. Among all these things, then, those only are the true objects of enjoy-ment which we have spoken of as eternal and unchangeable. The rest are for use, that we may be able to arrive at the full enjoyment of the former. We, however, who enjoy and use other things are things ourselves. For a great thing

truly is man, made after the image and similitude of God, not as respects the mortal body in which he is clothed, but as respects the rational soul by which he is exalted in honor above the beasts. And so it becomes an important question, whether men ought to enjoy, or to use, themselves, or to do both. For we are commanded to love one another: but it is a question whether man is to be loved by man for his own sake, or for the sake of something else. If it is for his own sake, we enjoy him; if it is for the sake of something else, we use him. It seems to me, then, that he is to be loved for the sake of something else. For if a thing is to be loved for its own sake, then in the enjoyment of it consists a happy life, the hope of which at least, if not yet the reality, is our comfort in the present time. But a curse is pronounced on him who places his hope in man (Jeremiah 17:5).

21. Neither ought any one to have joy in himself, if you look at the matter clearly, because no one ought to love even himself for his own sake, but for the sake of Him who is the true object of enjoyment. For a man is never in so good a state as when his whole life is a journey towards the unchangeable life, and his affections are entirely fixed upon that. If, however, he loves himself for his own sake, he does not look at himself in relation to God, but turns his mind in upon himself, and so is not occupied with anything that is unchangeable. And thus he does not enjoy himself at his best, because he is better when his mind is fully fixed upon, and his affections wrapped up in, the unchangeable good, than when he turns from that to enjoy even himself. Wherefore if you ought not to love even yourself for your own sake, but for His in whom your love finds its most worthy object, no other man has a right to be angry if you love him too for God's sake. For this is the law of love that has been laid down by Divine authority: You shall love your neighbor as yourself; but, You shall love God with all your heart, and with all your soul, and with all your mind: so that you are to concentrate all your thoughts, your whole life and your whole intelligence upon Him from whom you derive all that you bring. For when He says, "With all your heart, and with all your soul, and with all your mind," He means that no part of our life is to be unoccupied, and to afford room, as it were, for the wish to enjoy some other object, but that whatever else may suggest itself to us as an object worthy of love is to be borne into the same channel in which the whole current of our affections flows. Whoever, then, loves his neighbor aright, ought to urge upon him that he too should love God with his whole heart, and soul, and mind. For in this way, loving his neighbor as himself, a man turns the whole current of his love both for himself and his neighbor into the channel of the love of God, which suffers no stream to be drawn off from itself by whose diversion its own volume would be diminished.

Discussion Questions

1. How does Augustine connect a theme of "use" and "enjoyment" to a fundamental Christian doctrine?

2. Augustine's distinction between "use" and "enjoyment" implies a Platonic notion of the hierarchy of goods (lesser goods versus higher goods). How do you personally relate to Augustine's distinction between "use" and "enjoyment"?

3. Do you believe Augustine's distinction between "use" and "enjoyment" is a helpful way of thinking about the world? Why or why not?

4. How should one understand love in terms of use and enjoyment?

CHAPTER 9

Gregory the Great

Introduction to *Life of Saint Benedict*, Dialogues, Book 2

JOHN SKILLEN

Saint Benedict (c. 480–547) wrote a rule of life for the monastic communities he established in the early sixth century, first in the mountains east of Rome. With their rapid proliferation throughout the whole of Europe, this network of Benedictine monasteries formed a sort of archipelago of islands of civility, hospitality, care, devotion, and prayer. In the preface to his *Rule*, Benedict describes them as "schools for the service of the Lord."[1] Indeed, Benedict is often credited not only with the spiritual renewal of Europe but with the recovery of its social, cultural, educational, and even agricultural fabric amid the slow unraveling of the imperial Roman order.

The companion to the *Rule of Saint Benedict* is the account of Benedict's life composed only a few decades after his death by Pope Gregory—one of the four church fathers in Catholic tradition. Couched in the form of a dialogue with his young deacon Peter, Gregory comments toward the end that "anyone who wishes to know more about his life and character can discover in his Rule exactly what he was like as an abbot, for his life could not have differed from his teaching."[2]

One of the themes in Gregory's narration concerns education, a thread taken up at the outset when he reveals that Benedict quit his education in the liberal arts at the university in Rome because he was disturbed by the dissolute behavior of his peers. Benedict hiked up into the mountains to live as a hermit. It wasn't long before he found himself teaching the simple peasant folk who sought him out. His gradual discovery of God's call on his life came partly through mistakes—a lesson for us all. One monastery became twelve, and devout patricians from a decaying Rome began to send their children to Benedict "to be schooled in the service of God."[3]

Below, you will find a sequence of episodes from Gregory's narration that leads to Peter's "aha" moment. Without any prompting by Gregory, Peter

---

1. *St. Benedict's Rule for Monasteries*, trans. Leonard J. Doyle (Collegeville, MN: Liturgical, 1948), 5.
2. Pope St. Gregory the Great, *Life and Miracles of St. Benedict (Book Two of the Dialogues)*, trans. Odo J. Zimmerman and Benedict R. Avery (repr., Collegeville, MN: Liturgical, [1980]), 74.
3. *Life and Miracles of St. Benedict*, 16.

suddenly spots the parallels between the deeds of Benedict and those of several patriarchs and apostles, and exclaims, "This man must have been filled with the spirit of all the just."[4] Gregory affirms young Peter's comprehension of these parallels, but with an important correction: "Actually, Peter, blessed Benedict possessed the Spirit of only one Person, the Savior who fills the hearts of all the faithful by granting them the fruits of His Redemption."[5] Peter's discovery is twofold: not only does he learn how figures from the Old Testament point forward to the One to come, but he discovers how those Christ followers who more fully "imitate Christ"—like Benedict—point us back to Christ.

Indeed, Jesus himself drew several such parallels. "Just as Moses lifted up the snake in the wilderness," he said to Nicodemus, "so the Son of Man must be lifted up [on the cross]" (John 3:14). "For as Jonah was three days and three nights in the belly of a huge fish, so the Son of Man will be three days and three nights in the heart of the earth" (Matt. 12:40). "Our ancestors ate the manna in the wilderness. . . . It is not Moses who has given you the bread from heaven, but it is my Father who gives you the true bread from heaven. . . . I am the bread of life" (John 6:31–35).

In fact, this process of learning to read the Scriptures in the light of Christ became the core principle of schooling in Christianized Europe. How far might this principle of reading be fittingly applied to other texts of literature? This question has remained lively and contentious over the centuries, and it's something worth considering as you apply the reading below to your own studies.

From *Life of Saint Benedict*, Dialogues, Book 2
Prologue (spoken by Gregory to his interlocutor young deacon Peter):

There was a man of venerable life, blessed by grace, and blessed in name, for he was called "Benedictus" or Benedict. From his younger years, he always had the mind of an old man; for his age was inferior to his virtue. All vain pleasure he despised, and though he was in the world, and might freely have enjoyed such commodities as it yields, yet he esteemed it and its vanities as nothing.

He was born in the province of Norcia, of honorable parentage, and sent to Rome for an education in the liberal arts. When he found many of the students there abandoning themselves to vice, he withdrew himself from the world he had been preparing to enter, lest, entering too far in acquaintance with it, he likewise might have fallen into that dangerous and godless gulf.

Therefore, giving over his books, and forsaking his father's house and wealth, with a resolute mind only to serve God, he sought for some place,

---

4. *Life and Miracles of St. Benedict*, 25.
5. *Life and Miracles of St. Benedict*, 25–26.

where he might attain to the desire of his holy purpose. In this way he departed, instructed with learned ignorance, and furnished with unlearned wisdom.

[Chapter 1 recounts several episodes after Benedict leaves Rome, and begins life alone as a hermit in a cave high on the mountainside.]

From Chapter 2:

. . . About the same time, certain shepherds found him in that cave: and at the first, when they spied him through the bushes, and saw his apparel made of skins, they thought that it had been some beast. After they were acquainted with the servant of God, however, many of them were converted from their primitive life to grace, piety, and devotion. Thus his name in the country there about became famous, and many went to visit him, and in exchange for corporal meat which they brought him, they carried away spiritual food for their souls.

From Chapter 3:

As God's servant daily increased in virtue and became continually more famous for miracles, many were led by him to the service of almighty God in the same place. By Christ's assistance he built there twelve abbeys; over which he appointed governors, and in each of them placed twelve monks. A few he kept with himself; namely, those he thought would gain more profit and be better instructed by his own presence.

At that time also many noble and religious men of Rome came to him, and committed their children to be brought up under him for the service of God. Evitius delivered Maurus to him, and Tertullius, the Senator, brought Placidus. These were their sons of great hope and promise: of the two, Maurus, growing to great virtue, began to be his master's helper; but Placidus, as yet, was but a boy of tender years.

Chapter 5: Of a Fountain That Sprung Forth in the Top of a Mountain, by the Prayers of the Man of God.

Among the monasteries which he had built in those parts, three of them were situated on the rocks of a mountain, so that it was very painful for the monks to go down and fetch water, especially because the side of the hill was so steep that there was great fear of danger. Therefore the monks of those Abbeys with one consent came to the servant of God, Benedict, giving him to understand, how laborious it was for them daily to go down to the lake for water. They added that it was necessary for them to move to some other places.

The man of God, comforting them with sweet words, caused them to return. The next night, having with him only the little boy Placidus (of whom we spoke above), he ascended up to the rock of that mountain, and continued there a long time in prayer. When he had done, he took three stones, and laid them in the same place for a mark, and so, none of them being privy to what he had done, he returned to his own Abbey.

The next day, when the foresaid monks came again with their request, he said to them: "Go your way to the rock, and in the place where you find three stones laid one on another, dig a little hole, for almighty God is able to bring forth water in the top of that mountain, and so ease you of that great labor of fetching it so far." Away they went, and came to the rock of the mountain according to his directions. They found it as if it were sweating drops of water. After they had made a hollow place with a spade, it was immediately filled, and water flowed out abundantly. So plentifully, that even to this day, the water springs out and runs down from the top of that hill to the very bottom.

Chapter 6: How the Iron Head of a Bill, from the Bottom of the Water, Returned to the Handle Again.

At another time, a certain Goth, poor of spirit, that gave over the world, was received by the man of God. One day Benedict instructed him to take a brush hook, and to clear a certain plot of ground from briers, for the making of a garden, which ground was by the side of a lake. As the Goth was there laboring, by chance the iron blade slipped off, and fell into the water, which was so deep, that there was no hope ever to get it again. The poor Goth, in great fear, ran to Maurus and told him what he had lost, confessing his own fault and negligence. Maurus went right away to the servant of God, giving him to understand what had happened, who came immediately to the lake. He took the handle out of the Goth's hand, and put it into the water, and the iron head by and by ascended from the bottom and entered again into the handle of the brush hook, which he delivered to the Goth, saying: "Behold here is thy hook again, work on, and be sad no more."

[Editor's note: This is one of several episodes in the Life that correlate with chapters in the Rule of St. Benedict; in this case, chapter 32, concerning the importance of caring for "the tools and goods of the monastery" ("Whoever fails to keep the things belonging to the monastery clean or treats them carelessly should be reproved"), providing the context for the Goth's remorse for his carelessness.]

Chapter 7: How Maurus Walked upon the Water.

On a certain day, as venerable Benedict was in his cell, young Placidus, the holy man's monk, went out to take up water at the lake, and, putting down his pail carelessly, fell in after it. The current carried him away from the land as far as one may shoot an arrow. The man of God, being in his cell, by and by knew this. He called in haste for Maurus, saying: "Brother Maurus, run as fast as you can, for Placidus, who went to the lake to fetch water, has fallen in, and is carried a good way off."

A strange thing, and, since the time of Peter the Apostle, never heard of! Maurus asked his father's blessing and, departing in all haste at his command, ran to that spot on the water to which the young lad had been carried by the force of the water. Thinking that he had all that while been on the land, Maurus took fast hold of Placidus by the hair of his head, in all haste he returned with him. As soon as he was on land, coming to himself, he looked back, and then knew very well that he had run on the water. That which before he dared not to presume, being now done and past, he both marveled at, and was afraid of what he had done.

Coming back to the father, Benedict, and telling him what had happened, the venerable man did not attribute this to his own merits, but to the obedience of Maurus. Maurus, on the contrary, said that it was done only on his commandment, and that he had nothing to do with that miracle, not knowing at that time what he did. The friendly contention proceeded in mutual humility, but the youth himself that had been saved from drowning determined the fact. He said that when he was drawn out of the water, he saw the Abbot's garment on his head, affirming thereby that it was the man of God that had delivered him from that great danger.

Peter: Certainly these are wonderful things that you report, and they may serve for the edification of many. For my own part, the more that I hear of his miracles, the more do I desire to hear.

. . .

Chapter 8: How a Loaf Was Poisoned, and Carried Far Off by a Crow.

Gregory: When as the foresaid monasteries were zealous in the love of our Lord Jesus Christ, and their fame dispersed far and near, and many gave over the secular life, and subdued the passions of their soul, under the light yoke of our Savior, then (as the manner of wicked people is, to envy at that virtue which themselves desire not to follow) one Florentius, priest of a church nearby, and grandfather to Florentius our sub-deacon, possessed with diabolical malice, began to envy the holy man's virtues, to back-bite his manner of living, and to withdraw as many as he could from going to visit him.

When he saw that he could not hinder Benedict's virtuous proceedings, but that, on the contrary, the fame of his holy life increased, and many daily, on the very report of his sanctity, took themselves to a better state of life, Florentius burned more and more with the coals of envy. He became far worse; and though he desired not to imitate Benedict's commendable life, yet fain he would have had the reputation of his virtuous conversation.

In conclusion so much did malicious envy blind him, and so far did he wade in that sin, that he poisoned a loaf of bread and sent it to the servant of almighty God, as it were for a holy present. The man of God received it with great thanks, yet not ignorant of that which was hidden within. At dinner time, a crow used to come to him out of the nearby woods to receive bread at his hands. Coming that day after his manner, the man of God threw him the loaf which the priest had sent him, giving the crow this charge: "In the name of Jesus Christ our Lord, take up that loaf, and leave it in some such place where no man may find it." Then the crow, opening his mouth, and lifting up his wings, began to hop up and down about the loaf, and after his manner to cry out, as though he would have said that he was willing to obey, and yet could not do what he was commanded.

The man of God again and again bid him, saying: "Take it up without fear, and throw it where no man may find it." At length, with much ado, the crow took it up, and flew away, and after three hours, having dispatched the loaf, he returned again, and received his usual allowance from the man of God.

But the venerable father, perceiving the priest so wickedly bent against his life, was far more sorry for Florentius than grieved for himself. And Florentius, seeing that he could not kill the body of the master, attempts to do now what he can, to destroy the souls of Benedict's disciples. For that purpose he sent into the yard of the abbey before their eyes seven naked young women, which there took hands together, play and dance a long time before them, to the end that, by this means, they might inflame their minds to sinful lust. When the holy man beheld this damnable sight from his cell, and fearing the danger which thereby might ensue to his younger monks, and considering that all this was done only for his persecution, he let envy have its way. He appointed governors for those abbeys and oratories which he had built himself, and removed to another place in the company of a few monks.

And thus the man of God, in humility, gave place to the other's malice; but yet almighty God of justice severely punished Florentius' wickedness. For when the foresaid priest, being in his chamber, understood of the departure of holy Benedict, he was very glad of that news. Yet—behold—the chamber in the house in which he was, collapsed and Florentius was killed. When the holy man's disciple Maurus learned of this strange accident, he immediately sent Benedict word, for he was as yet scarce ten miles off, desiring him to return again, because the priest that persecuted him was slain. When Benedict heard, he was sorrowful, and lamented much, both because his enemy died in such sort, and also because one of his monks rejoiced. Therefore Benedict gave Maurus penance, because sending such news, he presumed to rejoice at his enemy's death.

Peter: The things you report are strange, and much to be wondered at. In making the rock to yield water, I see Moses; and in the iron, which came from the bottom of the lake, I behold Elisha; in the walking of Maurus on the water, I perceive Peter; in the obedience of the crow, I contemplate Elijah; and in lamenting the death of his enemy, I acknowledge David. Therefore, in my opinion, this one man was full of the spirit of all good men. [For biblical accounts, see Num. 20:1–13; 2 Kings 6:4–7; Matt. 14:22–33; 1 Kings 17:4–6; 2 Sam. 1:11–12.]

Gregory: Actually, Peter, Benedict had the spirit of the one true God, who, by the grace of our redemption, hath filled the hearts of his elect servants; of whom St. John says: "He was the true light, which does lighten every man coming into this world." Of whom, again, we find it written: "Of his fullness we have all received" [John 1:9, 16].

For God's holy servants might receive virtues from our Lord, but to bestow them on others they could not. Therefore it was he that gave the signs of miracles to his servants, who promised to give the sign of Jonah to his enemies [Matt. 12:40]. He died in the sight of the proud, to rise again before the eyes of the humble so that they might behold what they spurned, and those see that which they ought to worship and love. By reason of this mystery it comes to pass that, whereas the proud cast their eyes on the contempt of his death, the humble contrariwise, against death, lay hold of the glory of his power and might.

Discussion Questions

1. When young Peter spots the parallels between Benedict and Bible characters, is he "reading into" the text, or is he hearing the text truthfully with the eyes of faith?
2. Is it possible to take this way of reading Christ back into other stories of the Old Testament—modeled by Jesus himself—too far? Why or why not?
3. Perhaps you grew up reading C. S. Lewis's the Chronicles of Narnia and sensed the parallels between Aslan and Christ. Or maybe a pastor pointed out lessons for the Christian faith from J. R. R. Tolkien's the Lord of the

Rings series. Is it appropriate to read Christian messages into works of fiction such as these?

4. Art historian Matthew Milliner argues that characters in the television series *The Walking Dead* exhibit the four cardinal virtues.[6] Does this interpretation hold water if the script writers weren't consciously trying to draw this connection?

5. Gregory clearly presents Benedict as an imitator of Christ. Does that strike you as lifting up Benedict too high? What are we to make of the apostle Paul's exhortation in 1 Corinthians 11:1, "Imitate me, just as I also imitate Christ" (NKJV)?

---

6. "The Cardinal Virtues and *The Walking Dead*," *First Things* magazine, January 15, 2016. Available online at https://www.firstthings.com/web-exclusives/2016/01/the-cardinal-virtues-the-walking-dead.

Part 2

AD 600 to AD 1700

CHAPTER 10

Dante Alighieri

Introduction to *Divine Comedy: Inferno* 1

JASON M. BAXTER

The Middle Ages birthed all kinds of artistic representations of the afterlife: imaginative journeys in which peasants were led by saints or angels to see what hell was like (like the vision of Thurkill), sermons in which medieval preachers attempted to awaken their congregations to the presumed fate of the wicked (like Innocent III's "On the Misery of the Human Condition"), carvings over the main doors to churches (see the *Last Judgment* at St. Lazare, Autun, France), and paintings in private chapels (Giotto's Arena Chapel). All of these treatments had one thing in common: their shared conviction that "the fear of the LORD is the beginning of wisdom" (Prov. 9:10). And they took the term *fear* quite literally. Thus, the depictions were often terrifying, portraying demons inflicting horrible and humiliating suffering in the afterlife (see Hieronymus Bosch's *Last Judgment*).

Dante Alighieri's depiction of the afterlife, in some ways, follows this precedent. His *Inferno* (hell) has demons and tears and curses and screams, along with punishments and darkness and fear. Why, then, are students still regularly asked to read Dante's literary masterpiece but rarely assigned to read about poor old Thurkill? The reasons are many, but I'll give two here.

First, Dante's vision doesn't end with fear. His pilgrim, after being shocked, alarmed, and awakened to the gravity of the human situation—to our tendency to rationalize our evil proclivities, to our proclivity to hoard, lust, and covet—then goes on to a realm in which broken people who admit they need divine help are re-formed, rewritten, and made new (*Purgatorio*). It's a place of spring, green, and hope. In this second part of his trilogy, Dante emphasized freedom, love, and friendship as powers that can mend broken people. But then, for the third part of his trilogy, the medieval author used every ounce of artistic creativity in his body to make heaven as shockingly "painful" in its joy and goodness as hell was terrifying. As C. S. Lewis loved to say, it's one of the few artistic representations that makes heaven and goodness feel "heavy" and substantial, as opposed to some watery, sallow image of angels playing lutes and sitting on clouds (which seems really boring).

Second, Dante's literary portrayal has a new "psychological intensity"; that is, as opposed to some "everyman" who meets allegorical personifications of virtues and vices, this pilgrim meets real people and has real conversations. What is more, because Dante is the name of both the author and the main character (Dante-pilgrim), the author, like a modern film director, avails himself of multiple cinematic angles. Sometimes the author describes a situation objectively and in detail, but other times we experience the poem through the eyes of the pilgrim in an intense, pulse-throbbing, limited, point-of-view shot.

Although Dante's *Inferno* is composed of 100 small chapters (each of which Dante calls a "canto," a little song that takes about nine minutes to read), I can only give one: *Inferno* 1, the introductory moment in which we start, rather abruptly, right in the middle of things. In my translation of the Italian that follows, I try to capture the dreamlike feeling of anxiety and sorrow and the sense of loss that haunts real people who have lost the "right way" and can't quite remember what they were looking for.

Divine Comedy: Inferno 1
TRANSLATED BY JASON M. BAXTER

Midway in the journey of our life
I found myself in the midst of a dark wood—
the true way was lost.

Ah! How hard it is to tell!
How savage, harsh, and fierce was this wood,
so much that in my mind my fear returns.

It is so bitter that death is barely worse.
But to treat the good that I found there
I will speak about the other things I saw.

I cannot well recall how I came there.
I was so full of sleep at that time,
I had wandered off from the true way.

But when I had come to the foot of a hill,
There where that valley came to an end,
The one that had stabbed my heart with fear,

I lifted up my eyes and saw a mountain's shoulders
now clothed in the rays of the planet

who makes the way straight along any path.[1]

And then the fear within was, just a bit, calmed.
It had pooled up in my heart and oppressed me
For a whole night, one I passed in so much angst.
And like one who, with labored breath,
just escaped from the sea onto the shore,
turns toward the dangerous waters and stares,
just so did my mind, still in flight,
turn back to gaze at the pass
which never yet let out a man alive.

After I had let my flesh rest a while
I took up the way again through the deserted slope,
in this way: the firm foot was always lower down.

And behold, here, almost at the first rise:
A leopard, so light, nimble, and swift,
completely covered in a spotted pelt;

And she would not depart before my visage
But, rather, was impeded my path
So that I, I was just about to turn away, more than once.

The time was the first of the morning,
And the sun was climbing up, to be among those stars
who first were with him, when divine love

Moved all those gorgeous things at the great beginning;
And so, I had reason to maintain my hope—
Thought standing before the gaudy pelt of the savage beast—

given the hour of the day and the sweetness of the season;
But not for long: I now take fright
At the sight of . . . a lion! who flashed before me.

It seemed he came directly at me

---

1. A poetic (and roundabout) way of saying, "the sun."

With his head, high, and with a hunger so raw
it seemed the air trembled because of him.

And then: a she-wolf! Who, with every desire,
Seemed laden. Gaunt starvation.
Many are the men she has made to live in woe.

She put me in such a state of heavy sorrow,
due to the fear that was emanating from her face,
I lost all hope of the mountain's heights.

And like the man who wins with joy,
but then the moment arrives, and he loses all,
and then is miserable and weeps in all his thoughts,

Such was I, thanks to the beast who knows not peace.
And now, approaching, nearing, bit by bit,
She backed me back down to where the sun has no sound.

And so I was tumbling down toward my lowest point, and
There was given unto me, before my eyes,
Something, it seemed, which, for a long time, had been mute.

And when I saw him in that vast waste
"Have mercy on me!" I screamed to him:
"whatever you are, whether man or uncertain shade!"

And he replied to me: "No, not a man, though once I was.
My parents were from Lombardy
Mantuans, their native land, both.

"I was born *sub Julio*, and that was already late,
I lived in Rome under good Augustus
In the time of false and thieving gods.

"A poet, was I, and sang the just
Son of Anchises, who came from Troy
After proud Ilion burned to the ground.

"But you? Why do you return to such angst?
Why not ascend the mountain of delight
Which is the beginning and cause of all our joy?"

"Are you, then, Virgil? That spring and font
which gushed forth in a broad river of speech?"
I said this, and said it with a humbled brow.

"O! Pride and light of all poets,
let my long study and great love be merit for me,
It was love that drove me to search through your tome.

"You, you are my master! You are my authoritative guide!
You are the only from whom I drew
My beautiful style, the one that has brought me fame.

"You see the beast: she has turned me!
Now save me from her, O famous sage,
Because she makes my very veins and pulses tremble!"

"For you . . . you will have to take another road,"
he replied, after he saw me reduced to tears,
"if you want to escape this savage place.

"This beast, who makes you cry and wail
never lets a man pass along her way;
rather, she hinders him until the she takes his life.

"Her nature is so wicked and debased.
She cannot ever satisfy her clamorous desire.
After eating she has more hunger than before!

"Many are the animals with whom she mates.
And there will be others still, until the hound
Will come and make her die, with sorrow.

"This hound will not sup on lands, nor on possessions,
But on wisdom, love, and virtuous strength.

His nation will be between feltro and feltro.[2]

"And poor, beaten-down Italy! He will be her salvation!
For whom the virgin princess, Camilla, died.
So did Euryalus, Turnus, and Nisos, of those wounds.

"This hound will chase her through every village,
Until that he will have returned her to hell,
Whence primal envy first took off.

"Thus: I think and perceive that for your good
you follow me. I will be your guide.
I will take you from here, into an eternal place;

"There you will hear strident cries of those who have no hope.
You will see the souls of old, now in sorrow.
Each of them grieves his second death.

"Then you will see those who are content
in their flames, because they have the hope to come
among the blessed race—whenever that shall be.

"And then on those . . . if you want still to ascend, on
to them, there is a soul more worthy than I.
With her I will leave you when I need to depart.

"For the emperor who rules up there,
Given that I was a rebel against his law,
He does not wish there be any entry for me into his city.

"Every place is his demesne, but there, he rules;
There: that is his city. His lofty seat.
Oh! Blessed is the man who is chosen to be there!"

---

2. Literally, between "felt" and "felt." The prophecy, like other end-time predictions, is deliberately vague. It rhymes with "veltro," Dante's "hound." It might refer to a vague region, from which a just ruler would emerge, somewhere between two "feltros": Montefeltro (a region around modern-day San Marino) and Feltre (a town near Trento). It might also refer to homespun material—felted wool—and, thus, perhaps a mendicant preacher (a Franciscan?) in simple cloth (as opposed to silk or something exotic).

And I to him: "Poet, I beg you
By that God whom you did not know,
In order that I may flee this evil, and whatever could be worse,

"lead me to that place you have just described
so that I might see St. Peter's gate
as well as those you make out as so distraught."
And so he took his way, and I, I followed after.

Discussion Questions

1. Based on your own experience, does Dante's image of being lost in a seemingly endless dark wood accurately and successfully describe moments of the Christian life?
2. In the reading above, Dante is delighted to see Virgil. Why? Why do we need a guide on the Christian pilgrimage?
3. Who are the three animals? Why are there three of them? And what is the "mountain of delight"?
4. How should Christians respond when their hopes and dreams are ruined by the impediments of sin?

CHAPTER 11

Nezahualcoyotl

Introduction to "A Flower Song of Nezahualcoyotl"
TIMOTHY E. G. BARTEL

When we think of the great books of Mexico, we usually think of literature written in Spanish. And indeed, for the last five hundred years, most of the major literature from Latin America has been written in Spanish. But it is important to remember that Spanish has only been in Mexico as long as Europeans have been there, and there is a whole history of Mexico from before the first Europeans came—and a vivid literary tradition. Poetry was especially prized in pre-Columbian Mexico, and this poetry was written in a language called Nahuatl, the language of the Aztec Empire, whose capital city was Tenochtitlan (present-day Mexico City).

Arguably the greatest of the Nahuatl poets was Nezahualcoyotl, a fifteenth-century prince from a city to the east of Tenochtitlan: Texcoco, a powerful ally of the Aztecs with a tumultuous history. When Nezahualcoyotl was just a teenager, he witnessed the assassination of his father, the king. He fled into hiding and spent years gathering allies to help him take back his kingdom from his father's murderers. Once he had taken back his kingdom, Nezahualcoyotl gained renown as a lawgiver and a promoter of religion. He ordered a temple built to a deity called Ipalnemohuani (literally, "He in whom we live," or "Giver of Life"). Though animal and even human sacrifice was common in Texcoco, Nezahualcoyotl disallowed any taking of life in the temple of this Giver of Life.

From the time of his exile through his career as a revered king, Nezahualcoyotl wrote poems, and many compositions have been preserved under his name. Nezahualcoyotl's poems are beautiful examples of the richness of Nahuatl poetry in the last generations before the Spaniards came. Nahuatl poetry is not metered in the same way as English poetry; it is intentionally structured into stanzas that often end in the refrain of *Ohuaya* (pronounced Oh-WAH-ya) or a similar interjection. In addition to employing lovely refrains, Nezahualcoyotl is a master of vivid natural imagery. Flowers, feathers, cocoa, and music waft through his poetry. He celebrates the joys of life even as he contemplates the reality of death. For Nezahualcoyotl, flowers are an image of art, especially poems. Like flowers, poems can bloom and delight us, but also they will someday fade and be forgotten. This is the life of humans on the earth for Nezahualcoyotl. Yet there is something before and after life: the Giver of Life himself.

Scholars debate whether Nezahualcoyotl can be called a monotheist in the same sense as someone from the Jewish or Christian religion. What is more certain is that Nezahualcoyotl saw this Giver of Life as someone who tied all human and nonhuman life together, a divine source to whom both the lowliest peasant and the greatest king were accountable.

Though we often think of poets as fulfilling a different role in society than kings, Nezahualcoyotl is an example of the poet-ruler who shows us that leadership need not be divorced from a love of language and literature. Those of us who seek to be leaders in our communities can learn much from Nezahualcoyotl: how to celebrate the joy of the small pleasures in life—the plumage of a bird, the first sip of cocoa—while keeping in mind the eternal matters of death and judgment.

A Flower Song of Nezahualcoyotl[1]

These flowers are our only crowns,
These songs our only balm for pain,
Down here on earth—
Ohuaya, Ohuaya

All my possessions will likely be lost;
All my companions will likely be gone;
When I, Yoyontzin, lie down—*Ohuaye*—
In the realm of song and the Giver of Life—
Ohuaya, Ohuaya.

Oh, who is able to say where we go,
And who is the guide to His hidden home?
Down here on earth is where we live.
Ohuaya, Ohuaya.

Your heart must acknowledge, oh Princes,
Oh eagles and jaguars, this truth:
Companionship comes to an end,
For only a moment we're here
And afterwards gone—to His home.
Ohuaya.

---

1. Translated by Timothy E. G. Bartel and used with permission.

Discussion Questions

1. One of the poetic elements that ties this poem together is the refrain of "Ohuaya." How does this refrain shape the poem? What does the placement of the refrain tell us about what Nezahualcoyotl wants to emphasize in the poem?

2. How does Nezahualcoyotl's repeated use of the words "only," "earth," and "home" contribute to the meaning and shape of the poem?

3. Throughout the poem, Nezahualcoyotl contrasts the experience of those on earth with those who have died. How optimistic is the poet about the afterlife? How pessimistic is he about life on earth?

4. If we will surely die, how can we enjoy the things on earth? Does the fear of death make the joys of life more significant or less?

5. If God is real and we will go to him when we die, what is the worth of the things on earth that we enjoy, such as art, food, and friendship? If these things will fade, how much should they matter to us?

CHAPTER 12

Anonymous

Introduction to "The Peace Prayer of Saint Francis"
TUAN HOANG

Despite what its name suggests, there is no evidence that the prayer below was written by Francis of Assisi. It was most likely a product of the early twentieth century, since its wording has been traced to a small devotional Catholic magazine in France in 1912. The explosion of the two world wars fueled the prayer's popularity among Catholics, especially after the Vatican's official newspaper published a version in January 1916. It then spread among other Christians and even non-Christians. As Augustine Thompson points out in the introduction of his biography of Francis of Assisi, Francis "would not have written such a piece, focused as it is on the self, with its constant repetition of the pronouns 'I' and 'me,' the words 'God' and 'Jesus' never appearing once."[1]

Fair enough. But it is fair, too, to note that few if any people have complained loudly about the misattribution. Could it be because Francis's well-known love for nature and animals is not far removed from the desire for societal peace expressed in the prayer? Or could it be that the simple prayer reflects his simplicity in the popular imagination? Whatever the explanation for the peace prayer's association with Francis, its popularity suggests that Francis might be a man for all Christian seasons and epochs.

The words "peace" and "eternal life" bookend the popular prayer from Francis of Assisi you're about to read. The implication is that they are one and the same, that peace on earth would lead to life with God in the afterlife. More significant is the desire of the Christian supplicant to become an "instrument" of peace. Both verses carry the assumption that Christians encounter and even generate hatred, injury, doubt, despair, darkness, and sadness during their earthly journeys. The prayer admits, too, that they naturally desire consolation, understanding, love, forgiveness, and life from others in their society.

The peace prayer upturns and reverses this paradigm. Forcefully and rhythmically, it calls for activism in society—though not political activism,

---

1. Augustine Thompson, *Francis of Assisi: A New Biography* (Ithaca, NY: Cornell University Press, 2012), ix.

which involves organization among the like-minded and, likely, confrontation and opposition to the different-minded. The call of this prayer is broader than politics. It calls for conducting one's life according to the Gospels and in kindness towards others. It is an aspirational prayer since the supplicant asks to be a better Christian by living Christian values antithetical to many harsh realities in society.

It is to this ideal and desire that the repetition of "grant that I may not so much seek to be _____ as to _____" of the second verse proves appealing and powerful. It juxtaposes the passive tense and the active one, confirming the call to follow Jesus Christ, the Prince of Peace. This verse also names a hierarchy of sorts about human needs: the needs for consolation then understanding then love. It concludes with an affirmation about the paradoxes of being a Christian, showing two sides of the same coin: giving and receiving, death and eternal life, and forgiveness that goes both ways. The prayer not only lists the most important values; it also empowers the supplicant to pursue them actively and purposefully.

The Peace Prayer of Saint Francis

Lord, make me an instrument of your peace:
where there is hatred, let me sow love;
where there is injury, pardon;
where there is doubt, faith;
where there is despair, hope;
where there is darkness, light;
where there is sadness, joy.

O divine Master, grant that I may not so much seek
to be consoled as to console,
to be understood as to understand,
to be loved as to love.
For it is in giving that we receive,
it is in pardoning that we are pardoned,
and it is in dying that we are born to eternal life.
Amen.

Discussion Questions

1. Think of the word *injury* in the context of this prayer, and then name at least three kinds of *injury* in society. What are they, and what are their effects?

2. How could Christians "receive" when they give, as the prayer suggests? And what do they receive?

3. The words "love" and "pardon" (and related forms) appear more than other nouns or verbs in this prayer. What is the relationship between love and pardon?

4. Do you feel empowered by this prayer as you read it out loud? If yes, how? If no, why not?

CHAPTER 13

Margery Kempe

Introduction to *The Book of Margery Kempe*

BETH ALLISON BARR

Only a few years after Geoffrey Chaucer was laid to rest in 1400 in the south transept of Westminster Abbey, a woman cried out to God in desperation. Her name was Margery Kempe (1373–1440), and while her life overlapped with England's noble bard, she shared only a few things in common with him. Both lived in the aftermath of the Black Death, during the Hundred Years' War, and through the tumult of Richard II's murder and usurpation by Henry IV. Both had upwardly mobile and politically connected families; both married and became parents.

Yet, while Chaucer's career as a courtier, soldier, civil servant, and poet mostly took off—earning him royal favor, politically important friends, and even a burial in Westminster Abbey—Kempe's career did not. She failed twice as an entrepreneur, and her husband once called her a "no good wife." The aftermath of a dangerous bout of postpartum depression helped Kempe find her true vocation, which proved as unconventional as her life became. She felt called to the service of God. But because she was married, she could not take religious vows. Kempe instead became a self-proclaimed mystic and pilgrim.

In short, Margery Kempe was not a stereotypical late medieval woman.

Kempe's obstinate perseverance to fulfill God's calling on her life extended to furthering her education. While it is possible that Kempe was as illiterate as some scholars have assumed, lacking the ability to read or write even in the vernacular, it is not likely. As a well-to-do laywoman, she needed basic literacy skills to perform her tasks as housewife and business owner. However, she would not have needed the ability to read or write Latin. So while Chaucer probably attended a local school (such as at St. Paul's Cathedral) and learned to read Latin poetry as a child, Kempe lacked the skills needed to read religious texts. She found herself wholly dependent on the clergy around her to preach to her, read to her, and even write for her. This is why, in the early years of the fifteenth century, she found herself despondently crying out to God for help. She hungered for knowledge but could not feed herself.

As you read about Kempe's desire to learn, compare your own education journey to hers. She prayed for God's intercession in facing obstacles. Her learning required years of study in conversation with a devoted teacher. Ultimately, her education prepared her to be, as St. Peter advises, ready to give an answer for her faith. Kempe could never take for granted the ability to read religious texts and to learn from the wisdom of others. She had to diligently pursue them every day of her life.

From *The Book of Margery Kempe*

Once, when at her devotion, she hungered right so after God's word.[1]

She cried out, "Alas! Lord, as many clerks as you have in this world, that you would not send me one of them that might fill my soul with your word and with reading of Holy Scripture. For all the clerks in the world may not fill it, for I think my soul is ever hungry. If I had gold enough, I would give every day a noble to have every day a sermon, for Thy word is more worthy to me than all the good in this world. Therefore, blessed Lord, have pity on me, for you have taken away the anchorite from me who was my singular solace and comfort. He had many times refreshed me with Thine holy word."

Then answered our Lord Jesus Christ in her soul, saying, "One shall come from afar who shall fulfill your desire."

So, many days after this answer, there came a new priest to Lynn who had never known her before. When he saw her going in the streets, he was greatly moved to speak with her and asked other folk what sort of woman she was. They said they trusted God that she was a right, good woman. So the priest sent for her, praying for her to come and speak with him and his mother (he had hired rooms for his mother and himself and they lived together). Then the said creature came to see what he wanted. She spoke with him and his mother and had right good cheer of them both.

Then the priest took a book. He read therein how our Lord, seeing the city of Jerusalem, wept over it, rehearsing the mischiefs and sorrows that would come to it. . . . When the said creature heard read how our Lord wept, she too wept sore and cried loudly. Neither the priest nor his mother knew the cause of her weeping. When her crying and her weeping stopped, they rejoiced and were right merry in our Lord. Then she took her leave and parted from them. When she was gone, the priest said to his mother, "I marvel much of this woman, why she wept and cried so! Nevertheless, I think she is a good woman, and I desire greatly to speak more with her." His mother was well pleased and counseled that he should do so. Afterwards the same priest loved her and trusted her very much. He blessed the time that ever he knew her, for he found great ghostly comfort in her. She caused him to look up much good scripture and many a good

---

1. Translation by Beth Allison Barr. Chapters 58–60, 62.

doctor, which he would not have studied if she had not been there. He read to her many a good book about high contemplation as well as other books, such as the Bible (with the commentary of scholars), Saint Bride's book, Hilton's book, Bonaventure's *Stimulus Amoris*, the *Incendium Amoris*, and such others.

And then she knew that it was a spirit sent of God which said to her these words (as is written a little before, when she complained for lack of reading): "One shall come from afar who shall fulfill your desire." And, thus, she knew by experience that it was a right, true spirit. The foresaid priest then read her books for seven or eight years, to the great increase of his knowledge and merit. He suffered many an evil word for his love, inasmuch as he read to her so many books and supported her weeping and crying. But afterwards, when he received a benefice and had a large cure of souls [pastoral ministry], he was glad that he had read so much before.

Thus, through the hearing of holy books and the hearing of holy sermons, she increased in contemplation and holy meditation. It is impossible to record all the holy thoughts, holy speech, and the high revelations which our Lord showed to her—both of herself and of other men and women, also of many souls, some to be saved and some to be damned . . .

[Margery Kempe is brought before the archbishop on charges of heresy. Indeed, the archbishop calls her a "false heretic." Listen to how she responds as their conversation progresses.]

And then, anon, the Archbishop put to her the Articles of Faith. God gave her grace to answer well, truly, and readily without any great study, so that the archbishop might not find blame with her. Then the Archbishop turned to the clerks [in the room with him], "She knows her faith well enough. What shall I do with her"?

The clerks said, "We know well that she can say the Articles of Faith, but we will not suffer her to dwell among us, for the people have great faith in her dalliance, and peradventure she might pervert some of them.

Then the Archbishop said to her, "I am evil informed of you; I hear it said you are a right wicked woman." And she said to him, "Sir, so I hear that you are a wicked man. And if you be as wicked as men say, you shall never come to heaven unless you amend while you are still here."

The said he angrily, "Why, you, what say men of me?" She answered, "Other men, sir, can tell you well enough." Then said a great clerk with a furred hood, "Peace! You speak of yourself and let him be!"

Afterwards, the Archbishop said to her, "Lay your hand on the book here before me and swear that you shall go out of my diocese as soon as you may."

"Nay, sir," she replied. "I pray you, give me leave to go again into York to take leave of my friends." Then he gave her leave for one day or two. She thought it was too short a time, wherefore she said again. "Sir, I may not go out of this diocese so hastily, for I must tarry and speak with good men before I go. I must, sir, with your leave, go to Bridlington and speak with my confessor, a good man. He was the good prior's confessor, who is now canonized."

Then said the Archbishop to her, "You shall swear that you shall not teach nor challenge the people in my diocese."

"Nay, sir, I shall not swear," she said. "For I shall speak of God and rebuke those who swear great oaths wheresoever I go unto the time that the Pope and Holy Church proclaim that none may be so bold as to speak of God. For God almighty forbids not, sir, that we shall speak of him. Also, the Gospel makes mention that, when the woman had heard our Lord preach, she came before him with a loud voice and said, 'Blessed be the womb that bore you and the teats that gave you suck.' Then our Lord said again to her, 'Forsooth! So are they blessed that hear the word of God and keep it.' And, therefore, sir, I think that the Gospel gives me leave to speak of God."

"Ahh! Sir!," said the clerks. "Here we see that she has a devil in her, for she speaks of the Gospel." Quickly a great clerk brought forth a book and read Saint Paul for his part against her that no woman should preach. She answered thereto, saying, "I preach not, Sir, I come into no pulpit. I use but communication and good words, and that will I do while I live."

[After further conversation, the Archbishop successfully sends Margery Kempe from his court, paying a man five shillings to escort her out. Kempe remembers her confrontation with the Archbishop as a triumph.]

Then she, going back to York, was received by many people and important clerks. They rejoiced in the Lord who had given her, an illiterate woman, the wit and wisdom to answer so many learned men without villainy or blame. Thanks be to God!

Discussion Questions

1. What is Margery Kempe so hungry to learn? How should we imitate her hunger?
2. What do the "texts" Margery Kempe desires to learn from and were available to her tell us about her education?
3. What do Margery Kempe and the priest in Lynne gain from their sessions together?
4. In what ways did Margery Kempe's love of learning affect her faith?
5. In what ways did the people around Margery Kempe impact her ability to learn and develop her faith? How does her experience compare to our lives today?

CHAPTER 14

William Shakespeare

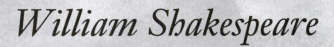

Introduction to *King Lear*

JULIANNE SANDBERG

In the play *King Lear*, William Shakespeare (1564–1616) staged the tragic story of a king who, through his own shortsighted choices, falls from power but acquires glimpses of wisdom and self-recognition through this experience of loss. The play opens with the elderly Lear asking his three daughters how much they love him. When the eldest two, Goneril and Regan, deceptively flatter him with lofty praise, he rewards them with a portion of his kingdom. But Cordelia, the youngest and only loyal daughter, refuses to play Lear's self-gratifying game and is banished from the kingdom. Everything Lear holds dear—crown, home, family, and companionship—quickly slips from his grasp when Goneril and Regan strip their father of all his power. Lear's tragedy is compounded by that of Gloucester, his friend and adviser, who experiences a similar reversal when his disloyal son, Edmund, orchestrates his father's demise, which ultimately leads to Gloucester having his eyes gouged out.

By the time we arrive at act 4, scene 6, Lear and Gloucester are a weep-worthy sight. Lear has been driven to madness, Gloucester has just barely escaped his own suicide, and they reunite in this scene of sorrow. They likely are wounded and bloody, barely upright, and dressed in rags, their bodies mirroring the depths of their brokenness. Along with Edgar, Gloucester's faithful son, we grieve their fates and grapple with the paths that led them to such tragedy.

But it is here, in this place of sorrow and confusion, that Lear learns wisdom. Where before he faulted only his daughters and saw himself as "a man more sinned against than sinning,"[1] he now turns the critique toward himself. When he asserts, "They told me I was everything; 'tis a lie, I am not ague-proof," he names more than his daughters' deception; he also identifies his own vulnerability. Despite what he preferred to think, he is not invincible but, in fact, weak and finite, not altogether different from a crying babe, lacking agency and perception. Perhaps more importantly, Lear recognizes that he, too, is capable of the very sins for which he has hypocritically chastised others.

This recognition of his own weakness and pride allows Lear to see with

---

1. William Shakespeare, *King Lear*, act 3, sc. 2, lines 59–60.

different eyes. He has lived his life convinced of his exceptionalism, as though his wealth and status could protect him from sorrow and suffering. His own vulnerability, he learns, connects him to the rest of humanity and allows him to see himself and others differently. He thus becomes an emblem of humility's necessity.

For the Christian student, Lear's example suggests that any act of learning requires that we first humbly recognize our limitations. We may not always see clearly; our untested certainty could be misdirected; our understanding of ourselves or others may be wrong or incomplete. Recognizing our proclivity to err and misperceive invites us to suspend hasty judgment and open ourselves up to a richer and truer understanding of ourselves and our world. We are then positioned for empathy, a virtue that literature—and perhaps study of all kinds—invites us to cultivate. For Lear, and no less for us, humility is the catalyst of wisdom.

From Shakespeare's *King Lear*, Act 4, Scene 6

Edgar: Bear free and patient thoughts. But who comes here?

Enter King Lear, fantastically dressed with wild flowers

> The safer sense will ne'er accommodate
> His master thus.

King Lear: No, they cannot touch me for coining;[2] I am the king himself.

Edgar: O thou side-piercing sight!

King Lear: Nature's above art in that respect. There's your press-money.[3] That fellow handles his bow like a crow-keeper:[4] draw me a clothier's yard.[5] Look, look, a mouse! Peace, peace; this piece of toasted cheese will do 't.[6] There's my gauntlet;[7] I'll prove it on a giant. Bring up the brown bills.[8] O, well flown, bird![9] i' the clout, i' the clout:[10] hewgh! Give the word.

Edgar: Sweet marjoram.

King Lear: Pass.

Gloucester: I know that voice.

King Lear: Ha! Goneril, with a white beard! They flattered me like a dog; and told me I had white hairs in my beard ere the black ones were there.

---

2. Counterfeiting.
3. Money paid in advance, often to a soldier.
4. Scarecrow.
5. A measure for clothing, or the length of a long arrow.
6. Will bait the mouse.
7. A glove worn with armor.
8. A speared weapon.
9. Arrow.
10. The mark shot at.

To say 'ay' and 'no' to every thing that I said 'ay' and 'no' too was no good divinity.[11] When the rain came to wet me once, and the wind to make me chatter; when the thunder would not peace at my bidding; there I found 'em, there I smelt 'em out. Go to, they are not men o' their words: they told me I was everything; 'tis a lie, I am not ague-proof.[12]

Gloucester: The trick[13] of that voice I do well remember:

Is 't not the king?

King Lear: Ay, every inch a king:

When I do stare, see how the subject quakes.

I pardon that man's life. What was thy cause?

Adultery? Thou shalt not die: die for adultery!

No: The wren goes to 't, and the small gilded fly

Does lecher in my sight. Let copulation thrive;

For Gloucester's bastard son was kinder to his father

Than my daughters got 'tween the lawful sheets.

To 't, luxury,[14] pell-mell! for I lack soldiers.

Behold yond simpering[15] dame,

Whose face between her forks presages snow;[16]

That minces[17] virtue, and does shake the head

To hear of pleasure's name;

The fitchew,[18] nor the soiled horse, goes to 't

With a more riotous appetite.

Down from the waist they are Centaurs,[19]

Though women all above:

But to the girdle[20] do the gods inherit,

Beneath is all the fiends'; There's hell, there's darkness,

There's the sulphurous pit, burning, scalding,

Stench, consumption; fie, fie, fie! pah, pah!

Give me an ounce of civet, good apothecary,

To sweeten my imagination: there's money for thee.

Gloucester: O, let me kiss that hand!

---

11. Poor theology.
12. Resistant to fever or disease.
13. A characteristic form.
14. Lasciviousness, lust.
15. Coy, smiling.
16. That is, the area between her legs suggests frigidity.
17. Performs, enacts.
18. A polecat; a term of contempt.
19. Mythological creatures that have the torso of a human and the body and legs of a horse.
20. Waist.

King Lear: Let me wipe it first; it smells of mortality.

Gloucester: O ruin'd piece of nature! This great world
    Shall so wear out to nought. Dost thou know me?

King Lear: I remember thine eyes well enough. Dost thou squiny[21] at me?
    No, do thy worst, blind Cupid! I'll not love.
    Read thou this challenge; mark but the penning of it.

Gloucester: Were all the letters suns, I could not see one.

Edgar: I would not take this from report; it is,
    And my heart breaks at it.

King Lear: Read.

Gloucester: What, with the case of eyes?

King Lear: O, ho, are you there with me? No eyes in your head, nor no money
    in your purse? Your eyes are in a heavy case, your purse in a light; yet you
    see how this world goes.

Gloucester: I see it feelingly.

King Lear: What, art mad? A man may see how this world goes with no eyes.
    Look with thine ears: see how yond justice[22] rails upon yond simple
    thief. Hark, in thine ear: change places; and, handy-dandy, which is
    the justice, which is the thief? Thou hast seen a farmer's dog bark at
    a beggar?

Gloucester: Ay, sir.

King Lear: And the creature run from the cur?[23] There thou mightst behold
    the great image of authority: a dog's obeyed in office.
    Thou rascal beadle,[24] hold[25] thy bloody hand!
    Why dost thou lash that whore? Strip thine own back;
    Thou hotly lust'st to use her in that kind
    For which thou whipp'st her. The usurer hangs the cozener.[26]
    Through tatter'd clothes small vices do appear;
    Robes and furr'd gowns hide all. Plate[27] sin with gold,
    And the strong lance of justice hurtless[28] breaks:
    Arm it in rags, a pigmy's straw does pierce it.
    None does offend, none, I say, none; I'll able 'em:

---

21. Squint.
22. Judge, magistrate.
23. An untamed dog.
24. A messenger of justice; an underbailiff.
25. Restrain.
26. A deceiver, cheat.
27. To cover or overlay.
28. Harmlessly.

Take that of me, my friend, who have the power
To seal the accuser's lips. Get thee glass eyes;
And like a scurvy politician,[29] seem
To see the things thou dost not. Now, now, now, now:
Pull off my boots: harder, harder: so.

Edgar: O, matter and impertinency[30] mix'd! Reason in madness!

King Lear: If thou wilt weep my fortunes, take my eyes.
I know thee well enough; thy name is Gloucester:
Thou must be patient; we came crying hither:
Thou know'st, the first time that we smell the air,
We wawl and cry. I will preach to thee: mark.

Gloucester: Alack, alack the day!

King Lear: When we are born, we cry that we are come
To this great stage of fools: this a good block;
It were a delicate stratagem, to shoe
A troop of horse with felt: I'll put 't in proof;
And when I have stol'n upon these sons-in-law,
Then, kill, kill, kill, kill, kill, kill!

Enter a Gentleman, with Attendants

Gentleman: O, here he is: lay hand upon him. Sir,
Your most dear daughter—

King Lear: No rescue? What, a prisoner? I am even
The natural fool of fortune. Use me well;
You shall have ransom. Let me have surgeons;
I am cut to the brains.

Gentleman: You shall have any thing.

King Lear: No seconds? all myself?
Why, this would make a man a man of salt,
To use his eyes for garden water-pots,
Ay, and laying autumn's dust.

Gentleman: Good sir,—

King Lear: I will die bravely, like a bridegroom. What!
I will be jovial: come, come; I am a king,
My masters, know you that.

Gentleman: You are a royal one, and we obey you.

---

29. A schemer or plotter.
30. Substance and irrelevancy.

King Lear: Then there's life in 't. Nay, if you get it, you
shall get it with running. Sa, sa, sa, sa.

Exit running; Attendants follow

Gentleman: A sight most pitiful in the meanest wretch,
Past speaking of in a king! Thou hast one daughter,
Who redeems nature from the general curse
Which twain have brought her to.

Edgar: Hail, gentle sir.

Gentleman: Sir, speed you: what's your will?

Edgar: Do you hear aught, sir, of a battle toward?

Gentleman: Most sure and vulgar: every one hears that,
Which can distinguish sound.

Edgar: But, by your favour,
How near's the other army?

Gentleman: Near and on speedy foot; the main descry[31]
Stands on the hourly thought.

Edgar: I thank you, sir: that's all.

Gentleman: Though that the queen on special cause is here,
Her army is moved on.

Edgar: I thank you, sir.

Exit Gentleman

Gloucester: You ever-gentle gods, take my breath from me:
Let not my worser spirit tempt me again
To die before you please!

Edgar: Well pray you, father.

Gloucester: Now, good sir, what are you?

Edgar: A most poor man, made tame to fortune's blows;
Who, by the art of known and feeling sorrows,
Am pregnant to good pity. Give me your hand,
I'll lead you to some biding.[32]

Gloucester: Hearty thanks:
The bounty and the benison[33] of heaven
To boot, and boot!

---

31. Discovery, appearance.
32. An abode.
33. Blessing.

Discussion Questions

1. Look back over the selection above and circle or underline all the words that relate to sight or blindness. Why might this emphasis be important to the narrative?

2. Much of what Lear says in this scene may seem crazed and nonsensical, but his words often have substance behind them. What truths about the human experience can be gleaned from Lear's seemingly erratic statements?

3. In what ways might the world be perceived as "a great stage of fools"? How do the characters in this passage embody this idea?

4. Humility is not a popular virtue. Why do you think that is?

5. What practical steps can we take to cultivate humility in our lives? How would humility affect the way we learn, read, and study?

CHAPTER 15

John Amos Comenius

Introduction to *The Labyrinth of the World and the Paradise of the Heart*

DAVID I. SMITH

The year 2020 marked the 350th anniversary of the death of John Amos Comenius (1592–1670). His life was not easy. He spent much of it as a refugee amid a series of European wars and associated plagues. He lost possessions and family members amid the conflict on more than one occasion. He was a pastor and later a bishop in a small Christian denomination from Moravia, an area now part of the Czech Republic. His flock was forced into exile by the Thirty Years' War. They were never restored to their homeland.

Comenius might have been excused for keeping his head down, but he set himself a visionary agenda that included translating Scripture, transforming politics, and reforming education. His more than two hundred written works include repeated reflections on how education needed to change. In one of them, toward the end of his life, he wrote, "It is desired that not just one particular person be fully formed into full humanity, or a few, or even many, but every single person, young and old, rich and poor, of high and low birth, men and women, in a word, every person who is born: so that in the end, in time, proper formation might be restored to the whole human race, throughout every age, class, sex, and nationality."[1]

Comenius demanded that education be available for everyone, regardless of age, ethnicity, status, means, or ability, simply because of their dignity and calling as beings made in God's image. He argued that this universal education should not be a narrow job training, but a broadly based formation in the task of being human. People called to image God needed to learn to live well in a complex world. Education should, he insisted, be founded on the recognition that everything that humans do demands thought, is shaped by virtue and vice, and unfolds before God. Rationality, virtue, and faith must not be separated. Education must, he warned, be cleansed of the various forms of violence endemic

---

1. John Amos Comenius, *Pampaedia* 1:6, translation mine. Latin text: Johann Amos Comenius, *Pampaedia: lateinischer Text und deutsche Übersetzung*, ed. Dmitrij Tschiżewkij (Heidelberg: Quelle & Meyer, 1960).

to schooling. Violence against God's living images—young or old, rich or poor, male or female—amounted to violence against God himself.

As well as making his mark in the history of educational thought, Comenius found time to become a significant figure in the development of Czech literature. His satirical allegory *The Labyrinth of the World and the Paradise of the Heart* was written in Czech decades before Bunyan contributed *Pilgrim's Progress* to English literature. The *Labyrinth of the World* follows a pilgrim as he is led through the various human groups and callings that make up society. He is led by deceitful guides who force him into a bit and bridle and give him special spectacles made from the glass of presumption and the frames of habit. These spectacles make the ugly seem beautiful and the beautiful ugly. They are supposed to make the fallen world look normal so the pilgrim will be docile and accept the way things are as the way they have to be.

Fortunately, the spectacles do not quite sit straight on his nose. By tilting his head and squinting, he is able to see past them and glimpse a reality that does not match what his guides are telling him. After some time exploring various human practices with his false guides and faulty spectacles, he arrives among those who teach and study. Here, he is assured, is a world of peace, nobility, and usefulness. Here scholars are pursuing and sharing knowledge, students are learning what they need to know and submitting to appropriate discipline, and the most devoted learners are increasing their store of wisdom—or are they?

From *Labyrinth of the World*, Chapter 10, "The Pilgrim Examines the Learned Class: A General Survey"

1. "I understand where your thoughts are pulling you," my guide said to me. "Among the learned with you, among the learned. You will surely be attracted by this easier, more peaceful, and more useful life for the mind."

"Indeed that is so," said the interpreter. "For what can be more delightful than ignoring and neglecting the toils of the physical body in order to engage only in the examination of all manner of noble things? That is truly what makes mortal people similar, indeed almost equal, to immortal God. For they hope to become omniscient, knowing and pursuing all that was or will be in heaven, on earth, or in the depths. It is true, however, that not everyone reaches the same level of perfection."

"Lead me there," I said. "Why do you hesitate?"

First of all, a difficult examination

2. We came to a gate called Discipline. It was long, narrow, and dark, full of armed guards, to whom each one who wished to enter the street of the learned

had to give account and seek their guidance. I saw that crowds of people, especially the young, came and immediately went through various rigorous examinations. The first examination for each person investigated what kind of purse, buttocks, head, brain (which they judged by the nasal mucus), and skin they brought. If the head were of steel, the brain inside it of mercury, the buttocks of lead, the skin of iron, and the purse of gold, they praised the person and readily conducted him further. If he lacked one of these five qualities, they either ordered him to return or, foreboding an unhappy outcome, admitted him at random. Wondering at this, I said, "Does so much depend on these five metals that they are sought so diligently?"

"Very much, indeed," the interpreter answered. "If one does not have a head of steel, it will burst; without a brain of mercury, he would not have a mirror; without skin of sheet iron, he would not endure the educational process; without a seat of lead, he would not endure sitting and would lose everything; and without a purse of gold, where would he obtain time and teachers, both living and dead? Or do you presume that such great things can be obtained without cost?"

I then understood the direction of his comments, that one must bring to this profession health, wits, perseverance, patience, and money. "It can be truly affirmed," I said. "*Non cuivis contingit adire Corinthum*. Not all wood is sufficiently solid."

Entrance is difficult and painful Memoria artificialis

3. We proceeded further to the gate, and I saw that each guard took one or more of the candidates and led them along. He blew something in their ears, rubbed their eyes, cleaned their noses and nostrils, pulled out and trimmed their tongues, folded and unfolded their hands and fingers, and I do not know what more. Some even tried to bore holes in their heads and pour something into them. Seeing me alarmed, my interpreter said, "Do not be amazed. The learned must possess hands, tongue, eyes, ears, brain, and all internal and external senses different from the masses of ignorant people. For this reason they are reshaped, and this cannot be done without toil and pain."

Then I looked and saw how much these poor wretches had to pay for their education. I am not talking about their purses, but about their skin, which they had to expose. Indeed, they were often struck with fists, pointers, rods, and canes on their face, head, back, and seat until they shed blood and were almost completely covered with stripes, scars, bruises, and calluses. Seeing this, before they surrendered themselves to the guards, some only looked through the gate and ran away. Others, tearing themselves free from the hands of their educators, also fled. A lesser number of them persevered until they were released. Desiring to enter this profession, I too underwent this education, though not without difficulty and bitterness.

Every scholar is given a password

4. When we went through the gate, I saw that they gave to each who had undergone the preliminary training a stamp by which he could be recognized as belonging among the learned: an inkwell under his belt, a pen behind his ear, and for the hand an empty book for collecting knowledge. I too received these items. Searchall then said to me, "We have here four paths: philosophy, medicine, law, and theology. Where shall we go first?"

"What do you consider best?" I asked.

"Let us first go to the square where everyone assembles so that you can look at them all together. Then we will go to their various lecture halls."

Deficiencies even among the learned

5. He led me to a certain square where there was a mob of students, teachers, doctors, and priests—both youths and gray-haired men. Some of them gathered in groups, discussing and disputing among themselves. Others squeezed into corners out of the sight of the rest. Some (as I clearly perceived, though I dared not speak of it) had eyes, but no tongues; others had tongues, but no eyes; still others had only ears, without eyes or tongues. Thus I realized that here too there were deficiencies. Seeing that all were going out from and coming into a certain place, like bees swarming in and out of a hive, I asked that we also might enter.

Description of a library

6. So we entered. Here was a great hall, the end of which I could not see, but on all sides it was full of shelves, compartments, boxes, and cartons. A hundred thousand wagons could not remove them and each had its own inscription and title. "Into what kind of apothecary shop have we come?" I asked.

"Into an apothecary shop where medicines against ailments of the mind are kept," said the interpreter. "This place is properly called a library. Just look at these endless stores of wisdom!"

I looked around and saw groups of scholars coming and walking around these items. Some, choosing the finest and most sophisticated, tore off a piece and ate it, slowly chewing and digesting. Approaching one of these scholars, I asked what he was doing.

"I am improving myself," he answered. "And how does it taste?" I inquired.

"As long as one chews, it tastes bitter or acidic, but later it turns sweet," he replied.

"But why are you doing this?" I asked.

"It is easier for me to carry it inside," he answered, "and in this way I am surer of it. Do you not see its use?" I looked at him more carefully, and I saw that he was stout and fat, had a healthy color, his eyes shone like candles, his speech was careful, and everything about him was lively.

"Just look at these people!" the interpreter said to me.

The evils of studies

7. I saw some people who behaved very greedily, stuffing themselves with whatever came into their hands. Observing them more carefully, I noticed that they neither improved their complexion nor gained flesh or fat, but their stomachs were swollen and never satisfied. I also saw that what they crammed into themselves came out of them again undigested, either from above or from below. Some of them fainted from dizziness or went mad. Others grew pale, pined, and died. Many who saw these people pointed at them, indicating how dangerous it was to use books (as they called the boxes). Thereupon some ran away, and others exhorted people to deal with those things cautiously. Hence this latter group did not eat the books. Rather they filled them in sacks and bags and carried them in front and in back. (Most of the titles selected were Vocabulary, Dictionary, Lexicon, *Promtuarium, Florilegium, Loci communes*, Postils, Concordances, Herbaria, and so forth, according to what each judged most appropriate.) They carried these about, and whenever they had to speak or to write, they pulled them out of their pockets and drew forth whatever was needed for their mouth or pen. Noticing this, I said, "These people carry their knowledge in their pockets."

"Memoriae subsidia," my interpreter replied. "Haven't you heard of them?"

I had indeed heard this custom praised by some people, for it is said that they brought forth only knowledge that was sanctioned. This may very well be, but I also noticed other inconveniences. It happened in my presence that some scattered and lost their boxes, while those of others, who had laid them aside, caught fire. Oh, what running about, wringing of hands, lamenting and crying for help ensued. For the moment, no one wanted to dispute, write, or preach anymore; rather they walked about with downcast head, cringed, blushed, and sought another container from whomever they knew, with entreaty or with money. Those who had an inner store of knowledge did not fear such an incident.

Students who do not study

8. Meanwhile, I saw others who did not bother carrying the boxes of books in their pockets but brought them to their rooms. Going in after them, I saw that

they prepared beautiful cases for them. They painted them in various colors, and some even adorned them with silver and gold. They looked at the books, putting them on and taking them off the shelves again. They packed and unpacked them, and approaching and withdrawing, they showed each other and strangers how beautiful they looked. All this was done superficially. Occasionally, some also looked at the titles so that they would know what they were called. "Why are these people playing such games?" I asked.

"Dear fellow," the interpreter answered, "it is a fine thing to have a beautiful library."

"Even if it is not used?" I questioned.

"Those who love libraries are reckoned among the learned," he explained.

I thought to myself, "This is like counting someone among blacksmiths who has heaps of hammers and tongs but doesn't know how to use them." But I did not dare say this for fear of suffering a blow.

Evils of writing books

9. Entering the hall again, I noticed that the apothecary containers on all sides were ever increasing, and I tried to see where they were coming from. I saw a certain closed off area. Entering it, I found many turners who vied with one another to shape more carefully and artistically the boxes from wood, bone, stone, and various other materials. They filled them with salve or medicine and offered them for general consumption. "These people are worthy of praise and all honor," the interpreter said to me, "for sparing no toil or effort for the increase of wisdom and knowledge, they share their glorious gifts with others."

I desired to examine how these potions (which are called gifts and wisdom) were made and prepared. I observed one or two people who gathered fragrant spices and herbs, then cut, ground, boiled, and distilled them, preparing various delightful remedies, cures, syrups, and other medicines useful for human life. On the other hand, I saw some who merely took from the vessels of others and transferred the contents to their own. Of these there were hundreds. "These people are only pouring water from one vessel into another," I exclaimed.

"And so is knowledge increased," my interpreter responded. "For is it not possible that one thing is prepared in different ways? And something can always be added to or improved in the original substance."

"And ruined as well," I answered angrily, seeing clearly that a fraud was being perpetrated. Indeed, some seized others' vessels in order to fill several of their own, then diluted the contents as much as possible, even with dirty dishwater. Still others thickened it with various odds and ends, even dust or refuse, so that it would appear as if something new had been made. Meanwhile, they added inscriptions more glorious than the original ones and, like other quacks, they shamelessly extolled their own work.

I was both amazed and angered (as I noted above) that few examined the true content of the substance, but took everything indiscriminately. And if they chose, they looked only at the outer appearance and inscriptions. Then I understood why it is that so few of them attained inner freshness of mind. For the more of these medicines a person gulped down, the more he vomited, turned pale, faded and wasted away.

I also observed that the great part of these fine remedies were never even used by human beings, but were only the portion of moths, worms, spiders and flies, dust and mildew, and were finally relegated to dusty shelves and back corners. Fearing this fate, some people, as soon as they had prepared their remedy (indeed some even before they had seriously begun to prepare it), ran to neighbors to beg for prefaces, verses, and anagrams. They also sought patrons who would lend their names and purses to the new preparations. They painted most ornate titles and inscriptions or embellished the various figures and engravings with decorative floral designs. They personally brought such potions to people, and crammed them down their throats against their will.

I saw, however, that this effort finally failed because the concoctions had been multiplied too much. Therefore, I pitied some who could have had complete peace, yet needlessly and uselessly gave themselves to this quackery, even at the risk of their own reputation and to the detriment of their neighbors. When I offered warnings in this regard, I gained only hatred, as if I had impeded the common good. I kept silent about how some prepared their quack remedies out of thoroughly toxic materials. As a result, as many poisons as medicines were being sold. Though I bore this evil with displeasure, there was no one to correct it.

Discord and strife

10. Then we returned to the square of the learned, and behold there were quarrels, strife, and fights between them. It was rare indeed for someone not to be involved in some type of scuffle. Not only the young (whose impudence could be attributed to their age), but also the old, were fighting each other. For the more learned one considered himself or was esteemed by others, the more quarrels he began; and he fought, hacked, threw, and shot those around him until it was frightful to behold. He based his honor and esteem on such behavior.

"But dear God, what is this?" I asked. "For I thought and you had promised me that this profession was the most peaceful, yet I find so many quarrels."

"You do not understand, my son," the interpreter answered. "They are merely sharpening their wits."

"Sharpening their wits?" I retorted. "But I see wounds, blood, anger, and murderous hatred of one toward another. Even among the working class, I have seen nothing like this."

"Doubtless," said he, "for the arts of such people are manual and slavish, whereas these others are concerned with the liberal arts. Therefore, what is not permitted or even tolerated by the former group is freely granted to the latter."

"But how that can be called orderly I do not know," I said. It is true that their weapons did not appear fearful. For the spears, swords, and daggers with which they hacked and stabbed each other were made of leather, and they did not hold them in their hands but in their mouths. Their artillery was made of reeds and sand, loaded with dust dissolved in water, and they shot at each other with paper. On the surface, as I said, none of this appeared fearful. However, seeing how one who was lightly wounded jerked, cried out, writhed, and fled, I clearly recognized that this was no joke, but a real fight. One individual was attacked by a great number of others until the clang of swords deafened the ears and paper bullets fell on him like hail. Defending himself courageously, one person drove off and dispersed all his assailants. Another fell, overcome by wounds. I observed here a cruelty unusual elsewhere. They spared neither the wounded nor the dead, but mercilessly hacked and lashed at them all the more, each more gladly proving his valor against one who did not defend himself. Some behaved more moderately, though they were not free from disputes and misunderstandings. For no sooner did someone utter a word than someone else immediately contradicted him. There were even arguments about whether snow was white or black, or whether fire was hot or cold.

Great confusion among them

11. Then some began to intervene in these quarrels and to counsel peace. This sight gladdened me. A rumor also arose that all quarrels were to be settled. The question remained as to who would bring about this reconciliation. The reply was that by the permission of Queen Wisdom, the most judicious people of all estates should be chosen and given authority, after hearing the opposing sides, to make a decision on each case and to declare which was the truer argument. Many of those who were chosen or who wished to be judges gathered together. There also assembled a great multitude of those who disputed among themselves over different views. Among them I saw Aristotle with Plato, Cicero with Sallust, Scotus with Aquinas, Bartolus with Bardus, Erasmus with the Sorbonnists, Ramus and Campanella with the Peripatetics, Copernicus

with Ptolemy, Theophrastus with Galen, Hus, Luther, and others with the pope and the Jesuits, Brenz with Beza, Bodin with Wier, Sleidanus with Surius, Schmiedlein with the Calvinists, Gomarus with Arminius, to the Rosicrucians with the philosophasters, and countless others. When the *conciliatores* ordered them to present their charges, complaints, arguments, and inferences in the shortest possible written form, they piled up such heaps of books that six thousand years would not suffice to survey them. They desired that this outline of their opinions be accepted at the moment. Later, as need arose, each should be given complete freedom to explain and defend their views more fully. Then they began to look at these books; and whatever book one scanned immediately intoxicated him, and he began to defend its ideas. So there arose among the arbiters and mediators great dissensions; for one defended one view, another something else. Consequently, they solved nothing and dispersed. The learned returned to their quarrels, and I was brought to tears.

Discussion Questions

1. How many different forms of violence afflict the educational world glimpsed by Comenius's pilgrim? Do they persist in your own present-day educational context?
2. As Comenius satirized the sin-soaked failings of education, what did he imply positively about the way things are supposed to be?
3. Even amid the chaos, some are showing signs of health. Who are they and why are they doing better than their fellows?
4. Which parts of Comenius's picture challenge your own practices as a student?
5. Later in the story, the pilgrim despairs but is visited by Christ and undergoes a profound personal transformation. He then turns back to the world with a Christian gaze. How do you think such a change might lead to different educational practices?

CHAPTER 16

George Herbert

Introduction to Five Poems of George Herbert

JASON CRAWFORD

What does prayer have to do with learning? Can our work as learners teach us how to pray? Can our practices of prayer guide our practices of academic inquiry? If biblical texts such as the Psalms are any indication, prayer can involve a lot of things: celebration, contemplation, thanksgiving, lament, complaint, confession, petition. Often, in the Scriptures, prayer takes the form of artistic making, of poetry and song. And often prayer, like learning, takes the form of conversation, of talking with a God who talks back. Can academic learning teach us to converse and create in cooperation with a speaking and creative God? Can our endeavors in learning—our research essays, piano scales, and physics experiments—be invitations to prayer, exercises in listening and love?

The poetry of George Herbert can help us reflect on the significance of prayer to our academic work. Herbert walked away from a brilliant public career at age thirty-one and spent years wrestling with questions about his own work and vocation, finally devoting himself to a humble pastoral appointment in the Church of England. In those troubled years, unknown to all but a few friends, Herbert was writing one of the most searching, spiritually intense bodies of lyric poetry in the English language. He called his poems "a picture of the conflicts that have passed between God and my soul,"[1] and they read like a modern book of psalms, the record of one believer's fiery conversations with a God he loves but cannot understand.

The five poems selected here exemplify the prayerful qualities of George Herbert's poetry. "Redemption" offers a parable about who the poet imagines God to be, where he goes searching for this imagined God, and what he discovers in the shocking moment when at last they meet. "Discipline" and "The Collar" record the poet's cries from places of failure and frustration. These poems capture the experience of searching for a God who seems far off, and they reflect on what happens when our best efforts seem futile, crippled by fear and self-regard.

---

1. For a detailed account of Herbert's life, see John Drury, *Music at Midnight: The Life and Poetry of George Herbert* (Chicago: University of Chicago Press, 2013); this quotation appears on p. 251.

In "Prayer (I)," the poet imagines prayer as a dynamic, surprising, life-giving encounter between God and his creation. And in "Love (III)" the poet dramatizes this encounter by imagining himself in conversation with a Love who finds him in error, sets out to show him something better, and bids him sit and eat.

In all these poems, Herbert asks who God is and who we are; they are poems of inquiry. In all of them, he finds fresh ways to lament, celebrate, and proclaim; they are poems of creative experimentation. And in all of them he enters into the discipline of listening; they are poems of conversation. These activities—inquiry, creativity, and conversation—are at the core of our work as learners. As Herbert discovers the possibilities of prayer, he can help us to discover the possibilities of learning. He might help us to see our academic work as a site of prayerful encounter, an invitation to gather at the table of grace.

Five Poems
Redemption

Having been tenant long to a rich Lord,[2]
> Not thriving, I resolved to be bold
> And make a suit unto him, to afford
A new small-rented lease, and cancel the old.

In heaven at his manor I him sought:
> They told me there that he was lately gone
> About some land, which he had dearly bought
Long since on earth, to take possession.

I straight returned and, knowing his great birth,
> Sought him accordingly in great resorts—
> In cities, theaters, gardens, parks, and courts.
At length I heard a ragged noise and mirth

> Of thieves and murderers: there I him espied,
> Who straight *Your suit is granted* said, and died.

---

2. I've edited the text of these poems from the first edition of Herbert's poetry collection, *The Temple* (1633), in a copy housed at the British Library. I have modernized spelling and punctuation but have otherwise retained Herbert's language and layout. I am grateful to the British Library for permission to use text from digital images of this volume: © British Library Board, Digital Store 1076.i.25, pp. 31–32, 43, 147, 173–74, 183.

Discipline

Throw away thy rod,
Throw away thy wrath,
         O my God,
Take the gentle path.

For my heart's desire
Unto thine is bent;
         I aspire
To a full consent.

Not a word or look
I affect to own,
         But by book,
And thy book alone.

Though I fail, I weep,
Though I halt in pace,
         Yet I creep
To the throne of grace.

Then let wrath remove;
Love will do the deed,
         For with love
Stony hearts will bleed.

Love is swift of foot,
Love's a man of war,
         And can shoot,
And can hit from far.

Who can 'scape his bow?
That which wrought on thee,
         Brought thee low,
Needs must work on me.

Throw away thy rod,
Though man frailties hath,

Thou art God:
Throw away thy wrath.

The Collar

I struck the board[3] and cried, "No more!
     I will abroad.
 What? Shall I ever sigh and pine?
My lines and life are free, free as the road,
 Loose as the wind, as large as store.
   Shall I be still in suit?
Have I no harvest but a thorn
To let me blood, and not restore
What I have lost with cordial[4] fruit?
     Sure, there was wine
  Before my sighs did dry it; there was corn
  Before my tears did drown it.
 Is the year only lost to me?
  Have I no bays[5] to crown it?
No flowers, no garlands gay? All blasted?
    All wasted?
 Not so, my heart: but there is fruit,
    And thou hast hands.
  Recover all thy sigh-blown age
On double pleasures; leave thy cold dispute
Of what is fit, and not; forsake thy cage,
    Thy rope of sands,
Which petty thoughts have made, and made to thee
 Good cable, to enforce and draw,
    And be thy law,
While thou didst wink[6] and wouldst not see.
   Away! Take heed:
   I will abroad.
Call in thy death's head[7] there; tie up thy fears.
   He that forbears

---

3. The table.
4. Restorative or medicinal.
5. Crowns of leaves from the bay laurel tree, a mark of military or poetic triumph.
6. Sleep.
7. A representation of a human skull, the emblem of mortality. In the seventeenth century, some people wore death's head rings; see *Oxford English Dictionary*, s.v., "death's head, n., sense 2," www.oed.com.

To suit and serve his need
            Deserves his load."
But as I raved and grew more fierce and wild
            At every word,
Me thoughts I heard one calling, *Child*:
            And I replied, *My Lord*.

Prayer (I)

Prayer, the church's banquet, angels' age,
            God's breath in man returning to his birth,
            The soul in paraphrase, heart in pilgrimage,
The Christian plummet sounding heaven and earth,

Engine[8] against the Almighty, sinners' tower,
            Reversed thunder, Christ-side-piercing spear,
            The six-days world transposing in an hour,
A kind of tune, which all things hear and fear,

Softness, and peace, and joy, and love, and bliss,
            Exalted manna, gladness of the best,
            Heaven in ordinary,[9] man well dressed,
The Milky Way,[10] the bird of paradise,

            Church bells beyond the stars heard, the soul's blood,
            The land of spices; something understood.

Love (III)

Love bade me welcome, yet my soul drew back,
            Guilty of dust and sin.
But quick-eyed Love, observing me grow slack
            From my first entrance in,
Drew nearer to me, sweetly questioning
            If I lacked any thing.

---

8. A war machine; a plot.

9. Probably a pun on multiple meanings. The noun *ordinary*, in seventeenth-century usage, can indicate (among other things) a regular custom or habit, a prayer book, a courier taking dispatches from place to place, a daily meal, and the room at a pub where the daily meal is served; see the *Oxford English Dictionary*, s.v. "ordinary, n.," www.oed.com.

10. It meant in the seventeenth century the same thing it means now: the band of stars in the night sky, our own galaxy.

"A guest," I answered, "worthy to be here."
    Love said, "you shall be he."
"I, the unkind, ungrateful? Ah, my dear,
    I cannot look on thee."
Love took my hand, and smiling did reply,
    "Who made the eyes but I?"

"Truth Lord, but I have marred them; let my shame
    Go where it doth deserve."
"And know you not," says Love, "who bore the blame?"
    "My dear, then I will serve."
"You must sit down," says Love, "and taste my meat."
    So I did sit and eat.

Discussion Questions

1. Consider the person who speaks these five poems. Who is he? How does he change from poem to poem?
2. Consider the God who looms over these five poems. What different guises and traits does he take on from poem to poem? How does he speak? When is he silent?
3. Think about how these poems ask to be performed. Which of them could be spoken in unison by a group of people? Which could be performed as a dialogue with two speakers? Which could be performed as a one-person show on stage? Which most lend themselves to reading in solitude?[11]
4. Several of these poems end with interruptions, outbursts, or surprises. Why?
5. Try to imagine the scene in "Love (III)." What sort of setting are we in? What sort of figure is "Love"? What does the speaker think is happening? In what ways is he wrong?

---

11. If you have time, consider performing the poems in some of these various modes.

CHAPTER 17

Matsuo Basho

Introduction to Three Haiku Poems

TIMOTHY E. G. BARTEL

One of the great joys of being alive in this world is attending to nature: the trees, the water, the mysterious ways of animals, and—perhaps most mysterious of all—our own relationship to these things. The poet and travel writer Matsuo Basho was the greatest of medieval Japan's poets, and the key to his greatness was his ability to explore and meditate on humans and the natural world in brief, elegant poems. In Basho's seventeenth-century Japan, poets were prized for their ability to write *hokku*, a type of poetic stanza that consists of three lines. These lines must contain five syllables, seven syllables, and five syllables respectively. Poets who could write hokku well were often the honored guests at parties in which the partygoers would write long series of linked hokku stanzas; the greatest poets were offered the privilege of writing the first hokku of the night—in effect, they got the party started.

Though some Japanese poets wrote hokku that were merely witty, Basho developed a hokku style that was unique in two ways: First, he was less interested in wit than insight, the ability to see the beauty and mystery in ordinary things, like the frog in springtime, the stone in a temple wall, the song of the cicadas in summer. Second, Basho's hokku were so well constructed, they began to be read as complete poems in their own right rather than merely the first stanza of many. Thus, Basho helped to invent the haiku as we know it today: a complete artwork in three short lines.

What can Christian students in the twenty-first century learn from Basho and his haiku? Basho's haiku teach us about attentiveness to the present moment: What do we see before us? What sounds can we discern? What smells, what sharp tastes? So often we are concerned with the far away, with the yet to come. What is here, now, before you? How can you be a mindful witness of what happened when and where you were alive?

This attentiveness was a concern of the early Christian monks as well. In their writings, they speak of the importance of mindfulness, of attending carefully to the internal world of thought and the external world of nature, seeking to find God and his grace in both worlds, undistracted by the regrets of the past and the worries of the future. In his own way, Basho trains us in mindfulness.

Like the Italian poet Dante, Basho liked to think of life as a journey. At the beginning of his travel journal *The Narrow Road to the Deep North*, he wrote,

> The moon and sun are on an eternal journey. The years are travelers too. The sailor on his ship, the rider on his horse: both eventually bow to the weight of ages, for the road has become their home. Many ancients before us met death on the path. I too have been driven by longing for travel—my heart is a wind-blown cloud.[1]

Movement and stillness, the body and the soul—these are Basho's concerns. He asks us to attend to our inner and outer lives, and diligent students who apprentice themselves to attend to the present as Basho does can begin to experience the same patience and the same desire to see the eternal in the patterns of the earth.

Selected Haiku[2]

Furuike ya
At the ancient pond,
Mr. frog hops in—he makes
The sound of water.

Shizukasa ya
The summer stillness—
These temple stones have absorbed
The cicada's song.

Tabi ni yande
Ill on this journey—
But through winter fields my dreams
Are marching onward.

Discussion Questions:

1. Pay attention to how Basho arranges the images in his lines. What is the effect of presenting the images in the order he does in each poem?
2. Basho is interested in more than just sight images. How does Basho use references to sound to create beauty in his poems?

---

1. From the opening paragraph of Basho's *Narrow Road to the Deep North*, translated by Timothy E. G. Bartel. Used with permission of the translator.
2. All three haiku have been translated by Timothy E. G. Bartel with his permission to publish.

3. Before Basho wrote his frog haiku, it was customary to speak of the croaking sound that frogs make, but Basho chose to focus on a different sound made by the frog. What is the effect of his drawing our attention away from the conventional sound to his new "sound of water"?

4. "Tabi ni yande" was likely the last haiku written by the dying Basho, and translators have disagreed about how hopeful the poem should sound. Do you think Basho's imagining that his dreams are "marching onward" is an image of futility or hope?

CHAPTER 18

René Descartes and Blaise Pascal

Introduction to *Meditations on First Philosophy* and *The Pensées*
RAVI JAIN

Blaise Pascal was born in France in 1623 and died at a young thirty-nine years old. While he was a polymath and gifted with literary flair, he is most celebrated for his unique achievements in mathematics, natural science, and philosophy. Pascal laid foundations for calculus, probability theory, fluid dynamics, and computing machines. Like many of his time, Pascal was more interested in arguments from sensible experience than from Aristotle. Yet by today's standards, his philosophy is at once more traditional and more contemporary than that of his seventeenth-century peers. His ideas often resemble the thought of Augustine ("Our hearts are restless, until they rest in You"[1]) and Thomas Aquinas ("Intellectual knowledge is caused by the senses"[2]). But he also influenced nineteenth- and twentieth-century postmodern philosophers like Friedrich Nietzsche, Søren Kierkegaard, and Martin Heidegger.

Pascal thus holds an interesting position in the history of thought. He was a younger contemporary of the renowned René Descartes, the father of modern philosophy. And while Pascal met Descartes to discuss Pascal's theory of the vacuum, the two never saw eye to eye. Ultimately Pascal thought Descartes's philosophy was not just incorrect but was deeply wrong. While Pascal and Descartes both championed the new mathematical and natural scientific advances of the time, Pascal would not tolerate what he believed were Descartes's theological-philosophical heresies. He fiercely criticized Descartes, especially in his final, unfinished posthumous work titled *The Pensées*, or "Thoughts." Thus, Blaise Pascal became the first critic of modern philosophy.

To understand Pascal's critique, we must first listen to Descartes. While Descartes was not himself a skeptic, he began with the skeptics' famous question: How do we know our senses do not deceive us? The seriousness with which modern philosophy treats the skeptical question is one of its chief hallmarks.

---

1. Augustine of Hippo, *Confessions* 1.1.
2. Thomas Aquinas, *Summa Theologica* 1.1.84.6.

Like Pascal, many later philosophers did not think Descartes had effectively escaped skepticism. Descartes did not establish so certainly what he sought to establish. So each modern philosopher has sought to escape the skeptical question anew. And thus Descartes' legacy was not that he had proven the reality of God and the reliability of the senses as he had hoped. Instead, it was the throwing off of tradition, faith, and embodied sense experience, and placing trust in autonomous reason alone.

Blaise Pascal recognized immediately that Descartes had entered the skeptical trap. And from that trap there is no way out. The skeptical trap is well illustrated by the character Mal in the 2010 movie *Inception*. Her husband, Cobb, seeded her mind with doubt about whether she was living in reality or a dream, and she had no way to shake that doubt. Cobb only realized the depth of the problem once it could not be remedied. Tragically, Mal never overcame her doubt in the substance of reality, and it led to her demise.

Pascal stood like Cobb, screaming at his generation: *Don't engage in radical doubt. No, our senses are not wholly reliable, and neither are tradition, custom, nor faith in friends. Nonetheless, they do give us knowledge—"Human-sized" knowledge, but knowledge nonetheless. If we doubt all these things and set aside God as well, we will not escape the skeptical trap. Don't jump!* Pascal pleaded with a world walking onto the window ledge, as is our own. His clarion call is still worth our rapt attention.

From *Meditations on First Philosophy*[3]

TRANSLATED BY JOHN COTTINGHAM
First Meditation: On what can be called into doubt

Some years ago I was struck by how many false things I had believed, and by how doubtful was the structure of beliefs that I had based on them. I realized that if I wanted to establish anything in the sciences that was stable and likely to last, I needed—just once in my life—to demolish everything completely and start again from the foundations. It looked like an enormous task, and I decided to wait until I was old enough to be sure that there was nothing to be gained from putting it off any longer. I have now delayed it for so long that I have no excuse for going on planning to do it rather than getting to work. So today I have set all my worries aside and arranged for myself a clear stretch of free time. I am here quite alone, and at last I will devote myself, sincerely and without holding back, to demolishing my opinions.

3. René Descartes, *Meditations on First Philosophy, with Selections from the Objections and Replies*, trans. John Cottingham, 2nd ed., Cambridge Texts in the History of Philosophy (Cambridge: Cambridge University Press, 2017).

I can do this without showing that all my beliefs are false, which is probably more than I could ever manage. My reason tells me that as well as withholding assent from propositions that are obviously false, I should also withhold it from ones that are not completely certain and indubitable. So all I need, for the purpose of rejecting all my opinions, is to find in each of them at least some reason for doubt. I can do this without going through them one by one, which would take forever: once the foundations of a building have been undermined, the rest collapses of its own accord; so I will go straight for the basic principles on which all my former beliefs rested.

Whatever I have accepted until now as most true has come to me through my senses. But occasionally I have found that they have deceived me, and it is unwise to trust completely those who have deceived us even once.

Yet although the senses sometimes deceive us about objects that are very small or distant, that doesn't apply to my belief that I am here, sitting by the fire, wearing a winter dressing-gown, holding this piece of paper in my hands, and so on. It seems to be quite impossible to doubt beliefs like these, which come from the senses.

Another example: how can I doubt that these hands or this whole body are mine? To doubt such things I would have to liken myself to brain-damaged madmen who are convinced they are kings when really they are paupers, or say they are dressed in purple when they are naked, or that they are pumpkins, or made of glass. Such people are insane, and I would be thought equally mad if I modelled myself on them.

What a brilliant piece of reasoning! As if I were not a man who sleeps at night and often has all the same experiences while asleep as madmen do when awake—indeed sometimes even more improbable ones. Often in my dreams I am convinced of just such familiar events—that I am sitting by the fire in my dressing-gown—when in fact I am lying undressed in bed! Yet right now my eyes are certainly wide open when I look at this piece of paper; I shake my head and it isn't asleep; when I rub one hand against the other, I do it deliberately and know what I am doing. This wouldn't all happen with such clarity to someone asleep.

Indeed! As if I didn't remember other occasions when I have been tricked by exactly similar thoughts while asleep! As I think about this more carefully, I realize that there is never any reliable way of distinguishing being awake from being asleep.

This discovery makes me feel dizzy, which itself reinforces the notion that I may be asleep! Suppose then that I am dreaming—it isn't true that I, with my eyes open, am moving my head and stretching out my hands. Suppose, indeed that I don't even have hands or any body at all.

Still, it has to be admitted that the visions that come in sleep are like paint-ings: they must have been made as copies of real things; so at least these general kinds of things—eyes, head, hands and the body as a whole—must be real and not imaginary. For even when painters try to depict sirens and satyrs with the most extraordinary bodies, they simply jumble up the limbs of different kinds of real animals, rather than inventing natures that are entirely new. If they do succeed in thinking up something completely fictitious and unreal—not remotely like anything ever seen before—at least the colours used in the picture must be real. Similarly, although these general kinds of things—eyes, head, hands and so on—could be imaginary, there is no denying that certain even simpler and more universal kinds of things are real. These are the elements out of which we make all our mental images of things—the true and also the false ones.

These simpler and more universal kinds include body, and extension; the shape of extended things; their quantity, size and number; the places things can be in, the time through which they can last, and so on.

So it seems reasonable to conclude that physics, astronomy, medicine, and all other sciences dealing with things that have complex structures are doubtful; while arithmetic, geometry and other studies of the simplest and most general things—whether they really exist in nature or not—contain something certain and indubitable. For whether I am awake or asleep, two plus three makes five, and a square has only four sides. It seems impossible to suspect that such obvious truths might be false.

However, I have for many years been sure that there is an all-powerful God who made me to be the sort of creature that I am. How do I know that he hasn't brought it about that there is no earth, no sky, nothing that takes up space, no shape, no size, no place, while making sure that all these things appear to me to exist? Anyway, I sometimes think that others go wrong even when they think they have the most perfect knowledge; so how do I know that I myself don't go wrong every time I add two and three or count the sides of a square? Well, you might say, God would not let me be deceived like that, because he is said to be supremely good. But, I reply, if God's goodness would stop him from letting me be deceived all the time, you would expect it to stop him from allowing me to be deceived even occasionally; yet clearly I sometimes am deceived.

Some people would deny the existence of such a powerful God rather than believe that everything else is uncertain. Let us grant them—for purposes of argument—that there is no God, and theology is fiction. On their view, then, I am a product of fate or chance or a long chain of causes and effects. But the less powerful they make my original cause, the more likely it is that I am so imperfect as to be deceived all the time—because deception and error seem to be imperfections. Having no answer to these arguments, I am driven back to the position that doubts can properly be raised about any of my former beliefs. I don't reach this conclusion in a flippant or casual manner, but on the basis of powerful and well thought-out reasons. So in future, if I want to discover any certainty, I must withhold my assent from these former beliefs just as carefully as I withhold it from obvious falsehoods.

It isn't enough merely to have noticed this, though; I must make an effort to remember it. My old familiar opinions keep coming back, and against my will they capture my belief. It is as though they had a right to a place in my belief-system as a result of long occupation and the law of custom. It is true that these habitual opinions of mine are highly probable; although they are in a sense doubtful, as I have shown, it is more reasonable to believe than to deny them. But if I go on viewing them in that light I shall never get out of the habit of confidently assenting to them. To conquer that habit, therefore, I had better switch right around and pretend (for a while) that these former opinions of mine are utterly false and imaginary. I shall do this until I have something to counter-balance the weight of old opinion, and the distorting influence of habit no longer prevents me from judging correctly. However far I go in my distrustful attitude, no actual harm will come of it, because my project won't affect how I act, but only how I go about acquiring knowledge.

So I shall suppose that some malicious, powerful, cunning demon has done all he can to deceive me—rather than this being done by God, who is supremely good and the source of truth. I shall think that the sky, the air, the earth, colours, shapes, sounds and all external things are merely dreams that the demon has contrived as traps for my judgment. I shall consider myself as having no hands or eyes, or flesh, or blood or senses, but as having falsely believed that I had all these things. I shall stubbornly persist in this train of thought; and even if I can't learn any truth, I shall at least do what I can do, which is to be on my guard against accepting any falsehoods, so that the deceiver—however powerful and cunning he may be—will be unable to affect me in the slightest. This will be hard work, though, and a kind of laziness pulls me back into my old ways.

Like a prisoner who dreams that he is free, starts to suspect that it is merely a dream, and wants to go on dreaming rather than waking up, so I am content to slide back into my old opinions; I fear being shaken out of them because I am afraid that my peaceful sleep may be followed by hard labor when I wake, and that I shall have to struggle not in the light but in the imprisoning darkness of the problems I have raised.

From *The Pensées*[4]

TRANSLATED BY W. F. TROTTER

282. We know truth, not only by the reason, but also by the heart, and it is in this last way that we know first principles; and reason, which has no part in it, tries in vain to impugn them. The sceptics, who have only this for their object, labor to no purpose. We know that we do not dream, and, however impossible it is for us to prove it by reason, this inability demonstrates only the weakness of our reason, but not, as they affirm, the uncertainty of all our knowledge. For the knowledge of first principles, as space, time, motion, number, is as sure as any of those which we get from reasoning. And reason must trust these intuitions of the heart, and must base them on every argument. (We have intuitive knowledge of the tri-dimensional nature of space and of the infinity of number, and reason then shows that there are no two square numbers one of which is double of the other. Principles are intuited, propositions are inferred, all with certainty, though in different ways.) And it is as useless and absurd for reason to demand from the heart proofs of her first principles, before admitting them, as it would be for the heart to demand from reason an intuition of all demonstrated propositions before accepting them.

This inability ought, then, to serve only to humble reason, which would judge all, but not to impugn our certainty, as if only reason were capable of instructing us. Would to God, on the contrary, that we had never need of it, and that we knew everything by instinct and intuition! But nature has refused us this boon. On the contrary, she has given us but very little knowledge of this kind; and all the rest can be acquired only by reasoning.

Therefore, those to whom God has imparted religion by intuition are very fortunate and justly convinced. But to those who do not have it, we can give it only by reasoning, waiting for God to give them spiritual insight, without which faith is only human and useless for salvation.

434. The chief arguments of the sceptics—I pass over the lesser ones—are that we have no certainty of the truth of these principles apart from faith and revelation, except in so far as we naturally perceive them in ourselves. Now this natural intuition is not a convincing proof of their truth; since, having no certainty, apart from faith, whether man was created by a good God, or by a wicked demon, or by chance, it is doubtful whether these principles given to us are true, or false, or uncertain, according to our origin. Again, no person is certain, apart from faith, whether he is awake or sleeps, seeing that during sleep we believe that we are awake as firmly as we do when we are awake; we believe that we see space,

---

4. Blaise Pascal, *The Pensées* (New York: Dutton, 1958).

figure, and motion; we are aware of the passage of time, we measure it; and in fact we act as if we were awake. So that half of our life being passed in sleep, we have on our own admission no idea of truth, whatever we may imagine. As all our intuitions are, then, illusions, who knows whether the other half of our life, in which we think we are awake, is not another sleep a little different from the former, from which we awake when we suppose ourselves asleep?

And who doubts that, if we dreamt in company, and the dreams chanced to agree, which is common enough, and if we were always alone when awake, we should believe that matters were reversed? In short, as we often dream that we dream, heaping dream upon dream, may it not be that this half of our life, wherein we think ourselves awake, is itself only a dream on which the others are grafted, from which we wake at death, during which we have as few principles of truth and good as during natural sleep, these different thoughts which disturb us being perhaps only illusions like the flight of time and the vain fancies of our dreams?

These are the chief arguments on one side and the other.

I omit minor ones, such as the skeptical talk against the impressions of custom, education, manners, country and the like. Though these influence the majority of common folk, who dogmatize only on shallow foundations, they are upset by the least breath of the sceptics. We have only to see their books if we are not sufficiently convinced of this, and we shall very quickly become so, perhaps too much.

I notice the only strong point of the dogmatists, namely, that, speaking in good faith and sincerely, we cannot doubt natural principles. Against this the sceptics set up in one word the uncertainty of our origin, which includes that of our nature. The dogmatists have been trying to answer this objection ever since the world began.

So there is open war among men, in which each must take a part and side either with dogmatism or skepticism. For he who thinks to remain neutral is above all a sceptic. This neutrality is the essence of the sect; he who is not against them is essentially for them. In this appears their advantage. They are not for themselves; they are neutral, indifferent, in suspense as to all things, even themselves being no exception.

What, then, shall man do in this state? Shall he doubt everything? Shall he doubt whether he is awake, whether he is being pinched, or whether he is being burned? Shall he doubt whether he doubts? Shall he doubt whether he exists? We cannot go so far as that; and I lay it down as a fact that there never has been a real complete sceptic. Nature sustains our feeble reason and prevents it raving to this extent.

Shall he, then, say, on the contrary, that he certainly possesses truth—he who, when pressed ever so little, can show no title to it and is forced to let go his hold?

What a chimera, then, is man! What a novelty! What a monster, what a chaos, what a contradiction, what a prodigy! Judge of all things, imbecile worm of the earth; depositary of truth, a sink of uncertainty and error; the pride and refuse of the universe!

Who will unravel this tangle? Nature confutes the sceptics, and reason confutes the dogmatists. What, then, will you become, O men! who try to find out by your natural reason what is your true condition? You cannot avoid one of these sects, nor adhere to one of them.

Know then, proud man, what a paradox you are to yourself. Humble yourself, weak reason; be silent, foolish nature; learn that man infinitely transcends man, and learn from your Master your true condition, of which you are ignorant. Hear God....

77. I cannot forgive Descartes. In all his philosophy he would have been quite willing to dispense with God. But he had to make Him give a fillip to set the world in motion; beyond this, he has no further need of God.

78. Descartes useless and uncertain.

79. Descartes.—We must say summarily: "This is made by figure and motion," for it is true. But to say what these are, and to compose the machine, is ridiculous. For it is useless, uncertain, and painful. And were it true, we do not think all philosophy is worth one hour of pain.

Discussion Questions

1. In your opinion, is Descartes's argument persuasive? Why or why not?
2. Did Descartes intend to let his program of radical doubt affect his behavior? Do you think that was a likely outcome?
3. According to Pascal, what is the relationship between reason and the heart?
4. Why did Pascal think reason ought to be humble?
5. What did Pascal think of Descartes's skepticism? What did he think of Descartes's discussion of God?
6. Have you ever read a book that upset you, as Descartes's book upset Pascal? Were you able to find any redeeming qualities in the book? Why or why not?

CHAPTER 19

Sor Juana Inés de la Cruz

Introduction to "Respuesta a Sor Filotea de la Cruz"

THERESA M. KENNEY

In late seventeenth-century Mexico, universities existed, but no women were admitted. Young Juana Inés de la Cruz begged for the chance to go in disguise as a boy, but her mother wouldn't hear of it. Juana spoke and wrote in Latin by the age of three, wrote poetry as an eight-year-old, trained herself in Greek philosophy in her teens, and was a true Renaissance woman when it came to the study of mathematics, music, and science. She chose to take all these gifts with her to a convent rather than to marry, and she became Mexico's greatest Baroque dramatist and poet. Modern critics attribute her choice to a rejection of men and marriage, but they tend to overlook Juana's self-confessed deep piety and religious motivations. When attacked for criticizing a Jesuit theologian as a mere woman, Juana wrote her famous "Respuesta" to the pretended "Sor Filotea de la Cruz," who commentators agree was a stand-in for the bishop of Puebla, Mexico.

In this letter, Sor ("Sister") Juana explained both why she entered the convent in the first place and why she pursued knowledge in general. On the one hand, she understood that she only *needed* to know what is necessary to gain salvation as a Christian. In fact, she said, some believe even knowledge aimed toward the salvation of the soul is harmful to a woman. Juana tried to deal with this view of women's pursuit of knowledge, painfully and purposefully wrenching herself away from her inclination to know. Juana's renunciation of her natural desire for the fame that might accompany her humanistic studies was also a deliberate sacrifice, as she said, to "the one who gave" to her the "immense love for the truth."

Although Juana seems at first to be arguing simply for a right to self-actualize, to pursue a deeply held desire regardless of what the church teaches, she was no hypocrite pretending to love truth and aspire to theology when what really absorbed her was science and philosophy. She explained that other fields of humanistic knowledge lead necessarily to theology, the study of God. Her capacity to know and her desire to seek truth were both gifts from him. Criticized not

129

so much for her stance as for being a woman expressing a theological opinion in public, Sor Juana demonstrated that Scripture itself shows women's ability to do intellectual and political work and even to prophesy and interpret Scripture. She cited the female figures of Scripture, including Deborah and the queen of Sheba, who exemplified not only intellectual but also moral virtues. In this she was like another great woman who dealt with male opposition to women's search for knowledge: the medieval author of the *Book of the City of Ladies*, Christine de Pizan. Juana also called upon the fathers of the church—Augustine, Thomas Aquinas, and John Chrysostom—whose views she vindicated in opposition to Jesuit Father Vieyra.

Juana ably defended women's ability to pursue truth as the pathway to knowledge of God, but that does not neatly align her with all defiant self-seekers. She asked her opponent what knowledge is for and why God gives human beings a thirst for truth. It is revealing that the treatise she commented on was about God's greatest gift to human beings. Juana argued it was Christ's death on the cross and his presence on earth in the Eucharist; thus human beings must reciprocate the love God has first shown to them.

Reply to Sor Filotea de la Cruz por Sor Juana Inés de la Cruz

I do not study in order to write, and even less to teach—which, in me, would be colossal arrogance—but rather only to see if by studying I can be less ignorant. This is my answer and this is what I feel. . . . God graced me with a gift of an immense love for the truth. . . . Since the first light of reason dawned on me my inclination toward letters was so intense and powerful that neither reprimands by others, of which I have had many, nor self-reflection, of which I have done not a little, have been sufficient for me to stop pursuing this natural impulse that God put in me. God Almighty knows why and for what purpose. And he knows I've asked him to snuff out the light of my mind and leave only what's necessary to keep his commandments. Some would say that any more is too much in a woman, and some even say that it is harmful. The Almighty also knows that, since my request failed, I have tried to bury my intellect along with my name and to sacrifice all this only to the one who gave it to me. For no other reason I entered a religious order even though its duties and fellowship were anathema to the unhindered quietude required by my studious intent. . . .

Later on, when I was six or seven years old, and already knowing how to read and write along with all the other skills that women learn, such as embroidery and sewing, I heard that in Mexico City there was a university and there were schools where people studied the sciences. As soon as I heard this I began to kill my mother by constantly and naggingly begging her to dress me in boy's clothes and to send me to live with some relatives of hers in Mexico City so that I could study by enrolling in the University. She refused, and she was quite right, but I assuaged my desire by reading many kinds of books belonging to my grandfather, notwithstanding the punishment and scolding intended to stop me. So, when I came to Mexico, people were amazed, not so much by my intelligence as by my memory and the facts that I had acquired at an age that seemed hardly enough just to be able to learn to speak. . . .

I entered a religious order because, although I was aware that that lifestyle had certain things (I'm talking about incidental not official ones), or rather, many things that were abhorrent to my character—given my total rejection of marriage—it was the least objectionable and the most respectable one I could choose with regard to my desire to safeguard my salvation. In the face of this primary concern (surely it is the most important one) all the stubborn little impertinences of my nature gave way and bowed: that is, wanting to live alone; wanting not to have any obligatory duties that would hinder my freedom to study; being free from community noises that would interrupt the peace and quiet of my books. . . .

I proceeded in this way, as I've said, always directing the path of my studies toward the summit of holy theology. In order to reach it, it seemed to me necessary to ascend the ladder of the sciences and the humanities, for how can one who does not first know the ancillary fields possibly understand the queen of the sciences? Without logic, how could I possibly know the general and specific methods by which the Holy Scriptures are written? Without rhetoric, how could I possibly understand its figures, tropes, and phrasing? Without the natural sciences, what about so many questions pertaining to the multiple natures of the animals used in biblical sacrifices . . . ? If Saul was cured by the sound of David's harp, was it by virtue of the natural power of music, or the supernatural power God chose to infuse in David? . . .

This habit or bent of mine is of such a nature that I never look at anything without giving it a second thought. Two little girls were in front of me playing with a top, and, given this proclivity of mine, no sooner had I seen its movement and shape than I began studying its easy spinning and spherical shape, and I saw how long the impulse of its momentum lasted independent of its cause, for, separated from the girl's hand, which was its motive cause, the little top went on dancing. Not content with this, I ordered someone to bring me some flour and to spread it around it so that, when the top was dancing in it, it could be discerned whether or not the circles it was making with its movement were perfect or not. I found that they were but spiral lines that gradually lost circularity as the momentum decreased. . . .

I have not lacked for support in the many examples I have read in both sacred as well as secular writings. For I see a Deborah issuing laws in military matters as well as political affairs while governing a people among whom there were so many learned men. I see the extremely wise Queen of Sheba, so learned that she dares test the wisdom of the greatest of all sages by posing riddles without being chastised for doing so; rather, because she did this she will become the judge of unbelievers. I see so many significant women: some adorned with the gift of prophecy, like Abigail; others with persuasion, like Esther; others, with piety, like Rahab; others with perseverance, like Hannah, Samuel's mother; and infinitely more with other types of talents and virtues. . . .

And this is so just that interpreting Holy Texts was forbidden not only to women (who are held to be so inept) but also to men (who simply for being men think they are sages). This holds for all save those who are most learned and virtuous and of meek temperament and well intentioned. . . .

It follows that many parents choose to keep their daughters uncouth and uneducated rather than expose them to such a notoriously perilous familiarity with men. But all this would be avoided if there were educated elderly women, as St. Paul desires, and if the teaching profession were passed from one generation of women to the next just as what happens with sewing and all other customary skills. . . .

If my crime lies in the Letter Worthy of Athena, was that piece anything more than simply relating my views with all of the sanctions for which I am grateful to our Holy Mother Church? For if she, with her most holy authority, does not forbid me so, why must others so forbid me? Was it too bold of me to express an opinion in opposition to Vieyra, while it wasn't so for his Reverend Father to express an opinion in opposition to the Church's three Holy Fathers? My understanding, such as it is, isn't it as free as his, since it comes from the same backyard? Is his opinion any one of the revealed principles of our Holy Faith such that we must believe it with our eyes shut? Besides, I neither showed any lack of respect due such an eminent man, like that which his defender has shown in this case. . . .

Therefore, if the evil lies in verses being used by a woman, we have already seen how many women have used them commendably. Then, what is the problem with me being one? Of course, I confess my baseness and my base, vile nature; but I maintain that no one has ever seen an indecent poem of mine. Moreover, I have never written anything of my own volition, but rather at the request or directive of others. As a result the only thing I recall writing for my own pleasure is a little piece called the *Dream*.

Discussion Questions

1. How did Sor Juana respond to the accusation that knowledge of secular subjects is a sinful distraction from religious knowledge?
2. What famous women did Juana invoke, and why are their examples significant?
3. What dangers did Juana see for those who participate in higher studies that might also afflict men?
4. What do you think of Juana's worries for the physical and moral safety of women in coeducation?
5. How did Sor Juana view her own work?

CHAPTER 20

John Milton

Introduction to *Areopagitica*

LOUIS MARKOS

Though best known for his poetry, John Milton (1608–1674) was also an important prose writer whose essays are fully engaged in the theological, political, and aesthetic controversies of his day. In many of those essays, Milton fought for freedom, particularly the freedom to read and engage with truth in all its manifestations. To this day, Milton's logical, eloquent, and deeply felt defense of the freedom of the press, *Areopagitica* (1644), remains one of the crowning expressions of the need for a Christian society, and especially a Christian university, to ensure liberty in the humanistic realms of thought. It offers a timeless meditation on the status of truth in a fallen world and issues a thunderous call to Christian students to think deeply about that truth and to wrestle boldly with its claims, its presuppositions, and its consequences.

In choosing his somewhat obscure title, Milton was calling readers back to the birthplace of humanism, fifth-century BC Athens, where a council of elders called the Areopagus would, like the Parliament of Milton's day, hear cases and render judgment. He also was calling readers back to the early days of Christianity, when the apostle Paul (Acts 17) invited the members of the Areopagus to open their hearts and minds and to make a smooth and natural transition from their limited pagan belief in an unknown God to a fuller faith in an invisible Father who has made himself known through the incarnation, crucifixion, and resurrection of his Son.

Milton could not condone any abridgment of a person's right to study and seek after truth; his at once Christian and humanist view of truth would not allow that. He believed that truth, like the Bible itself, is ever active and alive, sharper and swifter than any double-edged sword. To censor truth is to mingle it with error, to hide it even further from our view. Rather than suppress it, we must allow it to follow its own winding course; only then will we be able to seek it out in all its forms.

Milton did not merely study books; he dined, conversed, and struggled with them as he would with a living, breathing person. Reading the ancients was never a passive exercise for Milton. To the contrary, as he absorbed the ideas in each work, he would actively measure those ideas against the truths he knew from his personal encounters with the Bible and the God of the Bible.

Students who read Milton, and who want to read *like* Milton, must do more than think outside the box. They must pursue truth passionately and allow that truth to affect and even alter their beliefs and behaviors. According to Milton, we are thinking beings endowed with the will and the skill to seek out truth wherever it hides. Rather than bury our heads in the sand for fear we will be corrupted by the books we read, we must press on with faith and courage, using our God-given reason to discern the good from the bad, the true from the false.

From *Areopagitica*

But I have first to finish, as was propounded, what is to be thought in general of reading books, whatever sort they be, and whether be more the benefit or the harm that thence proceeds.

Not to insist upon the examples of Moses, Daniel, and Paul, who were skillful in all the learning of the Egyptians, Chaldeans, and Greeks, which could not probably be without reading their books of all sorts; in Paul especially, who thought it no defilement to insert into Holy Scripture the sentences of three Greek poets, and one of them a tragedian; the question was notwithstanding sometimes controverted among the primitive doctors, but with great odds on that side which affirmed it both lawful and profitable; as was then evidently perceived, when Julian the Apostate and subtlest enemy to our faith made a decree forbidding Christians the study of heathen learning: for, said he, they wound us with our own weapons, and with our own arts and sciences they overcome us. And indeed the Christians were put so to their shifts by this crafty means, and so much in danger to decline into all ignorance, that the two Apollinarii were fain, as a man may say, to coin all the seven liberal sciences out of the Bible, reducing it into divers forms of orations, poems, dialogues, even to the calculating of a new Christian grammar. But, saith the historian Socrates, the providence of God provided better than the industry of Apollinarius and his son, by taking away that illiterate law with the life of him who devised it. So great an injury they then held it to be deprived of Hellenic learning; and thought it a persecution more undermining, and secretly decaying the Church, than the open cruelty of Decius or Diocletian.

And perhaps it was the same politic drift that the devil whipped St. Jerome in a lenten dream, for reading Cicero; or else it was a phantasm bred by the fever which had then seized him. For had an angel been his discipliner, unless it were for dwelling too much upon Ciceronianisms, and had chastised the reading, not the vanity, it had been plainly partial; first to correct him for grave Cicero, and not for scurril Plautus, whom he confesses to have been reading, not long before; next to correct him only, and let so many more ancient fathers wax old in those pleasant and florid studies without the lash of such a tutoring apparition; insomuch that Basil teaches how some good use may be made of Margites, a sportful poem, not now extant, writ by Homer; and why not then of Morgante, an Italian romance much to the same purpose?

But if it be agreed we shall be tried by visions, there is a vision recorded by Eusebius, far ancienter than this tale of Jerome, to the nun Eustochium, and, besides, has nothing of a fever in it. Dionysius Alexandrinus was about the year 240 a person of great name in the Church for piety and learning, who had wont to avail himself much against heretics by being conversant in their books; until a certain presbyter laid it scrupulously to his conscience, how he durst venture himself among those defiling volumes. The worthy man, loath to give offence, fell into a new debate with himself what was to be thought; when suddenly a vision sent from God (it is his own epistle that so avers it) confirmed him in these words: READ ANY BOOKS WHATEVER COME TO THY HANDS, FOR THOU ART SUFFICIENT BOTH TO JUDGE ARIGHT AND TO EXAMINE EACH MATTER. To this revelation he assented the sooner, as he confesses, because it was answerable to that of the Apostle to the Thessalonians, PROVE ALL THINGS, HOLD FAST THAT WHICH IS GOOD. And he might have added another remarkable saying of the same author: TO THE PURE, ALL THINGS ARE PURE; not only meats and drinks, but all kind of knowledge whether of good or evil; the knowledge cannot defile, nor consequently the books, if the will and conscience be not defiled.

For books are as meats and viands are; some of good, some of evil substance; and yet God, in that unapocryphal vision, said without exception, RISE, PETER, KILL AND EAT, leaving the choice to each man's discretion. Wholesome meats to a vitiated stomach differ little or nothing from unwholesome; and best books to a naughty mind are not inapplicable to occasions of evil. Bad meats will scarce breed good nourishment in the healthiest concoction; but herein the difference is of bad books, that they to a discreet and judicious reader serve in many respects to discover, to confute, to forewarn, and to illustrate. Whereof what better witness can ye expect I should produce, than one of your own now sitting in Parliament, the chief of learned men reputed in this land, Mr. Selden; whose volume of natural and national laws proves, not only by great authorities brought together, but by exquisite reasons and theorems almost mathematically demonstrative, that all opinions, yea errors, known, read, and collated, are of main service and assistance toward the speedy attainment of what is truest. I conceive, therefore, that when God did enlarge the universal diet of man's body, saving ever the rules of temperance, he then also, as before, left arbitrary the dieting and repasting of our minds; as wherein every mature man might have to exercise his own leading capacity.

How great a virtue is temperance, how much of moment through the whole life of man! Yet God commits the managing so great a trust, without particular law or prescription, wholly to the demeanour of every grown man. And therefore when he himself tabled the Jews from heaven, that omer, which was every man's daily portion of manna, is computed to have been more than might have well sufficed the heartiest feeder thrice as many meals. For those actions which enter into a man, rather than issue out of him, and therefore defile not, God uses not to captivate under a perpetual childhood of prescription, but trusts him with the gift of reason to be his own chooser; there were but little work left for preaching, if law and compulsion should grow so fast upon those things which heretofore were governed only by exhortation. Solomon informs us, that much reading is a weariness to the flesh; but neither he nor other inspired author tells us that such or such reading is unlawful: yet certainly had God thought good to limit us herein, it had been much more expedient to have told us what was unlawful than what was wearisome. As for the burning of those Ephesian books by St. Paul's converts; 'tis replied the books were magic, the Syriac so renders them. It was a private act, a voluntary act, and leaves us to a voluntary imitation: the men in remorse burnt those books which were their own; the magistrate by this example is not appointed; these men practised the books, another might perhaps have read them in some sort usefully.

Good and evil we know in the field of this world grow up together almost inseparably; and the knowledge of good is so involved and interwoven with the knowledge of evil, and in so many cunning resemblances hardly to be discerned, that those confused seeds which were imposed upon Psyche as an incessant labour to cull out, and sort asunder, were not more intermixed. It was from out the rind of one apple tasted, that the knowledge of good and evil, as two twins cleaving together, leaped forth into the world. And perhaps this is that doom which Adam fell into of knowing good and evil, that is to say of knowing good by evil. As therefore the state of man now is; what wisdom can there be to choose, what continence to forbear without the knowledge of evil? He that can apprehend and consider vice with all her baits and seeming pleasures, and yet abstain, and yet distinguish, and yet prefer that which is truly better, he is the true warfaring Christian.

I cannot praise a fugitive and cloistered virtue, unexercised and unbreathed, that never sallies out and sees her adversary but slinks out of the race, where that immortal garland is to be run for, not without dust and heat. Assuredly we bring not innocence into the world, we bring impurity much rather; that which purifies us is trial, and trial is by what is contrary. That virtue therefore which is but a youngling in the contemplation of evil, and knows not the utmost that vice promises to her followers, and rejects it, is but a blank virtue, not a pure; her whiteness is but an excremental whiteness. Which was the reason why our sage and serious poet Spenser, whom I dare be known to think a better teacher than Scotus or Aquinas, describing true temperance under the person of Guion, brings him in with his palmer through the cave of Mammon, and the bower of earthly bliss, that he might see and know, and yet abstain. Since therefore the knowledge and survey of vice is in this world so necessary to the constituting of human virtue, and the scanning of error to the confirmation of truth, how can we more safely, and with less danger, scout into the regions of sin and falsity than by reading all manner of tractates and hearing all manner of reason? And this is the benefit which may be had of books promiscuously read.

But of the harm that may result hence three kinds are usually reckoned. First, is feared the infection that may spread; but then all human learning and controversy in religious points must remove out of the world, yea the Bible itself; for that ofttimes relates blasphemy not nicely, it describes the carnal sense of wicked men not unelegantly, it brings in holiest men passionately murmuring against Providence through all the arguments of Epicurus: in other great disputes it answers dubiously and darkly to the common reader.

––––––––––

Many there be that complain of divine Providence for suffering Adam to transgress; foolish tongues! When God gave him reason, he gave him freedom to choose, for reason is but choosing; he had been else a mere artificial Adam, such an Adam as he is in the motions. We ourselves esteem not of that obedience, or love, or gift, which is of force: God therefore left him free, set before him a provoking object, ever almost in his eyes; herein consisted his merit, herein the right of his reward, the praise of his abstinence. Wherefore did he create passions within us, pleasures round about us, but that these rightly tempered are the very ingredients of virtue?

They are not skilful considerers of human things, who imagine to remove sin by removing the matter of sin; for, besides that it is a huge heap increasing under the very act of diminishing, though some part of it may for a time be withdrawn from some persons, it cannot from all, in such a universal thing as books are; and when this is done, yet the sin remains entire. Though ye take from a covetous man all his treasure, he has yet one jewel left, ye cannot bereave him of his covetousness. Banish all objects of lust, shut up all youth into the severest discipline that can be exercised in any hermitage, ye cannot make them chaste, that came not hither so; such great care and wisdom is required to the right managing of this point. Suppose we could expel sin by this means; look how much we thus expel of sin, so much we expel of virtue: for the matter of them both is the same; remove that, and ye remove them both alike.

This justifies the high providence of God, who, though he command us temperance, justice, continence, yet pours out before us, even to a profuseness, all desirable things, and gives us minds that can wander beyond all limit and satiety. Why should we then affect a rigour contrary to the manner of God and of nature, by abridging or scanting those means, which books freely permitted are, both to the trial of virtue and the exercise of truth? It would be better done, to learn that the law must needs be frivolous, which goes to restrain things, uncertainly and yet equally working to good and to evil. And were I the chooser, a dream of well-doing should be preferred before many times as much the forcible hindrance of evil-doing. For God sure esteems the growth and completing of one virtuous person more than the restraint of ten vicious.

————

Well knows he who uses to consider, that our faith and knowledge thrives by exercise, as well as our limbs and complexion. Truth is compared in Scripture to a streaming fountain; if her waters flow not in a perpetual progression, they sicken into a muddy pool of conformity and tradition. A man may be a heretic in the truth; and if he believe things only because his pastor says so, or the Assembly so determines, without knowing other reason, though his belief be true, yet the very truth he holds becomes his heresy.

There is not any burden that some would gladlier post off to another than the charge and care of their religion. There be—who knows not that there be?—of Protestants and professors who live and die in as arrant an implicit faith as any lay Papist of Loretto. A wealthy man, addicted to his pleasure and to his profits, finds religion to be a traffic so entangled, and of so many piddling accounts, that of all mysteries he cannot skill to keep a stock going upon that trade. What should he do? Fain he would have the name to be religious, fain he would bear up with his neighbours in that. What does he therefore, but resolves to give over toiling, and to find himself out some factor, to whose care and credit he may commit the whole managing of his religious affairs; some divine of note and estimation that must be. To him he adheres, resigns the whole warehouse of his religion, with all the locks and keys, into his custody; and indeed makes the very person of that man his religion; esteems his associating with him a sufficient evidence and commendatory of his own piety.

———————

Truth indeed came once into the world with her divine Master, and was a perfect shape most glorious to look on: but when he ascended, and his Apostles after him were laid asleep, then straight arose a wicked race of deceivers, who, as that story goes of the Egyptian Typhon with his conspirators, how they dealt with the good Osiris, took the virgin Truth, hewed her lovely form into a thousand pieces, and scattered them to the four winds. From that time ever since, the sad friends of Truth, such as durst appear, imitating the careful search that Isis made for the mangled body of Osiris, went up and down gathering up limb by limb, still as they could find them. We have not yet found them all, Lords and Commons, nor ever shall do, till her Master's second coming; he shall bring together every joint and member, and shall mould them into an immortal feature of loveliness and perfection. Suffer not these licensing prohibitions to stand at every place of opportunity, forbidding and disturbing them that continue seeking, that continue to do our obsequies to the torn body of our martyred saint.

We boast our light; but if we look not wisely on the sun itself, it smites us into darkness. Who can discern those planets that are oft combust, and those stars of brightest magnitude that rise and set with the sun, until the opposite motion of their orbs bring them to such a place in the firmament, where they may be seen evening or morning? The light which we have gained was given us, not to be ever staring on, but by it to discover onward things more remote from our knowledge. It is not the unfrocking of a priest, the unmitring of a bishop, and the removing him from off the presbyterian shoulders, that will make us a happy nation. No, if other things as great in the Church, and in the rule of life both economical and political, be not looked into and reformed, we have looked so long upon the blaze that Zuinglius and Calvin hath beaconed up to us, that we are stark blind. There be who perpetually complain of schisms and sects, and make it such a calamity that any man dissents from their maxims. 'Tis their own pride and ignorance which causes the disturbing, who neither will hear with meekness, nor can convince; yet all must be suppressed which is not found in their Syntagma. They are the troublers, they are the dividers of unity, who neglect and permit not others to unite those dissevered pieces which are yet wanting to the body of Truth. To be still searching what we know not by what we know, still closing up truth to truth as we find it (for all her body is homogeneal and proportional), this is the golden rule in theology as well as in arithmetic, and makes up the best harmony in a Church; not the forced and outward union of cold, and neutral, and inwardly divided minds.

Discussion Questions

1. How did Moses, Daniel, and Paul make use of pagan learning?
2. How did Milton take the biblical injunction that to the pure all things are pure (Titus 1:15) and apply it to a Christian's study of non-Christian literature?
3. The forbidden fruit Adam and Eve ate was the fruit of the knowledge of good and of evil. What implications are there for learning and the pursuit of truth in that?
4. What do you think Milton meant when he said, in reference to Adam, that "reason is but choosing"?
5. How is truth like a streaming fountain, and what bearing does that have on how we read and study?
6. How can we do our part in reconstructing truth as Isis did the body of Osiris?

Part 3

AD 1700 to AD 1900

CHAPTER 21

Jonathan Edwards

Introduction to "Personal Narrative"
JONATHAN CALLIS

While most people today know Jonathan Edwards (1703–58) for his famous (or infamous) sermon "Sinners in the Hands of an Angry God," he was known in his time as the leading Christian intellectual and theologian of the American colonies. In his "Personal Narrative" (1739), Edwards narrated his gradually increasing knowledge of God's grace. Edwards's understanding of salvation stressed not only conversion, but the sanctification and supernatural light God brings to each redeemed soul. In every work he published, Edwards attempted to show the entire scope of God's saving work in human life.

Edwards was born into an illustrious New England preaching family. His grandfather, Solomon Stoddard, was one of the most famous preachers of the early eighteenth century. Yet the young and brilliant Edwards, who began his studies at Yale at the age of thirteen (shockingly young, even for that time), did not restrict his curiosity to theology and biblical studies. He developed a wide-ranging set of interests that included philosophy, psychology, biology, and physics. The philosophers John Locke and Sir Isaac Newton were particular inspirations for Edwards. Edwards, however, was not content merely to absorb and pass on the latest trends in scientific understanding. He wanted to illustrate how each individual area of knowledge pointed to God's sovereign and active love for his creation. As many eighteenth-century scientists and philosophers drifted toward Deism (the idea that God is a detached and impersonal order standing behind the world), Edwards directed Christians to understand God's personal love for His creatures. Enamored of the beauty of creation and the majesty of God's infinite character, Edwards developed a Christian philosophy that explained how God sustained his creation at every instant. In Edwards's vision, all creation testifies to God's glory, which is reflected in the particularity of every living thing.

In his "Personal Narrative," Edwards showed how reading Scripture and observing the natural world can lead to a direct and mystical experience of God's "divine and supernatural light." Edwards would often compare true knowledge of God to tasting honey for the first time. While a person could theoretically know that honey tastes sweet, a direct taste of honey obliterates mere theoretical knowledge. God's grace overwhelms our minds with its sweetness. The entrance of God's grace into the soul is like the sweetest honey you can imagine. (Perhaps this would be chocolate for us modern readers, but you have to imagine a world without abundant sugary products.) God's character overwhelms our senses and transforms our minds into receptacles of his goodness. Once Edwards had experienced God's grace, the whole world was imaginatively transformed into a new sacred garden.

Edwards's "Narrative" prompts us to pursue God in every human endeavor: our studies at college, our careers, and our enjoyment of the world outside us. Through the saving work of Christ on the cross, earthly creatures can participate in God's divine life. In this work, we see how the beauty of this world is a doorway to an even deeper and greater reality beyond us.

From "Personal Narrative"
Opening: Edwards's Growth in Grace

The first instance that I remember of that sort of inward, sweet delight in God and divine things, that I have lived much in since, was on reading those words, 1 Tim. 1:17, "Now unto the King, eternal, immortal, invisible, the only wise God, be honor and glory forever and ever, Amen." As I read the words, there came into my soul, and was as it were diffused through it, a sense of the glory of the Divine Being; a new sense, quite different from any thing I ever experienced before. Never any words of Scripture seemed to me as these words did. I thought with myself, how excellent a Being that was, and how happy I should be, if I might enjoy that God, and be rapt up to him in heaven; and be as it were swallowed up in him forever! I kept saying, and as it were singing, over these words of Scripture to myself; and went to pray to God that I might enjoy him; and prayed in a manner quite different from what I used to do, with a new sort of affection. But it never came into my thought, that there was any thing spiritual, or of a saving nature, in this.

From about that time, I began to have a new kind of apprehensions and ideas of Christ, and the work of redemption, and the glorious way of salvation by him. An inward, sweet sense of these things, at times, came into my heart; and my soul was led away in pleasant views and contemplations of them. And my mind was greatly encouraged to spend my time in reading and meditating on Christ, on the beauty and excellency of his person, and the lovely way of salvation by free grace in him. I found no books so delightful to me, as those that treated of these subjects. Those words, Song. 2:1, used to be abundantly with me, "I am the Rose of Sharon, and the Lily of the valleys." The words seemed to me sweetly to represent the loveliness and beauty of Jesus Christ. The whole book of Canticles used to be pleasant to me, and I used to be much in reading it, about that time; and found, from time to time, an inward sweetness, that would carry me away in my contemplations. This I know not how to express otherwise, than by a calm, sweet abstraction of soul from all the concerns of this world; and sometimes a kind of vision, or fixed ideas and imaginations, of being alone in the mountains, or some solitary wilderness, far from all mankind, sweetly conversing with Christ, and rapt and swallowed up in God. The sense I had of divine things, would often of a sudden kindle up, as it were, a sweet burning in my heart; an ardor of soul that I know not how to express.

Not long after I first began to experience these things, I gave an account to my father of some things that had passed in my mind. I was pretty much affected by the discourse we had together; and when the discourse was ended, I walked abroad alone, in a solitary place in my father's pasture, for contemplation. And as I was walking there, and looking up on the sky and clouds, there came into my mind so sweet a sense of the glorious majesty and grace of God, that I know not how to express. I seemed to see them both in a sweet conjunction; majesty and meekness joined together: it was a sweet and gentle, and holy majesty; and also a majestic meekness; an awful sweetness; a high, and great, and holy gentleness.

After this my sense of divine things gradually increased, and became more and more lively, and had more of that inward sweetness. The appearance of every thing was altered; there seemed to be, as it were, a calm, sweet cast, or appearance of divine glory, in almost every thing. God's excellency, his wisdom, his purity and love, seemed to appear in every thing; in the sun, and moon, and stars; in the clouds and blue sky; in the grass, flowers, trees; in the water, and all nature; which used greatly to fix my mind. I often used to sit and view the moon for a long time; and in the day, spent much time in viewing the clouds and sky, to behold the sweet glory of God in these things; in the mean time, singing forth, with a low voice, my contemplations of the Creator and Redeemer. And scarce any thing, among all the works of nature, was so sweet to me as thunder and lightning; formerly nothing had been so terrible to me. Before, I used to be uncommonly terrified with thunder, and to be struck with terror when I saw a thunderstorm rising; but now, on the contrary, it rejoiced me. I felt God, if I may so to speak, at the first appearance of a thunderstorm; and used to take the opportunity, at such times, to fix myself in order to view the clouds and see the lightnings play, and hear the majestic and awful voice of God's thunder, which oftentimes was exceedingly entertaining, leading me to sweet contemplations of my great and glorious God. While thus engaged, it always seemed natural to me to sing or chant forth my meditations; or, to speak my thoughts in soliloquies with a singing voice.

Conclusion

I have loved the doctrines of the gospel; they have been to my soul like green pastures. The gospel has seemed to me the richest treasure; the treasure that I have most desired, and longed that it might dwell richly in me. The way of salvation by Christ has appeared, in a general way, glorious and excellent, most pleasant and most beautiful. It has often seemed to me, that it would, in a great measure, spoil heaven, to receive it in any other way. That text has often been affecting and delightful to me, Isa. 32:2, "A man shall be a hiding place from the wind, and a covert from the tempest," etc.

It has often appeared to me delightful, to be united to Christ; to have him for my Head, and to be a member of his body; also to have Christ for my Teacher and Prophet. I very often think with sweetness, and longings, and pantings of soul, of being a little child, taking hold of Christ, to be led by him through the wilderness of this world. That text, Mat. 18:3, has often been sweet to me, "Except ye be converted and become as little children," etc. I love to think of coming to Christ, to receive salvation of him, poor in spirit, and quite empty of self, humbly exalting him alone; cut off entirely from my own root, in order to grow into, and out of Christ; to have God in Christ to be all in all; and to live by faith on the Son of God, a life of humble, unfeigned confidence in him. That Scripture has often been sweet to me, Psa. 115:1, "Not unto us, O Lord, not unto us, but unto thy name give glory, for thy mercy, and for thy truth's sake." And those words of Christ, Luke 10:21, "In that hour Jesus rejoiced in spirit, and said, I thank thee, O Father, Lord of heaven and earth, that thou hast hid these things from the wise and prudent, and hast revealed them unto babes: even so, Father, for so it seemed good in thy sight." That sovereignty of God which Christ rejoiced in, seemed to me worthy of such joy; and that rejoicing seemed to show the excellency of Christ, and of what spirit he was.

Sometimes, only mentioning a single word caused my heart to burn within me; or only seeing the name of Christ, or the name of some attribute of God. And God has appeared glorious to me, on account of the Trinity. It has made me have exalting thoughts of God, that he subsists in three persons; Father, Son, and Holy Ghost. The sweetest joys and delights I have experienced, have not been those that have arisen from a hope of my own good estate; but in a direct view of the glorious things of the gospel. When I enjoy this sweetness, it seems to carry me above the thoughts of my own estate; it seems, at such times, a loss that I cannot bear, to take off my eye from the glorious, pleasant object I behold without me, to turn my eye in upon myself, and my own good estate.

My heart has been much on the advancement of Christ's kingdom in the world. The histories of the past advancement of Christ's kingdom have been sweet to me. When I have read histories of past ages, the pleasantest thing, in all my reading, has been to read of the kingdom of Christ being promoted. And when I have expected, in my reading, to come to any such thing, I have rejoiced in the prospect all the way as I read. And my mind has been much entertained and delighted with the Scripture promises and prophecies, which relate to the future glorious advancement of Christ's kingdom upon earth.

I have sometimes had a sense of the excellent fullness of Christ, and his meetness and suitableness as a Savior; whereby he has appeared to me, far above all, the chief of ten thousands. His blood and atonement have appeared sweet, and his righteousness sweet; which was always accompanied with ardency of spirit; and inward strugglings and breathings, and groanings that cannot be uttered, to be emptied of myself, and swallowed up in Christ.

Once, as I rode out into the woods for my health, in 1737, having alighted from my horse in a retired place, as my manner commonly has been, to walk for divine contemplation and prayer, I had a view that for me was extraordinary, of the glory of the Son of God, as Mediator between God and man, and his wonderful, great, full, pure and sweet grace and love, and meek and gentle condescension. This grace that appeared so calm and sweet, appeared also great above the heavens. The person of Christ appeared ineffably excellent, with an excellency great enough to swallow up all thought and conception—which continued, as near as I can judge, about an hour; which kept me the greater part of the time in a flood of tears, and weeping aloud. I felt an ardency of soul to be, what I know not otherwise how to express, emptied and annihilated; to lie in the dust, and to be full of Christ alone; to love him with a holy and pure love; to trust in him; to live upon him; to serve and follow him; and to be perfectly sanctified and made pure, with a divine and heavenly purity. I have several other times had views very much of the same nature, and which have had the same effects.

I have many times had a sense of the glory of the Third Person in the Trinity, and his office of Sanctifier; in his holy operations, communicating divine light and life to the soul. God, in the communications of his Holy Spirit, has appeared as an infinite fountain of divine glory and sweetness; being full and sufficient to fill and satisfy the soul; pouring forth itself in sweet communications; like the sun in its glory, sweetly and pleasantly diffusing light and life. And I have sometimes had an affecting sense of the excellency of the Word of God, as the word of life; as the light of life; a sweet, excellent, life-giving, word; accompanied with a thirsting after that word, that it might dwell richly in my heart.

Often, since I lived in this town, I have had very affecting views of my own sinfulness and vileness; very frequently to such a degree as to hold me in a kind of loud weeping, sometimes for a considerable time together; so that I have often been forced to shut myself up. I have had a vastly greater sense of my own wickedness, and the badness of my heart, than ever I had before my conversion. It has often appeared to me, that if God should mark iniquity against me, I should appear the very worst of all mankind; of all that have been since the beginning of the world to this time; and that I should have by far the lowest place in the world to this time; and that I should have by far the lowest place in hell. When others, that have come to talk with me about their soul concerns, have expressed the sense they have had of their own wickedness by saying, that it seemed to them, that they were as bad as the devil himself; I thought their expressions seemed exceeding faint and feeble, to represent my wickedness.

My wickedness, as I am in myself, has long appeared to me perfectly ineffable, and swallowing up all thought and imagination; like an infinite deluge, or mountains over my head. I know not how to express better what my sins appear to me to be, than by heaping infinite upon infinite, and multiplying infinite by infinite. Very often, for these many years, these expressions are in my mind and in my mouth, "Infinite upon infinite—Infinite upon infinite!" When I look into my heart, and take a view of my wickedness, it looks like an abyss, infinitely deeper than hell. And it appears to me, that were it not for free grace, exalted and raised up to the infinite height of all the fullness and glory of the great Jehovah, and the arm of his power and grace stretched forth in all the majesty of his power, and in all the glory of his sovereignty, I should appear sunk down in my sins below hell itself; far beyond the sight of every thing, but the eye of sovereign grace, that can pierce even down to such a depth. And yet, it seems to me that my conviction of sin is exceeding small and faint; it is enough to amaze me, that I have very little sense of my sinfulness. I know certainly, that I have very little sense of my sinfulness. When I have had turns of weeping for my sins, I thought I knew at the time that my repentance was nothing to my sin.

I have greatly longed of late for a broken heart, and to lie low before God; and when I ask for humility, I cannot bear the thoughts of being no more humble than other Christians. It seems to me, that though their degrees of humility may be suitable for them, yet it would be a vile self-exaltation in me, not to be the lowest in humility of all mankind. Others speak of their longing to be "humbled in the dust"; that may be a proper expression for them, but I always think of myself, that I ought, and it is an expression that has long been natural for me to use in prayer, "to lie infinitely low before God." And it is affecting to think, how ignorant I was, when a young Christian, of the bottomless, infinite depths of wickedness, pride, hypocrisy and deceit, left in my heart.

I have a much greater sense of my universal, exceeding dependence on God's grace and strength, and mere good pleasure, of late, than I used formerly to have; and have experienced more of an abhorrence of my own righteousness. The very thought of any joy arising in me, on any consideration of my own amiableness, performances, or experiences, or any goodness of heart or life, is nauseous and detestable to me. And yet, I am greatly afflicted with a proud and self-righteous spirit, much more sensibly than I used to be formerly. I see that serpent rising and putting forth its head continually, every where, all around me.

Though it seems to me, that in some respects, I was a far better Christian, for two or three years after my first conversion, than I am now; and lived in a more constant delight and pleasure; yet of late years, I have had a more full and constant sense of the absolute sovereignty of God, and a delight in that sovereignty; and have had more of a sense of the glory of Christ, as a Mediator revealed in the gospel. On one Saturday night, in particular, I had such a discovery of the excellency of the gospel above all other doctrines, that I could not but say to myself, "This is my chosen light, my chosen doctrine"; and of Christ, "This is my chosen Prophet." It appeared sweet, beyond all expression to follow Christ, and to be taught, and enlightened, and instructed by him; to learn of him, and live to him. Another Saturday night (Jan. 1739) I had such a sense, how sweet and blessed a thing it was to walk in the way of duty; to do that which was right and meet to be done, and agreeable to the holy mind of God; that it caused me to break forth into a kind of loud weeping, which held me some time, so that I was forced to shut myself up, and fasten the doors. I could not but, as it were, cry out, "How happy are they who do that which is right in the sight of God! They are blessed indeed, they are the happy ones!" I had, at the same time, a very affecting sense, how meet and suitable it was that God should govern the world, and order all things according to his own pleasure; and I rejoiced in it, that God reigned, and that his will was done.

Discussion Questions

1. Edwards's growing knowledge of God makes him even more aware of the "bottomless infinite depths of human wickedness." Why does a greater awareness of one's own sin seem to follow his or her greater understanding of God's character?

2. How does the natural world lead Edwards to a deeper knowledge of God? How does Scripture?

3. How can a subject like biology or math help you understand God's goodness and grace?

4. If someone asked you to narrate your own journey of faith in God, what stories would you tell? What analogies or images would you use to explain your faith?

5. It is often said that Edwards's understanding of God is "aesthetic," focused on the beauty of God's creation. How can an appreciation of beauty lead you to believe in God, or perhaps to love him better? Think of particular places or works of music you enjoy because they are *beautiful* (not merely because they are useful or pleasant).

CHAPTER 22

Edmund Burke

Introduction to *Reflections on the Revolution in France*
BENJAMIN MYERS

Although Edmund Burke's *Reflections on the Revolution in France* was written to address specific developments in politics near the end of the eighteenth century, it has become a foundational book for all who cherish permanent human values and timeless, transcendent truths. As such, its implications for education are immense. Disturbed by what he saw as a reckless abandonment of hard-won wisdom and organic community in France, Burke laid out a clear argument for the value of tradition. Tradition, Burke insisted, rescues us from our own superficiality, from being subject to the whims of the moment. Without a rich tradition to guide us, we have only what is trendy and immediately accessible to inform our intellectual, aesthetic, and communal lives. Thus deprived of the past, we become what Burke memorably called "the flies of a summer."

Born in Dublin, Ireland, in 1729, Burke was educated at Trinity College Dublin. He moved to London with the intention of studying law but instead earned his living as a writer and went into politics. He entered the British House of Commons in 1765. As a member of parliament, Burke's commitment to what he saw as the traditional liberties of the English people led him both to sympathize with the American colonists in their dispute with the Crown and to oppose the slave trade. He was also a notable critic of British imperialism in India.

Reflections on the Revolution in France was published in 1790, at a relatively early stage in the French Revolution, yet Burke incisively predicted the excesses and violence that would mark later stages of the revolt. Such chaos and disruption, Burke suggested, are the inevitable result of attempts to overthrow inherited principles of social organization and replace them with rational planning. Skeptical of eighteenth-century Enlightenment claims about the ability of the reasoning individual to discern truth, Burke argued for the importance of what he called "prejudice" in making moral, social, cultural, and political judgments. For Burke, "prejudice" was not simply an irrational bias but was rather the individual's appropriation of the thought and experiences of his or her predecessors. As we are limited by the short span of our lives and by the limits of our own intelligence, no individual has the time or the ability to form a new understanding of the world from the ground up. We all must rely on judgments made before we lived, which were passed down to us in the form of tradition. We also have a responsibility to pass tradition down to those who come after us.

Over the course of the twentieth century, important thinkers—such as Christopher Dawson in *The Crisis of Western Education* and Michael Oakeshott in *The Voice of Liberal Learning*—applied the Burkean view of tradition to education and demonstrated how a true education is the receiving of an inheritance. Like inheriting a fine old house, a liberal education is a matter of both privilege and responsibility. Our inheritance gives us a beautiful and suitably roomy place to live, but it also obligates us to preserve this living place in good shape for future generations. When we study the political thought of ancient Athens, the plays of Shakespeare, or Newton's calculus, we are both learning to live in our inheritance and preserving that inheritance for those who come after us. That is what it means to be an "educated" person.

From *Reflections on the Revolution in France*

When ancient opinions and rules of life are taken away, the loss cannot possibly be estimated. From that moment we have no compass to govern us, nor can we know distinctly to what port we steer. Europe, undoubtedly, taken in a mass, was in a flourishing condition the day on which your Revolution was completed. How much of that prosperous state was owing to the spirit of our old manners and opinions is not easy to say; but as such causes cannot be indifferent in their operation, we must presume, that, on the whole, their operation was beneficial.

. . .

But one of the first and most leading principles on which the commonwealth and the laws are consecrated is lest the temporary possessors and life-renters in it, unmindful of what they have received from their ancestors, or of what is due to their posterity, should act as if they were the entire masters; that they should not think it amongst their rights to cut off the entail or commit waste on the inheritance, by destroying at their pleasure the whole original fabric of their society: hazarding to leave to those who come after them a ruin instead of an habitation,—and teaching these successors as little to respect their contrivances as they had themselves respected the institutions of their forefathers. By this unprincipled facility of changing the state as often and as much and in as many ways as there are floating fancies or fashions, the whole chain and continuity of the commonwealth would be broken; no one generation could link with the other; men would become little better than the flies of a summer.

And first of all, the science of jurisprudence, the pride of the human intellect, which, with all its defects, redundancies, and errors, is the collected reason of ages, combining the principles of original justice with the infinite variety of human concerns, as a heap of old exploded errors, would be no longer studied. Personal self-sufficiency and arrogance (the certain attendants upon all those who have never experienced a wisdom greater than their own) would usurp the tribunal. Of course no certain laws, establishing invariable grounds of hope and fear, would keep the actions of men in a certain course, or direct them to a certain end. Nothing stable in the modes of holding property or exercising function could form a solid ground on which any parent could speculate in the education of his offspring, or in a choice for their future establishment in the world. No principles would be early worked into the habits. As soon as the most able instructor had completed his laborious course of institution, instead of sending forth his pupil accomplished in a virtuous discipline fitted to pro- cure him attention and respect in his place in society, he would find everything altered, and that he had turned out a poor creature to the contempt and derision of the world, ignorant of the true grounds of estimation. Who would insure a tender and delicate sense of honor to beat almost with the first pulses of the heart, when no man could know what would be the test of honor in a nation continually varying the standard of its coin? No part of life would retain its acquisitions. Barbarism with regard to science and literature, unskilfulness with regard to arts and manufactures, would infallibly succeed to the want of a steady education and settled principle; and thus the commonwealth itself would in a few generations crumble away, be disconnected into the dust and powder of individuality, and at length dispersed to all the winds of heaven.

To avoid, therefore, the evils of inconstancy and versatility, ten thousand times worse than those of obstinacy and the blindest prejudice, we have con- secrated the state, that no man should approach to look into its defects or corruptions but with due caution; that he should never dream of beginning its reformation by its subversion; that he should approach to the faults of the state as to the wounds of a father, with pious awe and trembling solicitude. By this wise prejudice we are taught to look with horror on those children of their country who are prompt rashly to hack that aged parent in pieces and put him into the kettle of magicians, in hopes that by their poisonous weeds and wild incantations they may regenerate the paternal constitution and renovate their father's life.

Society is, indeed, a contract. Subordinate contracts for objects of mere occasional interest may be dissolved at pleasure; but the state ought not to be considered as nothing better than a partnership agreement in a trade of pepper and coffee, calico or tobacco, or some other such low concern, to be taken up for a little temporary interest, and to be dissolved by the fancy of the parties. It is to be looked on with other reverence; because it is not a partnership in things subservient only to the gross animal existence of a temporary and perishable nature. It is a partnership in all science, a partnership in all art, a partnership in every virtue and in all perfection. As the ends of such a partnership cannot be obtained in many generations, it becomes a partnership not only between those who are living, but between those who are living, those who are dead, and those who are to be born. Each contract of each particular state is but a clause in the great primeval contract of eternal society, linking the lower with the higher natures, connecting the visible and invisible world, according to a fixed compact sanctioned by the inviolable oath which holds all physical and all moral natures each in their appointed place. This law is not subject to the will of those who, by an obligation above them, and infinitely superior, are bound to submit their will to that law. The municipal corporations of that universal kingdom are not morally at liberty, at their pleasure, and on their speculations of a contingent improvement, wholly to separate and tear asunder the bands of their subordinate community, and to dissolve it into an unsocial, uncivil, unconnected chaos of elementary principles. It is the first and supreme necessity only, a necessity that is not chosen, but chooses, a necessity paramount to deliberation, that admits no discussion and demands no evidence, which alone can justify a resort to anarchy. This necessity is no exception to the rule; because this necessity itself is a part, too, of that moral and physical disposition of things to which man must be obedient by consent or force: but if that which is only submission to necessity should be made the object of choice, the law is broken, Nature is disobeyed, and the rebellious are outlawed, cast forth, and exiled, from this world of reason, and order, and peace, and virtue, and fruitful penitence, into the antagonist world of madness, discord, vice, confusion, and unavailing sorrow.

Discussion Questions

1. Burke suggested that a government, a society, or a civilization is a contract not only among the living but also with the dead and the yet to be born. In the realm of education, what responsibilities do today's students have to the past and to the future?

2. How might the conditions of our contemporary society—our consumerism and our technology, for example—encourage us to live like "the flies of a summer"?

3. What might a good education do to mitigate those conditions of contemporary society?

4. Burke objected to the desire among the French revolutionaries to wholly remake their form of government overnight. What role might good education play in maintaining the proper balance between social change and stability?

CHAPTER 23

Alfred Lord Tennyson

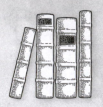

Introduction to "Ulysses"

SCOTT H. MOORE

Alfred Lord Tennyson's dramatic monologue "Ulysses" is one of the most famous poems of the Victorian era in British literature. Written in 1833 and published in 1842, the blank verse poem is often thought of as one of the most inspiring poems in the English language, and quotations from the poem are exceedingly popular. The poem is set in the mythological years after the Greek hero Ulysses (Odysseus) returned from two decades of fighting in the Trojan War and wandering throughout the Mediterranean Sea, returning home to Ithaca. In the monologue, Ulysses expresses his discontent with remaining at home with an "aged wife" and serving as an "idle king." He imagines that his son, Telemachus, is better suited to rule his island kingdom. He looks longingly to the sea and imagines sailing "beyond the sunset." The final stanza presents a rousing call to adventure and exploration. He calls to his mariners, "Come, my friends, / 'Tis not too late to seek a newer world." The poem ends with the heroic charge that though his body has been "made weak by time and fate," he remains "strong in will / To strive, to seek, to find, and not to yield."

Though Tennyson himself spoke of the poem and its narrator in heroic and positive terms, there is ample reason to question the virtue and the wisdom of the narrator. First, by choosing to call the character by his Roman name, Ulysses, rather than his Greek name, Odysseus, Tennyson associated him with the Roman and Latin traditions. For the great Roman poet Virgil, who spoke from the Trojan perspective, Ulysses was "cowardly," a "schemer," and a "mastermind of crime."[1]

Second, Tennyson specifically employed the Italian Renaissance poet Dante Alighieri's presentation of Ulysses. Dante popularized the idea that Ulysses set out on another, last adventure. In canto 26 of Dante's *Inferno*, the characters of Dante and Virgil encounter Ulysses in the ring of hell reserved for fraudulent counselors. There Ulysses tells Dante about his last trip and his attempt to conquer the mountain of Purgatory, which he discovered rising from the sea. In this foolish attempt to gain salvation by his own efforts and craftiness, Ulysses'

---

1. Virgil, *Aeneid*, trans. Robert Fagles (New York: Viking Penguin, 2006), 77, 79–80.

boat went down and the sea covered him for good. Ulysses was punished for the fraudulent counsel he gave during the Trojan War and, presumably, the bad advice he gave to his men to convince them to take one last adventure.

Students who read this famous poem are thus left with many questions. If Tennyson wanted to praise Ulysses, why did he not use Homer's more positive characterization? By using Dante's Ulysses, was Tennyson suggesting that the stirring words of the poem are really "fraudulent counsel" or bad advice?

"Ulysses"

It little profits that an idle king,
By this still hearth, among these barren crags,
Match'd with an aged wife, I mete and dole
Unequal laws unto a savage race,
That hoard, and sleep, and feed, and know not me.
I cannot rest from travel: I will drink
Life to the lees: All times I have enjoy'd
Greatly, have suffer'd greatly, both with those
That loved me, and alone, on shore, and when
Thro' scudding drifts the rainy Hyades
Vext the dim sea: I am become a name;
For always roaming with a hungry heart
Much have I seen and known; cities of men
And manners, climates, councils, governments,
Myself not least, but honour'd of them all;
And drunk delight of battle with my peers,
Far on the ringing plains of windy Troy.
I am a part of all that I have met;
Yet all experience is an arch wherethro'
Gleams that untravell'd world whose margin fades
For ever and forever when I move.
How dull it is to pause, to make an end,
To rust unburnish'd, not to shine in use!
As tho' to breathe were life! Life piled on life
Were all too little, and of one to me
Little remains: but every hour is saved
From that eternal silence, something more,
A bringer of new things; and vile it were
For some three suns to store and hoard myself,
And this gray spirit yearning in desire

To follow knowledge like a sinking star,
Beyond the utmost bound of human thought.

    This is my son, mine own Telemachus,
To whom I leave the sceptre and the isle,—
Well-loved of me, discerning to fulfil
This labour, by slow prudence to make mild
A rugged people, and thro' soft degrees
Subdue them to the useful and the good.
Most blameless is he, centred in the sphere
Of common duties, decent not to fail
In offices of tenderness, and pay
Meet adoration to my household gods,
When I am gone. He works his work, I mine.

    There lies the port; the vessel puffs her sail:
There gloom the dark, broad seas. My mariners,
Souls that have toil'd, and wrought, and thought with me—
That ever with a frolic welcome took
The thunder and the sunshine, and opposed
Free hearts, free foreheads—you and I are old;
Old age hath yet his honour and his toil;
Death closes all: but something ere the end,
Some work of noble note, may yet be done,
Not unbecoming men that strove with Gods.
The lights begin to twinkle from the rocks:
The long day wanes: the slow moon climbs: the deep
Moans round with many voices. Come, my friends,
'Tis not too late to seek a newer world.
Push off, and sitting well in order smite
The sounding furrows; for my purpose holds
To sail beyond the sunset, and the baths
Of all the western stars, until I die.
It may be that the gulfs will wash us down:
It may be we shall touch the Happy Isles,
And see the great Achilles, whom we knew.
Tho' much is taken, much abides; and tho'
We are not now that strength which in old days
Moved earth and heaven, that which we are, we are;

One equal temper of heroic hearts,
Made weak by time and fate, but strong in will
To strive, to seek, to find, and not to yield.

Discussion Questions

1. What is the underlying problem Ulysses faces in this poem? Is it a problem we face in today's world?
2. Are you, like Ulysses, tempted to believe that one more adventure will solve your problems? Why or why not?
3. What is the difference between confidence and hubris?
4. What are some ways to tell good advice from bad advice? Is it possible to learn to do this better?

CHAPTER 24

Frederick Douglass

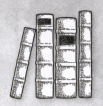

Introduction to *Narrative of the Life of Frederick Douglass, an American Slave*

H. COLLIN MESSER

Born on a Maryland plantation in 1818, Frederick Douglass was the son of an enslaved woman and an unknown white man. During his youth, Douglass witnessed the cruel, violent, and bloody depredations of American slavery, which his autobiography describes in vivid detail. In the opening chapter of his memoir, *Narrative of the Life of Frederick Douglass, an American Slave*, he poignantly recollected being separated from his mother at a very young age—a common practice in slaveholding that blunted "the child's affection toward its mother" and "destroyed the natural affection of the mother for the child."[1] Douglass was allowed to see his mother only four or five times during his childhood. She died when he was seven. Shortly after her death, Douglass was sent to Baltimore to serve in the household of his master's relatives. "Going to live at Baltimore," Douglass later recalled, "laid the foundation, and opened the gateway, to all my subsequent prosperity." Indeed, through a remarkable series of events and due mostly to his tenacious resourcefulness, Douglass learned to read and write in Baltimore. Moreover, in this bustling and prosperous city just south of the Mason-Dixon Line, Douglass began to imagine the possibility of freedom. After a failed escape attempt in 1836, Douglass successfully fled to New York City in 1838. Upon settling in New Bedford, Massachusetts, Douglass became involved in the antislavery movement as a passionate and dynamic speaker at abolitionist meetings. The story of freedom he so compellingly told on the platform became the basis for his *Narrative*, which was published in 1845.

In reading Douglass's life story, from his lurid childhood account to his often wry history of his years in Baltimore, we are immediately struck by his conviction that the institution of slavery is not only horrible for the slave but also deeply damaging to the slaveholder. Douglass wrote compellingly of his own suffering as a person born into slavery. Moreover, with great irony and even pity, he dramatized the moral and spiritual demise of the slaveholders themselves.

---

1. Frederick Douglass, *Narrative of the Life of Frederick Douglass, an American Slave. Written by Himself*, 1845; 1st electronic ed., University of North Carolina at Chapel Hill, 1999, https://docsouth.unc.edu/neh/douglass/douglass.html.

This realization is crucial to understanding Douglass's essential rhetorical purpose as an abolitionist speaker and author: convincing his audiences of the destructive and comprehensive evil of the institution of slavery. While the *Narrative* contains any number of villains—including the vile overseers Mr. Severe and Mr. Gore —Douglass was most insistent that slavery itself is the great enemy.

The story of how Douglass vanquished this enemy provides the Christian reader with an opportunity to grow in wisdom. Southern Catholic writer Walker Percy once quipped, "Bad books always lie. They lie most of all about the human condition, so that one never recognizes oneself, the deepest part of oneself in a bad book."[2] By Percy's definition, the *Narrative* is a very good book, chiefly because of Douglass's biblical understanding of human nature and the reality of systemic sin and evil in a fallen world. In the face of great suffering, Douglass did not despair. Rather, to borrow a phrase from Christian philosopher Francis Schaeffer, Douglass regarded human beings as "glorious ruins," capable of both great nobility and profound depravity. The people we meet in Douglass's narrative, including young Frederick himself, are most noble and heroic when they embrace their God-given capacity for language and learning, both for their own sake and for the sake of others. Conversely, they are most destructive and despicable when they abuse or withhold these same good gifts.

From *Narrative of the Life of Frederick Douglass, an American Slave. Written by Himself*
Chapter V.

As to my own treatment while I lived on Colonel Lloyd's plantation, it was very similar to that of the other slave children. I was not old enough to work in the field, and there being little else than field work to do, I had a great deal of leisure time. The most I had to do was to drive up the cows at evening, keep the fowls out of the garden, keep the front yard clean, and run of errands for my old master's daughter, Mrs. Lucretia Auld. The most of my leisure time I spent in helping Master Daniel Lloyd in finding his birds, after he had shot them. My connection with Master Daniel was of some advantage to me. He became quite attached to me, and was a sort of protector of me. He would not allow the older boys to impose upon me, and would divide his cakes with me.

I was seldom whipped by my old master, and suffered little from any thing else than hunger and cold. I suffered much from hunger, but much more from cold. In hottest summer and coldest winter, I was kept almost naked—no shoes, no stockings, no jacket, no trousers, nothing on but a coarse tow linen shirt,

---

2. Walker Percy, "Another Message in the Bottle," in Percy, *Signposts in a Strange Land*, ed. Patrick Samway (New York: Farrar, Straus and Giroux, 1991), 364.

reaching only to my knees. I had no bed. I must have perished with cold, but that, the coldest nights, I used to steal a bag which was used for carrying corn to the mill. I would crawl into this bag, and there sleep on the cold, damp, clay floor, with my head in and feet out. My feet have been so cracked with the frost, that the pen with which I am writing might be laid in the gashes.

We were not regularly allowanced. Our food was coarse corn meal boiled. This was called *mush*. It was put into a large wooden tray or trough, and set down upon the ground. The children were then called, like so many pigs, and like so many pigs they would come and devour the mush; some with oyster-shells, others with pieces of shingle, some with naked hands, and none with spoons. He that ate fastest got most; he that was strongest secured the best place; and few left the trough satisfied.

I was probably between seven and eight years old when I left Colonel Lloyd's plantation. I left it with joy. I shall never forget the ecstasy with which I received the intelligence that my old master (Anthony) had determined to let me go to Baltimore, to live with Mr. Hugh Auld, brother to my old master's son-in-law, Captain Thomas Auld. I received this information about three days before my departure. They were three of the happiest days I ever enjoyed. I spent the most part of all these three days in the creek, washing off the plantation scurf, and preparing myself for my departure.

The pride of appearance which this would indicate was not my own. I spent the time in washing, not so much because I wished to, but because Mrs. Lucretia had told me I must get all the dead skin off my feet and knees before I could go to Baltimore; for the people in Baltimore were very cleanly, and would laugh at me if I looked dirty. Besides, she was going to give me a pair of trousers, which I should not put on unless I got all the dirt off me. The thought of owning a pair of trousers was great indeed! It was almost a sufficient motive, not only to make me take off what would be called by pig-drovers the mange, but the skin itself. I went at it in good earnest, working for the first time with the hope of reward.

The ties that ordinarily bind children to their homes were all suspended in my case. I found no severe trial in my departure. My home was charmless; it was not home to me; on parting from it, I could not feel that I was leaving any thing which I could have enjoyed by staying. My mother was dead, my grandmother lived far off, so that I seldom saw her. I had two sisters and one brother, that lived in the same house with me; but the early separation of us from our mother had well nigh blotted the fact of our relationship from our memories. I looked for home elsewhere, and was confident of finding none which I should relish less than the one which I was leaving. If, however, I found in my new home hardship, hunger, whipping, and nakedness, I had the consolation that I should not have escaped any one of them by staying. Having already had more than a taste of them in the house of my old master, and having endured them there, I very naturally inferred my ability to endure them elsewhere, and especially at Baltimore.

. . .

We sailed out of Miles River for Baltimore on a Saturday morning. I remember only the day of the week, for at that time I had no knowledge of the days of the month, nor the months of the year. On setting sail, I walked aft, and gave to Colonel Lloyd's plantation what I hoped would be the last look. I then placed myself in the bows of the sloop, and there spent the remainder of the day in looking ahead, interesting myself in what was in the distance rather than in things nearby or behind.

. . .

Mr. and Mrs. Auld were both at home, and met me at the door with their little son Thomas, to take care of whom I had been given. And here I saw what I had never seen before; it was a white face beaming with the most kindly emotions; it was the face of my new mistress, Sophia Auld. I wish I could describe the rapture that flashed through my soul as I beheld it. It was a new and strange sight to me, brightening up my pathway with the light of happiness.

. . .

I look upon my departure from Colonel Lloyd's plantation as one of the most interesting events of my life. It is possible, and even quite probable, that but for the mere circumstance of being removed from that plantation to Baltimore, I should have to-day, instead of being here seated by my own table, in the enjoyment of freedom and the happiness of home, writing this Narrative, been confined in the galling chains of slavery. Going to live at Baltimore laid the foundation, and opened the gateway, to all my subsequent prosperity. I have ever regarded it as the first plain manifestation of that kind providence which has ever since attended me, and marked my life with so many favors. I regarded the selection of myself as being somewhat remarkable. There were a number of slave children that might have been sent from the plantation to Baltimore. There were those younger, those older, and those of the same age. I was chosen from among them all, and was the first, last, and only choice.

I may be deemed superstitious, and even egotistical, in regarding this event as a special interposition of divine Providence in my favor. But I should be false to the earliest sentiments of my soul, if I suppressed the opinion. I prefer to be true to myself, even at the hazard of incurring the ridicule of others, rather than to be false, and incur my own abhorrence. From my earliest recollection, I date the entertainment of a deep conviction that slavery would not always be able to hold me within its foul embrace; and in the darkest hours of my career in slavery, this living word of faith and spirit of hope departed not from me, but remained like ministering angels to cheer me through the gloom. This good spirit was from God, and to him I offer thanksgiving and praise.

Chapter VI.

My new mistress proved to be all she appeared when I first met her at the door,—a woman of the kindest heart and finest feelings. She had never had a slave under her control previously to myself, and prior to her marriage she had been dependent upon her own industry for a living. She was by trade a weaver; and by constant application to her business, she had been in a good degree preserved from the blighting and dehumanizing effects of slavery. I was utterly astonished at her goodness. I scarcely knew how to behave towards her. She was entirely unlike any other white woman I had ever seen. I could not approach her as I was accustomed to approach other white ladies. My early instruction was all out of place. The crouching servility, usually so acceptable a quality in a slave, did not answer when manifested toward her. Her favor was not gained by it; she seemed to be disturbed by it. She did not deem it impudent or unmannerly for a slave to look her in the face. The meanest slave was put fully at ease in her presence, and none left without feeling better for having seen her. Her face was made of heavenly smiles, and her voice of tranquil music.

But, alas! this kind heart had but a short time to remain such. The fatal poison of irresponsible power was already in her hands, and soon commenced its infernal work. That cheerful eye, under the influence of slavery, soon became red with rage; that voice, made all of sweet accord, changed to one of harsh and horrid discord; and that angelic face gave place to that of a demon.

Very soon after I went to live with Mr. and Mrs. Auld, she very kindly commenced to teach me the A, B, C. After I had learned this, she assisted me in learning to spell words of three or four letters. Just at this point of my progress, Mr. Auld found out what was going on, and at once forbade Mrs. Auld to instruct me further, telling her, among other things, that it was unlawful, as well as unsafe, to teach a slave to read. To use his own words, further, he said, "If you give a nigger an inch, he will take an ell. A nigger should know nothing but to obey his master—to do as he is told to do. Learning would *spoil* the best nigger in the world. Now," said he, "if you teach that nigger (speaking of myself) how to read, there would be no keeping him. It would forever unfit him to be a slave. He would at once become unmanageable, and of no value to his master. As to himself, it could do him no good, but a great deal of harm. It would make him discontented and unhappy." These words sank deep into my heart, stirred up sentiments within that lay slumbering, and called into existence an entirely new train of thought. It was a new and special revelation, explaining dark and mysterious things, with which my youthful understanding had struggled, but struggled in vain. I now understood what had been to me a most perplexing difficulty—to wit, the white man's power to enslave the black man. It was a grand achievement, and I prized it highly. From that moment, I understood the pathway from slavery to freedom. It was just what I wanted, and I got it at a time when I the least expected it. Whilst I was saddened by the thought of losing the aid of my kind mistress, I was gladdened by the invaluable instruction which, by the merest accident, I had gained from my master. Though conscious of the difficulty of learning without a teacher, I set out with high hope, and a fixed purpose, at whatever cost of trouble, to learn how to read. The very decided manner with which he spoke, and strove to impress his wife with the evil consequences of giving me instruction, served to convince me that he was deeply sensible of the truths he was uttering. It gave me the best assurance that I might rely with the utmost confidence on the results which, he said, would flow from teaching me to read. What he most dreaded, that I most desired. What he most loved, that I most hated. That which to him was a great evil, to be carefully shunned, was to me a great good, to be diligently sought; and the argument which he so warmly urged, against my learning to read, only served to inspire me with a desire and determination to learn. In learning to read, I owe almost as much to the bitter opposition of my master, as to the kindly aid of my mistress. I acknowledge the benefit of both.

. . .

Chapter VII

I lived in Master Hugh's family about seven years. During this time, I succeeded in learning to read and write. In accomplishing this, I was compelled to resort to various stratagems. I had no regular teacher. My mistress, who had kindly commenced to instruct me, had, in compliance with the advice and direction of her husband, not only ceased to instruct, but had set her face against my being instructed by any one else. It is due, however, to my mistress to say of her, that she did not adopt this course of treatment immediately. She at first lacked the depravity indispensable to shutting me up in mental darkness. It was at least necessary for her to have some training in the exercise of irresponsible power, to make her equal to the task of treating me as though I were a brute.

My mistress was, as I have said, a kind and tender-hearted woman; and in the simplicity of her soul she commenced, when I first went to live with her, to treat me as she supposed one human being ought to treat another. In entering upon the duties of a slaveholder, she did not seem to perceive that I sustained to her the relation of a mere chattel, and that for her to treat me as a human being was not only wrong, but dangerously so. Slavery proved as injurious to her as it did to me. When I went there, she was a pious, warm, and tender-hearted woman. There was no sorrow or suffering for which she had not a tear. She had bread for the hungry, clothes for the naked, and comfort for every mourner that came within her reach. Slavery soon proved its ability to divest her of these heavenly qualities. Under its influence, the tender heart became stone, and the lamblike disposition gave way to one of tiger-like fierceness. The first step in her downward course was in her ceasing to instruct me. She now commenced to practise her husband's precepts. She finally became even more violent in her opposition than her husband himself. She was not satisfied with simply doing as well as he had commanded; she seemed anxious to do better. Nothing seemed to make her more angry than to see me with a newspaper. She seemed to think that here lay the danger. I have had her rush at me with a face made all up of fury, and snatch from me a newspaper, in a manner that fully revealed her apprehension. She was an apt woman; and a little experience soon demonstrated, to her satisfaction, that education and slavery were incompatible with each other.

From this time I was most narrowly watched. If I was in a separate room any considerable length of time, I was sure to be suspected of having a book, and was at once called to give an account of myself. All this, however, was too late. The first step had been taken. Mistress, in teaching me the alphabet, had given me the *inch*, and no precaution could prevent me from taking the *ell*.

The plan which I adopted, and the one by which I was most successful, was that of making friends of all the little white boys whom I met in the street. As many of these as I could, I converted into teachers. With their kindly aid, obtained at different times and in different places, I finally succeeded in learning to read. When I was sent of errands, I always took my book with me, and by going one part of my errand quickly, I found time to get a lesson before my return. I used also to carry bread with me, enough of which was always in the house, and to which I was always welcome; for I was much better off in this regard than many of the poor white children in our neighborhood. This bread I used to bestow upon the hungry little urchins, who, in return, would give me that more valuable bread of knowledge. I am strongly tempted to give the names of two or three of those little boys, as a testimonial of the gratitude and affection I bear them; but prudence forbids;—not that it would injure me, but it might embarrass them; for it is almost an unpardonable offence to teach slaves to read in this Christian country. It is enough to say of the dear little fellows, that they lived on Philpot Street, very near Durgin and Bailey's ship-yard. I used to talk this matter of slavery over with them. I would sometimes say to them, I wished

I could be as free as they would be when they got to be men. "You will be free as soon as you are twenty-one, *but I am a slave for life*! Have not I as good a right to be free as you have?" These words used to trouble them; they would express for me the liveliest sympathy, and console me with the hope that something would occur by which I might be free.

Discussion Questions

1. How did Douglass understand God's providential care and action in the circumstances surrounding his move to Baltimore? What was his frame of mind as he left the plantation and headed to the city?
2. What do you find most striking about Douglass's portrayal of his "kind and tender-hearted" mistress, Sophia Auld? Was she a victim or a villain?
3. A theme Douglass returned to again and again is the importance of education, beginning with literacy. How is learning to read related to his larger quest for freedom?
4. What did Douglass learn from Mr. Auld in Baltimore? According to Douglass and Auld, why does the inability to read keep people enslaved?
5. In using the phrase "bread of knowledge," what did Douglass imply about the power of the written word as well as of literacy and education more generally?

CHAPTER 25

Elizabeth Barrett Browning

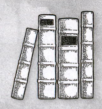

Introduction to *Aurora Leigh*

LANTA DAVIS

The Bible is filled with metaphors of sight and searching. We know Jesus healed the blind, but perhaps even more importantly, his parables heal us of a spiritual blindness, our inability to see the heavenly truths hidden in the earthly. Jesus' parables, which use ordinary objects, events, and relationships to reveal spiritual truths, teach us that if we are looking for God, a good place to begin is by looking at the world around us.

Many Christians today often think of God as being above and outside us (his transcendence) and neglect God's presence within our world (his immanence). Yet, as with other beautiful truths of the Christian faith, we must embrace a paradox: God is both transcendent and immanent. God became flesh and entered the world in the incarnation, infusing the material with the immaterial, the ordinary with the sacred, and the temporal with the eternal.

Imagination is required to see glimpses of the sacred in the ordinary. This imagination may seem, at first glance, like the opposite of reality, but properly understood, it is actually the faculty that equips us to see reality not as it merely appears on the surface, but as it truly is. Our imaginations exercise and shape our spiritual sight. They allow human beings to penetrate the surface of physical reality and begin to divine its greater meaning and beauty.

Similar to Jesus' parables, poetry helps us to see the ordinary anew and trains our imagination to pay closer attention to the hidden beauty all around us. Elizabeth Barrett Browning, for instance, believed art to be inseparable from faith, and she understood poetry as intrinsically connected to Christianity. She even wrote that Christianity is "poetry—poetry glorified," and exclaimed, "Oh what unspeakable poetry there is in Christ's religion!"

A nineteenth-century English poet who started writing and translating poetry at a very young age, Barrett Browning was a popular and prolific writer during her lifetime. She is perhaps best known today for poems like "Sonnet 43" ("How Do I Love Thee?"); for her courtship and marriage to poet Robert Browning, who first wrote to her in admiration of her poetry; and for *Aurora*

Leigh, an epic poem she styled as "a novel in verse" about a female poet trying to balance life, art, and love.

This selection from book 7 of *Aurora Leigh* provides a glimpse into Barrett Browning's understanding of faith as poetry. The poem challenges our tendency to divide the spiritual from the natural. It bluntly reminds us that a dichotomy between the earthly and the heavenly "is wrong, in short, at all points." Everything natural is also spiritual, Barrett Browning said, so that every tiny leaf, stone, bird, bee, and drop of blood has "eterne significance / Through the open arms of God." Nothing is truly temporal, for everything—even "a cup, column, or candlestick"—is a "pattern of what shall be in the Mount" of heaven. Each seemingly ordinary thing is not ordinary at all, but "clamour[s]" and "utter[s] itself distinct."

The last few lines in this selection from Barrett Browning's poem remind us that if we look with our spiritual eyes, we will start to see that "Earth's crammed with heaven / And every common bush afire with God." Not all will see these glimpses of the divine, however, and many will only see the bush for its utility, "pluck[ing] blackberries," "unaware" of the bush's "twofold" nature. Barrett Browning said that to reject God's presence in the material world is to reject ourselves, to deny our "first similitude": being created *imago Dei*, in God's image. Her words remind us that our very bodies are a living testament to seeing God within the world.

For Christians who train their eyes to see it, the ordinary world is in fact a treasure chest filled with delights. Some medieval thinkers thought of creation as a speculum for God, a mirror that shows us fragments of God's character. Julian of Norwich found spiritual consolation in a hazelnut, and Francis of Assisi considered the sun his brother and the moon his sister. As you read Barrett Browning's poem, allow it to train your eyes to see glimpses of eternity in the temporal and recognize just how much of heaven is "cramm'd" in the earth.

From *Aurora Leigh*

TRUTH, so far, in my book;—the truth which draws
Through all things upwards,—that a twofold world
Must go to a perfect cosmos. Natural things
And spiritual,—who separates those two
In art, in morals, or the social drift   5
Tears up the bond of nature and brings death,
Paints futile pictures, writes unreal verse,
Leads vulgar days, deals ignorantly with men,
Is wrong, in short, at all points. We divide
This apple of life, and cut it through the pips,—10
The perfect round which fitted Venus' hand

Has perished as utterly as if we ate
Both halves. Without the spiritual, observe,
The natural's impossible,—no form,
No motion: without sensuous, spiritual   15
Is inappreciable,—no beauty or power:
And in this twofold sphere the twofold man
(For still the artist is intensely a man)
Holds firmly by the natural, to reach
The spiritual beyond it,—fixes still   20
The type with mortal vision, to pierce through,
With eyes immortal, to the antetype
Some call the ideal,—better call the real,
And certain to be called so presently
When things shall have their names. Look long enough   25
On any peasant's face here, coarse and lined,
You'll catch Antinous somewhere in that clay,
As perfect featured as he yearns at Rome
From marble pale with beauty; then persist,
And, if your apprehension's competent,   30
You'll find some fairer angel at his back,
As much exceeding him as he the boor,
And pushing him with empyreal disdain
For ever out of sight. Aye, Carrington
Is glad of such a creed: an artist must,   35
Who paints a tree, a leaf, a common stone
With just his hand, and finds it suddenly
A-piece with and conterminous to his soul.
Why else do these things move him, leaf, or stone?
The bird's not moved, that pecks at a spring-shoot;   40
Nor yet the horse, before a quarry, a-graze:
But man, the twofold creature, apprehends
The twofold manner, in and outwardly,
And nothing in the world comes single to him,
A mere itself,—cup, column, or candlestick,   45
All patterns of what shall be in the Mount;
The whole temporal show related royally,
And built up to eterne significance
Through the open arms of God. 'There's nothing great
Nor small', has said a poet of our day,   50

Whose voice will ring beyond the curfew of eve
And not be thrown out by the matin's bell:
And truly, I reiterate, nothing's small!
No lily-muffled hum of a summer-bee,
But finds some coupling with the spinning stars;   55
No pebble at your foot, but proves a sphere;
No chaffinch, but implies the cherubim;
And (glancing on my own thin, veinèd wrist),
In such a little tremor of the blood
The whole strong clamour of a vehement soul   60
Doth utter itself distinct. Earth's crammed with heaven,
And every common bush afire with God;
But only he who sees, takes off his shoes,
The rest sit round it and pluck blackberries,
And daub their natural faces unaware   65
More and more from the first similitude.

Discussion Questions

1. What did Elizabeth Barrett Browning mean by her multiple uses of the word "twofold" in the first twenty lines of this poem? How does her description of this "twofold" sphere relate to the doctrine of the incarnation?

2. Browning's poem suggests that all temporal, material things have eternal significance. How does a "mere cup" point to a sacred truth? A column? A candlestick? What qualities or characteristics do these objects have that we frequently associate with the divine?

3. In this poem, Barrett Browning affirmed, "Truly, I reiterate, nothing's small." How does attentiveness to "small" details cultivate a kind of spiritual sight?

4. How can our attitude toward and interactions with the natural world shape our attitude toward and interactions with God?[1]

5. Reflect on an ordinary object of your choice. (For example, Barrett Browning mentioned a finch, a pebble, a drop of blood.) How does it reveal something about God's nature, character, or relationship with us?

---

1. Consider extending Barrett Browning's emphasis on training the eyes by reflecting on other poets and artists. Consider, for instance, Mary Oliver's declaration that our "work is loving the world . . . [our work] is mostly learning to stand still and be astonished." Or ponder William Blake's words, "To see a World in a Grain of Sand / And a Heaven in a Wild Flower / Hold Infinity in the palm of your hand / And Eternity in an hour." Art can provide excellent training in attention. Contemporary artist Makoto Fujimura, for instance, uses Japanese nihonga materials, including layers of pulverized metal. This technique requires a viewer to look at an artwork for at least fifteen minutes so that the eyes can adjust to see all the colors present in the work. Monet's famous water lilies are another exercise in seeing carefully. He painted the same subject over 150 times in an effort to capture them truthfully, through the way they appeared in different angles, lights, and shades.

CHAPTER 26

Henry David Thoreau

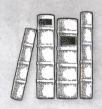

Introduction to "Life without Principle"

JEFFREY BILBRO

Henry David Thoreau (1817–62) wrote "Life without Principle" as a sort of follow-up to his well-known book *Walden*. The two years he spent living at Walden Pond provided him time to hone his critique of the rapidly industrializing American economy. This lecture critiques industrial standards of value, and Thoreau invites his hearers to "consider the way in which we spend our lives," measuring our lives not by quantitative or monetary standards but by whether we live up to our stated principles.[1] The lecture's second half in particular focuses on how we spend our attention, and Thoreau pulls no punches in describing the dangers that an industrialized society poses to a principled life. In particular, Thoreau challenges his readers to use their freedom well and to devote their attention to eternal goods.

Anticipating more recent discoveries about neuroplasticity, Thoreau notes that where and how we direct our attention alters our minds. It is this transformative power of attention that leads him to a startling and profound metaphor. He claims that attending to trivia (imagine, say, your social media feeds, Netflix, or TV news) "macadamizes" our intellect. This is a term for a method of road construction named after its inventor, John McAdam, a Scottish engineer. While most roads were built on a foundation of large stones, McAdam used small, hand-broken stones to surface roads; supervisors actually measured the stones to be sure that no large ones slipped through. The angular edges of these rocks would bind together and form a smooth, long-lasting surface for traffic. McAdam's name lives on today in the word *tarmac*, which refers to macadam roads that were sprayed with tar to cut the dust. While this is a positive development for road construction, it's not a feature of a well-formed intellect, as Thoreau elaborates.

Thoreau's metaphor compares our minds to temples. *Fane* is the Latin word for temple, so *profane* literally means before or outside the temple. Hence Thoreau suggests there are lasting, even eternal, consequences for what we give

---

1. Henry David Thoreau, *Civil Disobedience, Solitude and Life without Principle* (Amherst, NY: Prometheus, 1998), 64.

our attention to. This is why Paul instructed the Colossians, "Set your minds on things above, not on earthly things" (Col. 3:2).

Habit emphasizes the repetitive, formative nature of attention. What does our daily reading look like? What do we turn to when we're bored? Thoreau's use of "trivial" is of course an indictment of the frivolous distractions that consume our time, but this word also continues Thoreau's road metaphor. *Trivia* comes from a Latin word meaning an intersection of three roads, a place that is well traveled. Thoreau imagines our minds as conduits or roadways for ideas, and we are responsible to choose what we want rolling down these streets. Yet when we habitually attend to trivial things, our minds turn into gravel and become susceptible to whatever ads or slogans or memes other people send spinning down our macadamized intellects.

Thoreau goes on to propose a two-part remedy for this condition. We have all, to one degree or another, "desecrated" our minds by attending to trivia, but Thoreau hopes that through wariness and devotion we can reconsecrate our minds and make them into temples (*fanes*) again. If the problem is habitual attention to things outside the temple, the solution is habitual attention to things inside the temple. This includes a movement away from—of wariness toward—the gossip and trivia of "the Times" and a movement toward—of devotion to—the good, beautiful, and complex truth of "the Eternities."

From "Life without Principle"

When our life ceases to be inward and private, conversation degenerates into mere gossip. We rarely meet a man who can tell us any news which he has not read in a newspaper, or been told by his neighbor; and, for the most part, the only difference between us and our fellow is, that he has seen the newspaper, or been out to tea, and we have not. In proportion as our inward life fails, we go more constantly and desperately to the post-office. You may depend on it, that the poor fellow who walks away with the greatest number of letters, proud of his extensive correspondence, has not heard from himself this long while.

I do not know but it is too much to read one newspaper a week. I have tried it recently, and for so long it seems to me that I have not dwelt in my native region. The sun, the clouds, the snow, the trees say not so much to me. You cannot serve two masters. It requires more than a day's devotion to know and to possess the wealth of the day.

We may well be ashamed to tell what things we have read or heard in our day. I do not know why my news should be so trivial,—considering what one's dreams and expectations are, why the developments should be so paltry. The news we hear, for the most part, is not news to our genius. It is the stalest repetition. You are often tempted to ask, why such stress is laid on a particular experience which you have had,—that, after twenty-five years, you should meet Hobbins, Registrar of Deeds, again on the sidewalk. Have you not budged an inch then? Such is the daily news. Its facts appear to float in the atmosphere, insignificant as the sporules of fungi, and impinge on some neglected *thallus*, or surface of our minds, which affords a basis for them, and hence a parasitic growth. We should wash ourselves clean of such news. Of what consequence, though our planet explode, if there is no character involved in the explosion? In health we have not the least curiosity about such events. We do not live for idle amusement. I would not run round a corner to see the world blow up.

All summer, and far into the autumn, perchance, you unconsciously went by the newspapers and the news, and now you find it was because the morning and the evening were full of news to you. Your walks were full of incidents. You attended, not to the affairs of Europe, but to your own affairs in Massachusetts fields. If you chance to live and move and have your being in that thin stratum in which the events that make the news transpire,—thinner than the paper on which it is printed,—then these things will fill the world for you; but if you soar above or dive below that plane, you cannot remember nor be reminded of them. Really to see the sun rise or go down every day, so to relate ourselves to a universal fact, would preserve us sane forever. Nations! What are nations? Tartars, and Huns, and Chinamen! Like insects, they swarm. The historian strives in vain to make them memorable. It is for want of a man that there are so many men. It is individuals that populate the world. Any man thinking may say with the Spirit of Lodin,—

> I look down from my height on nations,
> And they become ashes before me;—
> Calm is my dwelling in the clouds;
> Pleasant are the great fields of my rest.

Pray, let us live without being drawn by dogs, Esquimaux-fashion, tearing over hill and dale, and biting each other's ears.

Not without a slight shudder at the danger, I often perceive how near I had come to admitting into my mind the details of some trivial affair,—the news of the street; and I am astonished to observe how willing men are to lumber their minds with such rubbish,—to permit idle rumors and incidents of the most insignificant kind to intrude on ground which should be sacred to thought. Shall the mind be a public arena, where the affairs of the street and the gossip of the tea-table chiefly are discussed? Or shall it be a quarter of heaven itself,—an hypæthral temple, consecrated to the service of the gods? I find it so difficult to dispose of the few facts which to me are significant, that I hesitate to burden my attention with those which are insignificant, which only a divine mind could illustrate. Such is, for the most part, the news in newspapers and conversation. It is important to preserve the mind's chastity in this respect. Think of admitting the details of a single case of the criminal court into our thoughts, to stalk profanely through their very *sanctum sanctorum* for an hour, ay, for many hours! to make a very bar-room of the mind's inmost apartment, as if for so long the dust of the street had occupied us,—the very street itself, with all its travel, its bustle, and filth had passed through our thoughts' shrine! Would it not be an intellectual and moral suicide? When I have been compelled to sit spectator and auditor in a court-room for some hours, and have seen my neighbors, who were not compelled, stealing in from time to time, and tiptoeing about with washed hands and faces, it has appeared to my mind's eye, that, when they took off their hats, their ears suddenly expanded into vast hoppers for sound, between which even their narrow heads were crowded. Like the vanes of wind-mills, they caught the broad, but shallow streams of sound, which, after a few titillating gyrations in their coggy brains, passed out the other side. I wondered if, when they got home, they were as careful to wash their ears as before their hands and faces. It has seemed to me, at such a time, that the auditors and the witnesses, the jury and the counsel, the judge and the criminal at the bar,—if I may presume him guilty before he is convicted,—were all equally criminal, and a thunderbolt might be expected to descend and consume them all together.

By all kinds of traps and sign-boards, threatening the extreme penalty of the divine law, exclude such trespassers from the only ground which can be sacred to you. It is so hard to forget what it is worse than useless to remember! If I am to be a thoroughfare, I prefer that it be of the mountain-brooks, the Parnassian streams, and not the town-sewers. There is inspiration, that gossip which comes to the ear of the attentive mind from the courts of heaven. There is the profane and stale revelation of the bar-room and the police court. The same ear is fitted to receive both communications. Only the character of the hearer determines to which it shall be open, and to which closed. I believe that the mind can be permanently profaned by the habit of attending to trivial things, so that all our thoughts shall be tinged with triviality. Our very intellect shall be macadamized, as it were,—its foundation broken into fragments for the wheels of travel to roll over; and if you would know what will make the most durable pavement, surpassing rolled stones, spruce blocks, and asphaltum, you have only to look into some of our minds which have been subjected to this treatment so long.

If we have thus desecrated ourselves,—as who has not?—the remedy will be by wariness and devotion to reconsecrate ourselves, and make once more a fane of the mind. We should treat our minds, that is, ourselves, as innocent and ingenuous children, whose guardians we are, and be careful what objects and what subjects we thrust on their attention. Read not the Times. Read the Eternities. Conventionalities are at length as bad as impurities. Even the facts of science may dust the mind by their dryness, unless they are in a sense effaced each morning, or rather rendered fertile by the dews of fresh and living truth. Knowledge does not come to us by details, but in flashes of light from heaven. Yes, every thought that passes through the mind helps to wear and tear it, and to deepen the ruts, which, as in the streets of Pompeii, evince how much it has been used. How many things there are concerning which we might well deliberate, whether we had better known them,—had better let their peddling-carts be driven, even at the slowest trot or walk, over that bridge of glorious span by which we trust to pass at last from the farthest brink of time to the nearest shore of eternity! Have we no culture, no refinement,—but skill only to live coarsely and serve the Devil?—to acquire a little worldly wealth, or fame, or liberty, and make a false show with it, as if we were all husk and shell, with no tender and living kernel to us? Shall our institutions be like those chestnut-burs which contain abortive nuts, perfect only to prick the fingers?

America is said to be the arena on which the battle of freedom is to be fought; but surely it cannot be freedom in a merely political sense that is meant. Even if we grant that the American has freed himself from a political tyrant, he is still the slave of an economical and moral tyrant. Now that the republic—the *res-publica*—has been settled, it is time to look after the *res-privata*,—the private state,—to see, as the Roman senate charged its consuls, "*ne quid res-*PRIVATA *detrimenti caperet,*" that the *private* state receive no detriment.

Do we call this the land of the free? What is it to be free from King George and continue the slaves of King Prejudice? What is it to be born free and not to live free? What is the value of any political freedom, but as a means to moral freedom? Is it a freedom to be slaves, or a freedom to be free, of which we boast? We are a nation of politicians, concerned about the outmost defences only of freedom. It is our children's children who may perchance be really free. We tax ourselves unjustly. There is a part of us which is not represented. It is taxation without representation. We quarter troops, we quarter fools and cattle of all sorts upon ourselves. We quarter our gross bodies on our poor souls, till the former eat up all the latter's substance.

With respect to a true culture and manhood, we are essentially provincial still, not metropolitan,—mere Jonathans. We are provincial, because we do not find at home our standards,—because we do not worship truth, but the reflection of truth,—because we are warped and narrowed by an exclusive devotion to trade and commerce and manufactures and agriculture and the like, which are but means, and not the end.

So is the English Parliament provincial. Mere country-bumpkins, they betray themselves, when any more important question arises for them to settle, the Irish question, for instance,—the English question why did I not say? Their natures are subdued to what they work in. Their "good breeding" respects only secondary objects. The finest manners in the world are awkwardness and fatuity, when contrasted with a finer intelligence. They appear but as the fashions of past days,—mere courtliness, knee-buckles and small-clothes, out of date. It is the vice, but not the excellence of manners, that they are continually being deserted by the character; they are cast-off clothes or shells, claiming the respect which belonged to the living creature. You are presented with the shells instead of the meat, and it is no excuse generally, that, in the case of some fishes, the shells are of more worth than the meat. The man who thrusts his manners upon me does as if he were to insist on introducing me to his cabinet of curiosities, when I wished to see himself. It was not in this sense that the poet Decker called Christ "the first true gentleman that ever breathed." I repeat that in this sense the most splendid court in Christendom is provincial, having authority to consult about Transalpine interests only, and not the affairs of Rome. A prætor or proconsul would suffice to settle the questions which absorb the attention of the English Parliament and the American Congress.

Government and legislation! these I thought were respectable professions. We have heard of heaven-born Numas, Lycurguses, and Solons, in the history of the world, whose *names* at least may stand for ideal legislators; but think of legislating to *regulate* the breeding of slaves, or the exportation of tobacco! What have divine legislators to do with the exportation or the importation of tobacco? what humane ones with the breeding of slaves? Suppose you were to submit the question to any son of God,—and has He no children in the century? is it a family which is extinct?—in what condition would you get it again? What shall a State like Virginia say for itself at the last day, in which these have been the principal, the staple productions? What ground is there for patriotism in such a State? I derive my facts from statistical tables which the States themselves have published.

A commerce that whitens every sea in quest of nuts and raisins, and makes slaves of its sailors for this purpose! I saw, the other day, a vessel which had been wrecked, and many lives lost, and her cargo of rags, juniper-berries, and bitter almonds were strewn along the shore. It seemed hardly worth the while to tempt the dangers of the sea between Leghorn and New York for the sake of a cargo of juniper-berries and bitter almonds. America sending to the Old World for her bitters! Is not the sea-brine, is not shipwreck, bitter enough to make the cup of life go down here? Yet such, to a great extent, is our boasted commerce; and there are those who style themselves statesmen and philosophers who are so blind as to think that progress and civilization depend on precisely this kind of interchange and activity,—the activity of flies about a molasses-hogs-head. Very well, observes one, if men were oysters. And very well, answer I, if men were mosquitoes.

Lieutenant Herndon, whom our Government sent to explore the Amazon, and, it is said, to extend the area of Slavery, observed that there was wanting there "an industrious and active population, who know what the comforts of life are, and who have artificial wants to draw out the great resources of the country." But what are the "artificial wants" to be encouraged? Not the love of luxuries, like the tobacco and slaves of, I believe, his native Virginia, nor the ice and granite and other material wealth of our native New England; nor are "the great resources of a country" that fertility or barrenness of soil which produces these. The chief want, in every State that I have been into, was a high and earnest purpose in its inhabitants. This alone draws out "the great resources" of Nature, and at last taxes her beyond her resources; for man naturally dies out of her. When we want culture more than potatoes, and illumination more than sugar-plums, then the great resources of a world are taxed and drawn out, and the result, or staple production, is, not slaves, nor operatives, but men,—those rare fruits called heroes, saints, poets, philosophers, and redeemers.

In short, as a snow-drift is formed where there is a lull in the wind, so, one would say, where there is a lull of truth, an institution springs up. But the truth blows right on over it, nevertheless, and at length blows it down.

What is called politics is comparatively something so superficial and inhuman, that, practically, I have never fairly recognized that it concerns me at all. The newspapers, I perceive, devote some of their columns specifically to politics or government without charge; and this, one would say, is all that saves it; but, as I love literature, and, to some extent, the truth also, I never read those columns at any rate. I do not wish to blunt my sense of right so much. I have not got to answer for having read a single President's Message. A strange age of the world this, when empires, kingdoms, and republics come a-begging to a private man's door, and utter their complaints at his elbow! I cannot take up a newspaper but I find that some wretched government or another, hard pushed, and on its last legs, is interceding with me, the reader, to vote for it,—mere importunate than an Italian beggar; and if I have a mind to look at its certificate, made, perchance, by some benevolent merchant's clerk, or the skipper that brought it over, for it cannot speak a word of English itself, I shall probably read of the eruption of some Vesuvius, or the overflowing of some Po, true or forged, which brought it into this condition. I do not hesitate, in such a case, to suggest work, or the almshouse; or why not keep its castle in silence, as I do commonly? The poor President, what with preserving his popularity and doing his duty, is completely bewildered. The newspapers are the ruling power. Any other government is reduced to a few marines at Fort Independence. If a man neglects to read the Daily Times, government will go down on its knees to him, for this is the only treason in these days.

Those things which now most engage the attention of men, as politics and the daily routine, are, it is true, vital functions of human society, but should be unconsciously performed, like the corresponding functions of the physical body. They are *infra*-human, a kind of vegetation. I sometimes awake to a half-consciousness of them going on about me, as a man may become conscious of some of the processes of digestion in a morbid state, and so have the dyspepsia, as it is called. It is as if a thinker submitted himself to be rasped by the great gizzard of creation. Politics is, as it were, the gizzard of society, full of grit and gravel, and the two political parties are its two opposite halves,—sometimes split into quarters, it may be, which grind on each other. Not only individuals, but States, have thus a confirmed dyspepsia, which expresses itself, you can imagine by what sort of eloquence. Thus our life is not altogether a forgetting, but also, alas! to a great extent, a remembering of that which we should never have been conscious of, certainly not in our waking hours. Why should we not meet, not always as dyspeptics, to tell our bad dreams, but sometimes as *eu*peptics, to congratulate each other on the ever glorious morning? I do not make an exorbitant demand, surely.

Discussion Questions

1. What forms of relaxation restore your mind, and what forms macadamize them—that is, grind them down to allow any trivial thought to pass along unhindered?

2. What streams of trivia most tempt you (for example, social media, Netflix, YouTube)? What limits can you set on these streams to reconsecrate yourself?

3. What books, people, and questions deserve your devoted attention now? What practices or habits can help you appropriately train your attention?

4. What are you free *for*? If you are enrolled in college, you have an incredible freedom to pursue truth. How might you pursue ultimate goods through the ways in which you spend your time and attention?

CHAPTER 27

Gerard Manley Hopkins

Introduction to "As Kingfishers Catch Fire"

JENNIFER L. HOLBERG

How do we know who we are? How do we know who we're supposed to be? And how do we know what we're supposed to do with our lives? For Victorian poet Gerard Manley Hopkins (1844–89), our identity and our calling are inextricably tied together. Indebted to the medieval philosopher Duns Scotus's *haecceitas* (or "thisness"), Hopkins used the term *inscape* (short for "inner landscape") for the unique God-given design of every created thing. Hopkins believed this inner landscape was projected out to others' view by an energy he called *instress*. Together inscape and instress point to and celebrate God as the giver and enabler of a person's divinely made identity.

The interplay between inscape/instress and identity is at the heart of Hopkins's poem "As Kingfishers Catch Fire." At first glance, the poem can seem a little daunting because of all the stress marks, the imagery, and the diction. But Hopkins's poems all exhibit a kind of inscape themselves, a design best discovered by reading aloud (itself a kind of instress). Inspired by Welsh and Old English prosody, Hopkins invented a poetic style called "sprung rhythm" to more closely approximate natural speech. It is characterized by syncopation and a rhyme scheme that doesn't conform to the iambic pentameter you might be more used to.

One of the keys, then, to successfully understanding this poem is to break it down and paraphrase it. Think about the opening images: As the kingfisher bird dives for its food, it exposes its red coloring; the dragonfly beating its wings looks as if it is flickering. Different kinds of "fire" come from actions distinct to each creature. In lines 2–4, Hopkins says that when you throw a rock into a well, it announces, "I'm a rock." The same is true with the plucking of a string or the ringing of a bell. The bell never sounds like the rock. It can't, because the bell's interior is different from the rock's, so when they do their particular "thing," they are simply expressing who they are. More importantly, they do it because, as the eighth line wonderfully asserts, they were made for that purpose: "*Whát I dó is me: for that I came.*"

What's more exciting is that the same can be said for human beings. In stanza 2, Hopkins applied this idea to the Christ follower. Our actions—just and grace-filled—should reflect the inner landscape of someone for whom justice and grace have been accomplished (notice how Hopkins simply made up the word *justices* to emphasize this connection between inner and outer). Christ's redemptive work has transformed our inner landscape so radically that when God looks down on us, God sees Christ, not us. Indeed, God witnesses Christ's work beautifully happening everywhere Christians live fully into their Christ-given identity. In other words, the work loveliest to God, our highest vocation, is being a faithful disciple. To walk like Christ, to see like Christ, to do Christ's work—for that we came.

As Kingfishers Catch Fire

As kingfishers catch fire, dragonflies draw flame;
As tumbled over rim in roundy wells
Stones ring; like each tucked string tells, each hung bell's
Bow swung finds tongue to fling out broad its name;
Each mortal thing does one thing and the same:
Deals out that being indoors each one dwells;
Selves—goes itself; *myself* it speaks and spells,
Crying *Whát I dó is me: for that I came.*

I say móre: the just man justices;
Keeps grace: thát keeps all his goings graces;
Acts in God's eye what in God's eye he is—
Chríst—for Christ plays in ten thousand places,
Lovely in limbs, and lovely in eyes not his
To the Father through the features of men's faces.

Discussion Questions

1. Read the poem aloud. Think of the accent marks as akin to musical notation. Pretend the poem is like a piece of jazz or reggae. How does hearing the poem change your sense of it? What do the sounds bring forward in your interpretation?
2. Look at all the stressed words with the accent mark on them. Why did Hopkins emphasize those words for both sound and meaning?
3. Think about the phrase "Christ plays in ten thousand places." How many definitions of *play* can you see at work? Why do you think Hopkins chose this word instead of some other?
4. How can your God-given identity in Christ provide peace and confidence in understanding your calling and vocation?

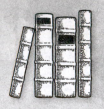

CHAPTER 28

Jarena Lee

Introduction to *Religious Experience*

PATRICIA BROWN

Welcoming a female preacher in a Christian pulpit can be an uncomfortable concept to embrace because we are accustomed to seeing males in leadership positions in the church. Sometimes our feelings about women preachers and pastors are wrought with misguided assumptions concerning the headship of the church. Thankfully, God will give us the courage to enter these spaces of discomfort and do the demanding work of reshaping our perceptions about gender roles in the church.

Gender inequity, the "glass ceiling," and sexual harassment are some of the persistent challenges with which females have had to contend for centuries. Part of what makes these struggles particularly painful is that many gender biases are rooted in the church. It is undeniable that religion, specifically Christianity, traditionally has been conceived of, by some, as a sexist and delimiting institution for women. In light of the women's suffrage movement during the 1880s and the women's liberation movement in the 1960s, American women found it difficult to reconcile their devotion to Christianity and their desire for gender equality and liberation.

To complicate matters further, nineteenth century African American women had to face the bitter reality that their race and caste made it nearly impossible to be a leader in the church. Jarena Lee, one of the pioneering African American female preachers, documented the trials that she endured as an itinerate preacher in her 1849 autobiography, *Religious Experience and Journal of Mrs. Jarena Lee, Giving an Account of Her Call to Preach the Gospel*. Although Lee focused primarily on gender disparities in the Christian tradition, she was well aware that her gender identity was unique because African American women were the only women expected to accept their social caste as chattel while espousing the supposed legitimization of slavery in the Bible. Lee used nonconventional interpretive strategies and pulpit rhetoric to contribute to a growing discourse of freedom and empowerment—for women and African Americans. Lee challenged traditional theological interpretations of the Bible in an effort to broaden the pulpit to fit her divine calling.

As Christian learners, we can take our cue from Christ regarding gender

183

equality. On several occasions, he aligned himself with the plight women. For example, he took compassion on the woman with the issue of blood and stood beside the woman caught in the act of adultery. Jarena Lee, like many theologians, argued that it was a woman, Mary Magdalene, whom Christ first commissioned to preach the gospel. In fact, Paul declared in Galatians 3:28, "There is neither Jew nor Gentile, neither slave nor free, nor is there male and female, for you are all one in Christ Jesus." This scriptural reference is not to suggest that there are no distinguishable differences between males and females; rather, those differences should not elevate one over the other. If we are to be unbiased Christian scholars, we must reshape our perspective about gender equality and become allies of those who have been traditionally subjugated and marginalized in the church.

Ultimately, *Religious Experience and Journal of Mrs. Jarena Lee, Giving an Account of Her Call to Preach the Gospel* is a text that every Christian should read for several reasons. It is a historical account of how a multiminoritized (race, caste, and gender) Christian broke ground for women to preach the gospel in the nineteenth century church, it offers a different reading of the Scriptures regarding gender equality, and it challenges the reader to sit in uncomfortable spaces to learn and grow.

From *Religious Experience*

Between four and five years after my sanctification, on a certain time, an impressive silence fell upon me, and I stood as if someone was about to speak to me, yet I had no such thought in my heart. But to my utter surprise there seemed to sound a voice which I thought I distinctly heard, and most certainly understood, which said to me, "Go preach the Gospel!" I immediately replied aloud "No one will believe me." Again, I listened, and again the same voice seemed to say, "Preach the Gospel; I will put words in your mouth, and will turn your enemies to become your friends."

At first, I supposed that Satan had spoken to me, for I had read that he could transform himself into an angel of light for the purpose of deception. Immediately I went into a secret place, and called upon the Lord to know if he had called me to preach, and whether I was deceived or not; when there appeared to my view the form and figure of a pulpit, with a Bible lying thereon, the back of which was presented to me as plainly as if it had been a literal fact.

In consequence of this, my mind became so exercised that during the night following, I took a text and preached in my sleep. I thought there stood before me a great multitude, while I expounded to them the things of religion. So violent were my exertions and so loud were my exclamations, that I awoke from the sound of my own voice, which also awoke the family of the house where I resided. Two days after, I went to see the preacher in charge of the African Society, who was the Rev. Richard Allen, the same before named in these pages, to tell him that I felt it my duty to preach the gospel. But as I drew near the street in which his house was, which was in the city of Philadelphia, my courage began to fail me; so terrible did the cross appear, it seemed that I should not be able to bear it. Previous to my setting out to go to see him, so agitated was my mind, that my appetite for my daily food failed me entirely. Several times on my way there, I turned back again; but as often I felt my strength again renewed, and I soon found that the nearer I approached to the house of the minister, the less was my fear. Accordingly, as soon as I came to the door, my fears subsided, the cross was removed, all things appeared pleasant—I was tranquil.

I now told him, that the Lord had revealed it to me, that I must preach the gospel. He replied, by asking, in what sphere I wished to move in. I said, among the Methodists. He then replied, that a Mrs. Cook, a Methodist lady, had also some time before requested the same privilege; who, it was believed, had done much good in the way of exhortation, and holding prayer meetings; and who had been permitted to do so by the verbal license of the preacher in charge at the time. But as to women preaching, he said that our Discipline knew nothing at all about it—that it did not call for women preachers. This I was glad to hear, because it removed the fear of the cross—but no sooner did this feeling cross my mind, than I found that a love of souls had in a measure departed from me; that holy energy which burned within me, as a fire, began to be smothered. This I soon perceived.

O how careful ought we to be, lest through our by-laws of church government and discipline, we bring into disrepute even the word of life. For as unseemly as it may appear now-a-days for a woman to preach, it should be remembered that nothing is impossible with God. And why should it be thought impossible, heterodox, or improper for a woman to preach? seeing the Saviour died for the woman as well as for the man.

If the man may preach, because the Saviour died for him, why not the woman? seeing he died for her also. Is he not a whole Saviour, instead of a half one? as those who hold it wrong for a woman to preach, would seem to make it appear.

Did not Mary *first* preach the risen Saviour, and is not the doctrine of the resurrection the very climax of Christianity—hangs not all our hope on this, as argued by St. Paul? Then did not Mary, a woman, preach the gospel? for she preached the resurrection of the crucified Son of God.

But some will say that Mary did not expound the Scripture, therefore, she did not preach, in the proper sense of the term. To this I reply, it may be that the term *preach* in those primitive times, did not mean exactly what it is now *made* to mean; perhaps it was a great deal more simple then, than it is now:—if it were not, the unlearned fishermen could not have preached the gospel at all, as they had no learning.

To this it may be replied, by those who are determined not to believe that it is right for a woman to preach, that the disciples, though they were fishermen and ignorant of letters too, were inspired so to do. To which I would reply, that though they were inspired, yet that inspiration did not save them from showing their ignorance of letters, and of man's wisdom: this the multitude soon found out, by listening to the remarks of the envious Jewish priests. If then, to preach the gospel, by the gift of heaven, comes by inspiration solely, is God straitened; must he take the man exclusively? May he not, did he not, and can he not inspire a female to preach the simple story of the birth, life, death, and resurrection of our Lord, and accompany it too with power to the sinner's heart. As for me, I am fully persuaded that the Lord called me to labor according to what I have received, in his vineyard. If he has not, how could he consistently bear testimony in favor of my poor labors, in awakening and converting sinners?

In my wanderings up and down among men, preaching according to my ability, I have frequently found families who told me that they had not for several years been to a meeting, and yet, while listening to hear what God would say by his poor coloured female instrument, have believed with trembling—tears rolling down their cheeks, the signs of contrition and repentance towards God. I firmly believe that I have sown seed, in the name of the Lord, which shall appear with its increase at the great day of accounts, when Christ shall come to make up his jewels.

At a certain time, I was beset with the idea, that soon or late I should fall from grace, and lost my soul at last. I was frequently called to the throne of grace about this matter, but found no relief; the temptation pursued me still. Being more and more afflicted with it, till at a certain time when the spirit strongly impressed it on my mind to enter into my closet, and carry my case once more to the Lord; the Lord enabled me to draw nigh to him, and to his mercy seat, at this time, in an extraordinary manner; for while I wrestled with him for the victory over this disposition to doubt whether I should persevere, there appeared a form of fire, about the size of a man's hand, as I was on my knees; at the same moment, there appeared to the eye of faith a man robed in a white garment, form the shoulders down to the feet; from him a voice proceeded, saying: "Thou shalt never return from the cross." Since that time I have never doubted, but believe that god will keep me until the day of redemption. Now I could adopt the very language of St. Paul, and say that nothing could have separated my soul from the love of god, which is in Christ Jesus [Rom. 8:35–39]. From that time, 1807, until the present, 1833, I have not yet doubted the power and goodness of God to keep me from falling, through sanctification of the spirit and belief of the truth.

Discussion Questions

1. Analyze Jarena Lee's scriptural support for women to be permitted to preach in the church. What are the strengths and/or weaknesses in her argument?
2. Jarena Lee primarily focused on oppositions to her gender; she rarely mentioned racial obstacles that were highly likely to arise during this era. Discuss possible reasons for Lee's desire to highlight gender disparities rather than racial inequities.
3. How does Jarena Lee's autobiography address ethical issues and matters of faith? How does this reading help or challenge your understanding of Christianity? How does it affect your Christian walk?

CHAPTER 29

Friedrich Nietzsche

Introduction to *Use and Abuse of History*

SCOTT HUELIN

Why should we study cultures that are remote in time and space from our own? Put another way, what is the goal of a liberal arts education? Friedrich Nietzsche was passionately committed to the study of the liberal arts, so it may seem strange, at first, that he wrote *The Use and Abuse of History* as a critique of liberal arts education in nineteenth-century Germany. Yet it was precisely his appreciation for the value of liberal arts that invoked such a strong response when he saw them being taught so poorly.

Nietzsche thought the purpose of a liberal arts education was to "serve life"—that is, vigorous and creative activity in the real world—but he believed students in his day were poorly served by schools and teachers who thought of humanistic knowledge as an end in itself. They required students to memorize large tables of historical facts and long passages of ancient poetry. Nietzsche pictured this type of rote memorization as a student being stuffed with "indigestible knowledge-stones," factoids incapable of nourishing the student's soul for authentic living. Those useless stones "rattle together in his body," producing speech to which "nothing external corresponds." In other words, a student may win applause at school by reciting from memory the first fifteen lines of Virgil's *Aeneid* in Latin, but in a time when the Muses' songs, Juno's rage, and the high walls of Rome are absent or irrelevant, it will not aid in the task of living well. This conflict between useless knowledge within a student and real life on the outside—what Nietzsche called the "opposition of inner and outer"—cripples the individual and divides the nation between "educated" stone swallowers and "uneducated" people with little inner life, leaving the two groups largely incapable of meaningful conversation.

Education today often runs the opposite risk to that of Nietzsche's day: focusing too little on the history and cultures of other times and places. Instead, many see the goal of education as little more than career preparation, a series of bland assignments leading to good grades to earn the right degree needed for a well-paying job. Maybe you've wondered during a test, *When am I ever going to use this information after I graduate?* On the surface, this may sound like a Nietzschean turn toward "real life," but he would likely howl at the association.

"Every man and nation needs a certain knowledge of the past," he wrote, lest we limit our capacity for reflecting on what it means to be human and to live well. According to Nietzsche, "uneducated" college graduates—those who have merely acquired skills without also learning the art of living well—run the risk of being well-paid sheep who are thoughtlessly ensnared by their society's system of values. For him, the "true path of education" does not abolish the liberal arts but makes them subservient to a larger goal: living authentically, creatively, and vigorously in the world.

On this point, a Christian reader might hear a certain echo of the New Testament: "Be doers of the word, and not hearers only" (James 1:22 NKJV). Whether in theology or in the humanities, the truth is not merely for our contemplation. It is meant to be lived.

From *Use and Abuse of History,* Section 4[1]

This is how history can serve life. Every man and nation needs a certain knowledge of the past, whether it be through monumental, antiquarian, or critical history, according to his objects, powers, and necessities. The need is not that of the mere thinkers who only look on at life, or the few who desire knowledge and can only be satisfied with knowledge; but it has always a reference to the end of life, and is under its absolute rule and direction. This is the natural relation of an age, a culture and a people to history; hunger is its source, necessity its norm, the inner plastic power assigns its limits. The knowledge of the past is only desired for the service of the future and the present, not to weaken the present or undermine a living future. All this is as simple as truth itself, and quite convincing to any one who is not in the toils of "historical deduction."

And now to take a quick glance at our time! We fly back in astonishment. The clearness, naturalness, and purity of the connection between life and history has vanished; and in what a maze of exaggeration and contradiction do we now see the problem! Is the guilt ours who see it, or have life and history really altered their conjunction and an inauspicious star risen between them? Others may prove we have seen falsely; I am merely saying what we believe we see. There is such a star, a bright and lordly star, and the conjunction is really altered—by science, and the demand for history to be a science. Life is no more dominant, and knowledge of the past no longer its thrall: boundary marks are overthrown and everything bursts its limits. The perspective of events is blurred, and the blur extends through their whole immeasurable course. No generation has seen such a panoramic comedy as is shown by the "science of universal evolution,"

---

1. Friedrich Nietzsche, *The Use and Abuse of History*, trans. Adrian Collins (New York: Macmillan/Library of Liberal Arts, 1957).

history; that shows it with the dangerous audacity of its motto—*"Fiat veritas, pereat vita* [Truth endures, life ends]."

Let me give a picture of the spiritual events in the soul of the modern man. Historical knowledge streams on him from sources that are inexhaustible, strange incoherencies come together, memory opens all its gates and yet is never open wide enough, nature busies herself to receive all the foreign guests, to honour them and put them in their places. But they are at war with each other: violent measures seem necessary, in order to escape destruction one's self. It becomes second nature to grow gradually accustomed to this irregular and stormy home-life, though this second nature is unquestionably weaker, more restless, more radically unsound than the first. The modern man carries inside him an enormous heap of indigestible knowledge-stones that occasionally rattle together in his body, as the fairy-tale has it. And the rattle reveals the most striking characteristic of these modern men, the opposition of something inside them to which nothing external corresponds; and the reverse. The ancient nations knew nothing of this. Knowledge, taken in excess without hunger, even contrary to desire, has no more the effect of transforming the external life; and remains hidden in a chaotic inner world that the modern man has a curious pride in calling his "real personality." He has the substance, he says, and only wants the form; but this is quite an unreal opposition in a living thing. Our modern culture is for that reason not a living one, because it cannot be understood without that opposition. In other words, it is not a real culture but a kind of knowledge about culture, a complex of various thoughts and feelings about it, from which no decision as to its direction can come. Its real motive force that issues in visible action is often no more than a mere convention, a wretched imitation, or even a shameless caricature. The man probably feels like the snake that has swallowed a rabbit whole and lies still in the sun, avoiding all movement not absolutely necessary. The "inner life" is now the only thing that matters to education, and all who see it hope that the education may not fail by being too indigestible. Imagine a Greek meeting it; he would observe that for modern men "education" and "historical education" seem to mean the same thing, with the difference that the one phrase is longer. And if he spoke of his own theory, that a man can be very well educated without any history at all, people would shake their heads and think they had not heard aright. The Greeks, the famous people of a past still near to us, had the "unhistorical sense" strongly developed in the period of their greatest power. If a typical child of his age were transported to that world by some enchantment, he would probably find the Greeks very "uneducated." And that discovery would betray the closely guarded secret of modern culture to the laughter of the world. For we moderns have nothing of our own. We only become worth notice by filling ourselves to overflowing with foreign customs, arts, philosophies, religions and sciences: we are wandering encyclopaedias, as an ancient Greek who had strayed into our time would probably call us. But the only value of an encyclopaedia lies in the inside, in the contents, not in what is written outside, in the binding or the wrapper. And so the whole of modern culture is essentially internal; the bookbinder prints something like this on the cover: "Manual of internal culture for external barbarians." The opposition of inner and outer makes the outer side still more barbarous, as it would naturally be, when the outward growth of a rude people merely developed its primitive inner needs. For what means has nature of repressing too great a luxuriance from without? Only one,—to be affected by it as little as possible, to set it aside and stamp it out at the first opportunity. And so we have the custom of no longer taking real things seriously, we get the feeble personality on which the real and the permanent make so little impression. Men become at last more careless and accommodating in external matters, and the considerable cleft between substance and form is widened; until they have no longer any feeling for barbarism, if only their memories be kept continually titillated, and there flow a constant stream of new things to be known, that can be neatly packed up in the cupboards of their memory. The culture of a people as against this barbarism, can be, I think, described with justice as the "unity of artistic style in every outward expression of the people's life." This must not be misunderstood, as though it were merely a question of the opposition between barbarism and "fine style." The people that can be called cultured, must be in a real sense a living unity, and not be miserably cleft asunder into form and substance. If one wish to promote a people's culture, let him try to promote this higher unity first, and work for the destruction of the modern educative system for the sake of a true education. Let him dare to consider how the health of a people that has been destroyed by history may be restored, and how it may recover its instincts with its honour.

I am only speaking, directly, about the Germans of the present day, who have had to suffer more than other people from the feebleness of personality and the opposition of substance and form. "Form" generally implies for us some convention, disguise or hypocrisy, and if not hated, is at any rate not loved. We have an extraordinary fear of both the word convention and the thing. This fear drove the German from the French school; for he wished to become more natural, and therefore more German. But he seems to have come to a false conclusion with his "therefore." First he ran away from his school of convention, and went by any road he liked: he has come ultimately to imitate voluntarily in a slovenly fashion, what he imitated painfully and often successfully before. So now the lazy fellow lives under French conventions that are actually incorrect:

his manner of walking shows it, his conversation and dress, his general way of life. In the belief that he was returning to Nature, he merely followed caprice and comfort, with the smallest possible amount of self-control. Go through any German town; you will see conventions that are nothing but the negative aspect of the national characteristics of foreign states. Everything is colourless, worn out, shoddy and ill-copied. Every one acts at his own sweet will—which is not a strong or serious will—on laws dictated by the universal rush and the general desire for comfort. A dress that made no head ache in its inventing and wasted no time in the making, borrowed from foreign models and imperfectly copied, is regarded as an important contribution to German fashion. The sense of form is ironically disclaimed by the people—for they have the "sense of substance": they are famous for their cult of "inwardness."

But there is also a famous danger in their "inwardness": the internal substance cannot be seen from the outside, and so may one day take the opportunity of vanishing, and no one notice its absence, any more than its presence before. One may think the German people to be very far from this danger: yet the foreigner will have some warrant for his reproach that our inward life is too weak and ill-organised to provide a form and external expression for itself. It may in rare cases show itself finely receptive, earnest and powerful, richer perhaps than the inward life of other peoples: but, taken as a whole, it remains weak, as all its fine threads are not tied together in one strong knot. The visible action is not the self-manifestation of the inward life, but only a weak and crude attempt of a single thread to make a show of representing the whole. And thus the German is not to be judged on any one action, for the individual may be as completely obscure after it as before. He must obviously be measured by his thoughts and feelings, which are now expressed in his books; if only the books did not, more than ever, raise the doubt whether the famous inward life is still really sitting in its inaccessible shrine. It might one day vanish and leave behind it only the external life,—with its vulgar pride and vain servility,—to mark the German. Fearful thought!—as fearful as if the inward life still sat there, painted and rouged and disguised, become a play-actress or something worse; as his theatrical experience seems to have taught the quiet observer Grillparzer, standing aside as he did from the main press. "We feel by theory," he says. "We hardly know any more how our contemporaries give expression to their feelings: we make them use gestures that are impossible nowadays. Shakespeare has spoilt us moderns."

This is a single example, its general application perhaps too hastily assumed. But how terrible it would be were that generalisation justified before our eyes! There would be then a note of despair in the phrase, "We Germans feel by theory, we are all spoilt by history;"—a phrase that would cut at the roots of any hope for a future national culture. For every hope of that kind grows from the belief in the genuineness and immediacy of German feeling, from the belief in an untarnished inward life. Where is our hope or belief, when its spring is muddied, and the inward quality has learned gestures and dances and the use of cosmetics, has learned to express itself "with due reflection in abstract terms," and gradually to lose itself? And how should a great productive spirit exist among a nation that is not sure of its inward unity and is divided into educated men whose inner life has been drawn from the true path of education, and uneducated men whose inner life cannot be approached at all? How should it exist, I say, when the people has lost its own unity of feeling, and knows that the feeling of the part calling itself the educated part and claiming the right of controlling the artistic spirit of the nation, is false and hypocritical? Here and there the judgment and taste of individuals may be higher and finer than the rest, but that is no compensation: it tortures a man to have to speak only to one section and be no longer in sympathy with his people. He would rather bury his treasure now, in disgust at the vulgar patronage of a class, though his heart be filled with tenderness for all. The instinct of the people can no longer meet him half-way; it is useless for them to stretch their arms out to him in yearning. What remains but to turn his quickened hatred against the ban, strike at the barrier raised by the so-called culture, and condemn as judge what blasted and degraded him as a living man and a source of life? He takes a profound insight into fate in exchange for the godlike desire of creation and help, and ends his days as a lonely philosopher, with the wisdom of disillusion. It is the painfullest comedy: he who sees it will feel a sacred obligation on him, and say to himself,—"Help must come: the higher unity in the nature and soul of a people must be brought back, the cleft between inner and outer must again disappear under the hammer of necessity." But to what means can he look? What remains to him now but his knowledge? He hopes to plant the feeling of a need, by speaking from the breadth of that knowledge, giving it freely with both hands. From the strong need the strong action may one day arise. And to leave no doubt of the instance I am taking of the need and the knowledge, my testimony shall stand, that it is German unity in, its highest sense which is the goal of our endeavour, far more than political union: it is the unity of the German spirit and life after the annihilation of the antagonism between form and substance, inward life and convention.

Discussion Questions

1. Has your learning ever left you feeling like you had swallowed some "indigestible knowledge-stones"? If so, what about the subject matter or the teaching approach left you feeling that way?

2. In this section, Nietzsche complained that because of the way modern students are educated, "we moderns have nothing of our own." What do you think he means by this?

3. What might a better approach to liberal arts education look like?

4. Nietzsche is rather vague in this essay about what he means by "life." What does the Christian faith have to offer those thinking about what it means to live a fully flourishing human life?

CHAPTER 30

Anna Julia Cooper

Introduction to *Womanhood: A Vital Element in the Regeneration and Progress of a Race*

ANIKA T. PRATHER

Many view Anna Julia Cooper as a black feminist, but that limits our knowledge of who she was and the philosophy that motivated her work. Few emphasize her strong Christian faith: "The idea of the radical amelioration of womankind, reverence for woman as woman regardless of rank, wealth, or culture, was to come from that rich and bounteous fountain from which flow all our liberal and universal ideas—the Gospel of Jesus Christ." She simply wanted all men and women to be treated equally, as Jesus Christ calls us, and she saw classical education as a means toward this great end.

Anna Julia Haywood was born into slavery in 1858 to an enslaved mother and her master in North Carolina. She remained on the Haywood plantation until emancipation. At around ten years old, she was enrolled in St. Augustine's Normal School, a school for the newly freed people that followed the classical tradition. Anna thrived under this type of education. She excelled so much that she was made a student teacher to help teach other newly freed people in the classical tradition. Her love for classical studies motivated her to ask if she could take the same rigorous classical courses as the male students. After finishing her courses at St. Augustine's, she went to Oberlin and earned her bachelor's and master's degrees in mathematics. At Oberlin as well, she asked to take "the Gentlemen's course," which allowed for her to take more rigorous classes in classics. At Oberlin she met and married a minister, George A. C. Cooper, who died soon after they were married. This did not cause her to give up on her passion for classical studies, however. From Oberlin, she went on to teach and eventually become the principal at the M Street School in Washington, DC, where she taught all of her students in the classical tradition; and those African American students went on to attend some of the top colleges in the United States. At age sixty-five, she earned a PhD from the Sorbonne in France, the fourth African American woman to do so.

Cooper had a passion for seeing the progress of the African American people through classical studies. She felt this type of education was for every human being who wanted it. Through her work at the M Street School and as president of Frelinghuysen University, she was dedicated to providing classical education to all students, no matter their socioeconomic status or background. In her work, we witness a woman who always remembered how far she had come from being enslaved to being in a position to help those less fortunate. She was humble, committed, and passionate about the uplift of her people through an education that would continue their liberation.

From *Womanhood: A Vital Element in the Regeneration and Progress of a Race*

The idea of the radical amelioration of womankind, reverence for woman as woman regardless of rank, wealth, or culture, was to come from that rich and bounteous fountain from which flow all our liberal and universal ideas—the Gospel of Jesus Christ.

And yet the Christian Church at the time of which we have been speaking would seem to have been doing even less to protect and elevate woman than the little done by secular society. The Church as an organization committed a double offense against woman in the Middle Ages. Making of marriage a sacrament and at the same time insisting on the celibacy of the clergy and other religious orders, she gave an inferior if not an impure character to the marriage relation, especially fitted to reflect discredit on woman. Would this were all or the worst! But the Church by licentiousness of its chosen servants invaded the household and established too openly and in good faith. . . .

Christ gave ideals not formulae. The Gospel is a germ requiring millennia for its growth and ripening. It needs and at the same time helps to form around itself a soil enriched in civilization and perfected in culture and insight without which the embryo can neither be unfolded or comprehended. With all the strides our civilization has made from the first to the nineteenth century, we can boast not an idea, not a principle of action, not a progressive social force but was already mutely foreshadowed, or directly enjoined in that simple tale of a meek and lowly life. The quiet face of the Nazarene is ever seen a little way ahead, never too far to come down to and touch the life of the lowest in days the darkest, yet ever leading onward, still onward, the tottering childish feet of our strangely boastful civilization.

By laying down for woman the same code of morality, the same standard of purity, as for man; by refusing to countenance the shameless and equally guilty monsters who were gloating over her fall,—graciously stooping in all the majesty of his own spotlessness to wipe away the filth and grime of her guilty past and bid her go in peace and sin no more; and again in the moments of her own careworn and footsore dejection, turning from the cruel malignity of mobs and prelates in the dusty marts of Jerusalem to the ready of sympathy, loving appreciation and unfaltering friendship of that quiet home at Bethany; and even at the last, by this dying bequest to the disciple whom he loved, signifying the protection and tender regard to be extended to that sorrowing mother and ever afterward to the sex she represented;—throughout his life and in his death he has given to men a rule and guide for the estimation of woman as an equal, as a helper, as a friend, and as a sacred charge to be sheltered and cared for with a brother's love and sympathy, lessons which nineteen centuries' gigantic strides in knowledge, arts and sciences, in social and ethical principles have not been able to probe to their depth or to exhaust in practice.

. . .

Woman, mother,—your responsibility is one that might make angels tremble and fear to take hold! To trifle with it, to ignore or misuse it, is to treat lightly the most sacred and solemn trust ever confided by God to humankind. The training of children is a task on which an infinity of weal or woe depends. Who does not covet it? Yet who does not stand awestruck before its momentous issues! It is a matter of small moment, it seems to me, whether that lovely girl in whose accomplishments you take such pride and delight, can enter the gay and crowded salon with the ease and elegance of this or that French or English gentlewoman, compared with the decision as to whether her individuality is going to reinforce the good or the evil elements of the world. The lace and the diamonds, the dance and the theater, gain new significance when scanned in their bearings on such issues. Their influence on the individual personality, and through her on the society and civilization which she vitalizes and inspires—all this and more must be weighed in the balance before the jury can return a just and intelligent verdict as to the innocence or banefulness of these apparently simple amusements. . . .

The vital agency of womanhood in the regeneration and progress of a race, as a general question, is conceded almost before it is fairly stated. I confess one of the difficulties for me in the subject assigned lay in its obviousness. . . .

"Women's influence on social progress"—who in Christendom doubts or questions it? One may as well be called on to prove that the sun is the source of light and heat and energy to this many-sided little world.

. . .

Only the Black Woman can say, "When and where I enter, in the quiet, undisputed dignity of my womanhood, without violence and without suing or special patronage, then and there the whole Negro race enters with me." Is it not evident then that as individual workers for this race we must address ourselves with no half-hearted zeal to this feature of our mission. The need is felt and must be recognized by all. There is a call for workers, for missionaries, for men and women with the double consecration of a fundamental love of humanity and a desire for its melioration through the Gospel; but superadded to this we demanded an intelligent and sympathetic comprehension of the interests and special needs of the Negro.

Discussion Questions

1. How did Cooper see the gospel as part of her work of activism?
2. What biblical female examples did Cooper use to support her understanding of the place of women in God's purpose for humanity?
3. Based on these excerpts, how are the views on women's rights that Cooper shared different from the current beliefs of the predominant twenty-first-century feminist movement?
4. What kind of activist would you describe Cooper to be?
5. How did Cooper see the humanitarian work of Jesus Christ as an example to learn from?

Part 4

AD 1900 to Present Day

CHAPTER 31

W. E. B. DuBois

Introduction to *The Souls of Black Folk*

ANGEL ADAMS PARHAM

W. E. B. DuBois was a prominent African American writer and social researcher who lived from 1868 to 1963. He was born into a family that had been free for generations before the official end of slavery in the United States and grew up in the town of Great Barrington, Massachusetts, where he was surrounded by a supportive family and interacted freely with white and black children and families from the community. In this sense, he had an unusual, relatively privileged childhood compared to the typical African American boy born in the mid- to late nineteenth century.

DuBois's great intelligence was noted early on by both black and white members of the Great Barrington community, and he was strongly encouraged and supported in his studies. Following his graduation from high school at the age of sixteen, several local Congregational churches raised money to send him to college at Fisk University. He was so advanced that he entered Fisk as a sophomore, graduated in three years, and then entered Harvard as a junior, where his studies were supported by funding from an academic prize. DuBois went on to complete a philosophy degree with honors and a master's degree while at Harvard. When technical issues with his residency documents prevented him from completing a doctorate in Germany, he returned to finish his studies at Harvard, becoming the first African American to be awarded the PhD from that institution. Although his degrees were in philosophy and history, DuBois had begun studying the new field of sociology during his time in Germany. Once he returned to the United States, he began his life's work of research and writing by combining historical and sociological methods to explain and address racial oppression and inequality.

In 1903 DuBois published a landmark work titled *The Souls of Black Folk*, which provided a moving and insightful meditation on black life in the decades following the Civil War and emancipation. The aim of the book was to make clear to American readers the internal and external struggles of black people who were seeking to make their way in the world without the benefit of adequate resources or education.

In the excerpt provided here, DuBois made reference to the "Veil," a metaphor he used to describe the separation between blacks and whites that kept black people from experiencing full membership in the national community. He explained that he first learned about the existence of this veil when he was a young boy and another child refused to accept a greeting card from him because he was black. In the opening pages of *The Souls of Black Folk*, he reflected on this experience: "It dawned upon me with a certain suddenness that I was different from the others; or like, mayhap, in heart and life and longing, but shut out from their world by a vast veil."[1] This concept of the veil is revisited in the excerpt below, where DuBois recounted the time he spent living and teaching poor black students in the countryside just a few years following the end of slavery.

From *The Souls of Black Folk*
Chapter 4. Of the Meaning of Progress

Once upon a time I taught school in the hills of Tennessee, where the broad dark vale of the Mississippi begins to roll and crumple to greet the Alleghanies. I was a Fisk student then, and all Fisk men thought that Tennessee—beyond the Veil—was theirs alone, and in vacation time they sallied forth in lusty bands to meet the county school-commissioners. Young and happy, I too went, and I shall not soon forget that summer, seventeen years ago.

First, there was a Teachers' Institute at the county-seat; and there distinguished guests of the superintendent taught the teachers fractions and spelling and other mysteries,—white teachers in the morning, Negroes at night. A picnic now and then, and a supper, and the rough world was softened by laughter and song. I remember how—But I wander.

There came a day when all the teachers left the Institute and began the hunt for schools. I learn from hearsay (for my mother was mortally afraid of firearms) that the hunting of ducks and bears and men is wonderfully interesting, but I am sure that the man who has never hunted a country school has something to learn of the pleasures of the chase. I see now the white, hot roads lazily rise and fall and wind before me under the burning July sun; I feel the deep weariness of heart and limb as ten, eight, six miles stretch relentlessly ahead; I feel my heart sink heavily as I hear again and again, "Got a teacher? Yes." So I walked on and on—horses were too expensive—until I had wandered beyond railways, beyond stage lines, to a land of "varmints" and rattlesnakes, where the coming of a stranger was an event, and men lived and died in the shadow of one blue hill.

Sprinkled over hill and dale lay cabins and farmhouses, shut out from the world by the forests and the rolling hills toward the east. There I found at last

---

1. W. E. B. DuBois, "Of Our Spiritual Strivings," in *The Souls of Black Folk*, in *W. E. B. DuBois: Writings*, ed. Nathan Huggins (New York: Library of America, 1986), 364

a little school. Josie told me of it; she was a thin, homely girl of twenty, with a dark-brown face and thick, hard hair. I had crossed the stream at Watertown, and rested under the great willows; then I had gone to the little cabin in the lot where Josie was resting on her way to town. The gaunt farmer made me welcome, and Josie, hearing my errand, told me anxiously that they wanted a school over the hill; that but once since the war had a teacher been there; that she herself longed to learn,—and thus she ran on, talking fast and loud, with much earnestness and energy.

Next morning I crossed the tall round hill, lingered to look at the blue and yellow mountains stretching toward the Carolinas, then plunged into the wood, and came out at Josie's home. It was a dull frame cottage with four rooms, perched just below the brow of the hill, amid peach-trees. The father was a quiet, simple soul, calmly ignorant, with no touch of vulgarity. The mother was different,—strong, bustling, and energetic, with a quick, restless tongue, and an ambition to live "like folks." There was a crowd of children. Two boys had gone away. There remained two growing girls; a shy midget of eight; John, tall, awkward, and eighteen; Jim, younger, quicker, and better looking; and two babies of indefinite age. Then there was Josie herself. She seemed to be the centre of the family: always busy at service, or at home, or berry-picking; a little nervous and inclined to scold, like her mother, yet faithful, too, like her father. She had about her a certain fineness, the shadow of an unconscious moral heroism that would willingly give all of life to make life broader, deeper, and fuller for her and hers. I saw much of this family afterwards, and grew to love them for their honest efforts to be decent and comfortable, and for their knowledge of their own ignorance. There was with them no affectation. The mother would scold the father for being so "easy"; Josie would roundly berate the boys for carelessness; and all knew that it was a hard thing to dig a living out of a rocky side-hill.

I secured the school. I remember the day I rode horseback out to the commissioner's house with a pleasant young white fellow who wanted the white school. The road ran down the bed of a stream; the sun laughed and the water jingled, and we rode on. "Come in," said the commissioner,—"Come in. Have a seat. Yes, that certificate will do. Stay to dinner. What do you want a month?" "Oh," thought I, "this is lucky"; but even then fell the awful shadow of the Veil, for they ate first, then I—alone.

The schoolhouse was a log hut, where Colonel Wheeler used to shelter his corn. It sat in a lot behind a rail fence and thorn bushes, near the sweetest of springs. There was an entrance where a door once was, and within, a massive rickety fireplace; great chinks between the logs served as windows. Furniture was scarce. A pale blackboard crouched in the corner. My desk was made of three boards, reinforced at critical points, and my chair, borrowed from the landlady, had to be returned every night. Seats for the children—these puzzled me much. I was haunted by a New England vision of neat little desks and chairs, but, alas! the reality was rough plank benches without backs, and at times without legs. They had the one virtue of making naps dangerous,—possibly fatal, for the floor was not to be trusted.

It was a hot morning late in July when the school opened. I trembled when I heard the patter of little feet down the dusty road, and saw the growing row of dark solemn faces and bright eager eyes facing me. First came Josie and her brothers and sisters. The longing to know, to be a student in the great school at Nashville, hovered like a star above this child-woman amid her work and worry, and she studied doggedly. There were the Dowells from their farm over toward Alexandria,—Fanny, with her smooth black face and wondering eyes; Martha, brown and dull; the pretty girl-wife of a brother, and the younger brood.

There were the Burkes,—two brown and yellow lads, and a tiny haughty-eyed girl. Fat Reuben's little chubby girl came, with golden face and old-gold hair, faithful and solemn. 'Thenie was on hand early,—a jolly, ugly, good-hearted girl, who slyly dipped snuff and looked after her little bow-legged brother. When her mother could spare her, 'Tildy came,—a midnight beauty, with starry eyes and tapering limbs; and her brother, correspondingly homely. And then the big boys,—the hulking Lawrences; the lazy Neills, unfathered sons of mother and daughter; Hickman, with a stoop in his shoulders; and the rest.

There they sat, nearly thirty of them, on the rough benches, their faces shading from a pale cream to a deep brown, the little feet bare and swinging, the eyes full of expectation, with here and there a twinkle of mischief, and the hands grasping Webster's blue-black spelling-book. I loved my school, and the fine faith the children had in the wisdom of their teacher was truly marvellous. We read and spelled together, wrote a little, picked flowers, sang, and listened to stories of the world beyond the hill. At times the school would dwindle away, and I would start out. I would visit Mun Eddings, who lived in two very dirty rooms, and ask why little Lugene, whose flaming face seemed ever ablaze with the dark-red hair uncombed, was absent all last week, or why I missed so often the inimitable rags of Mack and Ed. Then the father, who worked Colonel Wheeler's farm on shares, would tell me how the crops needed the boys; and the thin, slovenly mother, whose face was pretty when washed, assured me that Lugene must mind the baby. "But we'll start them again next week." When the Lawrences stopped, I knew that the doubts of the old folks about book-learning had conquered again, and so, toiling up the hill, and getting as far into the cabin as possible, I put Cicero "pro Archia Poeta" into the simplest English with local applications, and usually convinced them—for a week or so.

On Friday nights I often went home with some of the children,—sometimes
to Doc Burke's farm. He was a great, loud, thin Black, ever working, and trying
to buy the seventy-five acres of hill and dale where he lived; but people said that
he would surely fail, and the "white folks would get it all." His wife was a magnificent Amazon, with saffron face and shining hair, uncorseted and barefooted,
and the children were strong and beautiful. They lived in a one-and-a-half-room
cabin in the hollow of the farm, near the spring. The front room was full of great
fat white beds, scrupulously neat; and there were bad chromos on the walls, and
a tired centre-table. In the tiny back kitchen I was often invited to "take out and
help" myself to fried chicken and wheat biscuit, "meat" and corn pone, string-
beans and berries. At first I used to be a little alarmed at the approach of bedtime
in the one lone bedroom, but embarrassment was very deftly avoided. First, all
the children nodded and slept, and were stowed away in one great pile of goose
feathers; next, the mother and the father discreetly slipped away to the kitchen
while I went to bed; then, blowing out the dim light, they retired in the dark. In
the morning all were up and away before I thought of awaking. Across the road,
where fat Reuben lived, they all went outdoors while the teacher retired, because
they did not boast the luxury of a kitchen.

I liked to stay with the Dowells, for they had four rooms and plenty of good
country fare. Uncle Bird had a small, rough farm, all woods and hills, miles from
the big road; but he was full of tales,—he preached now and then,—and with his
children, berries, horses, and wheat he was happy and prosperous. Often, to keep
the peace, I must go where life was less lovely; for instance, 'Tildy's mother was
incorrigibly dirty, Reuben's larder was limited seriously, and herds of untamed
insects wandered over the Eddingses' beds. Best of all I loved to go to Josie's, and
sit on the porch, eating peaches, while the mother bustled and talked: how Josie
had bought the sewing-machine; how Josie worked at service in winter, but that
four dollars a month was "mighty little" wages; how Josie longed to go away to
school, but that it "looked like" they never could get far enough ahead to let her;
how the crops failed and the well was yet unfinished; and, finally, how "mean"
some of the white folks were.

For two summers I lived in this little world; it was dull and humdrum.
The girls looked at the hill in wistful longing, and the boys fretted and haunted
Alexandria. Alexandria was "town,"—a straggling, lazy village of houses,
churches, and shops, and an aristocracy of Toms, Dicks, and Captains. Cuddled
on the hill to the north was the village of the colored folks, who lived in three-
or four-room unpainted cottages, some neat and homelike, and some dirty.
The dwellings were scattered rather aimlessly, but they centred about the twin
temples of the hamlet, the Methodist, and the Hard-Shell Baptist churches.

These, in turn, leaned gingerly on a sad-colored schoolhouse. Hither my little world wended its crooked way on Sunday to meet other worlds, and gossip, and wonder, and make the weekly sacrifice with frenzied priest at the altar of the "old-time religion." Then the soft melody and mighty cadences of Negro song fluttered and thundered.

I have called my tiny community a world, and so its isolation made it; and yet there was among us but a half-awakened common consciousness, sprung from common joy and grief, at burial, birth, or wedding; from a common hardship in poverty, poor land, and low wages; and, above all, from the sight of the Veil that hung between us and Opportunity. All this caused us to think some thoughts together; but these, when ripe for speech, were spoken in various languages. Those whose eyes twenty-five and more years before had seen "the glory of the coming of the Lord," saw in every present hindrance or help a dark fatalism bound to bring all things right in His own good time. The mass of those to whom slavery was a dim recollection of childhood found the world a puzzling thing: it asked little of them, and they answered with little, and yet it ridiculed their offering. Such a paradox they could not understand, and therefore sank into listless indifference, or shiftlessness, or reckless bravado. There were, however, some—such as Josie, Jim, and Ben—to whom War, Hell, and Slavery were but childhood tales, whose young appetites had been whetted to an edge by school and story and half-awakened thought. Ill could they be content, born without and beyond the World. And their weak wings beat against their barriers,—barriers of caste, of youth, of life; at last, in dangerous moments, against everything that opposed even a whim.

The ten years that follow youth, the years when first the realization comes that life is leading somewhere,—these were the years that passed after I left my little school. When they were past, I came by chance once more to the walls of Fisk University, to the halls of the chapel of melody. As I lingered there in the joy and pain of meeting old school-friends, there swept over me a sudden longing to pass again beyond the blue hill, and to see the homes and the school of other days, and to learn how life had gone with my school-children; and I went.

Josie was dead, and the gray-haired mother said simply, "We've had a heap of trouble since you've been away." I had feared for Jim. With a cultured parentage and a social caste to uphold him, he might have made a venturesome merchant or a West Point cadet. But here he was, angry with life and reckless; and when Fanner Durham charged him with stealing wheat, the old man had to ride fast to escape the stones which the furious fool hurled after him. They told Jim to run away; but he would not run, and the constable came that afternoon. It grieved Josie, and great awkward John walked nine miles every day to see his little brother through the bars of Lebanon jail. At last the two came back together in the dark night. The mother cooked supper, and Josie emptied her purse, and the boys stole away. Josie grew thin and silent, yet worked the more. The hill became steep for the quiet old father, and with the boys away there was little to do in the valley. Josie helped them to sell the old farm, and they moved nearer town. Brother Dennis, the carpenter, built a new house with six rooms; Josie toiled a year in Nashville, and brought back ninety dollars to furnish the house and change it to a home.

When the spring came, and the birds twittered, and the stream ran proud and full, little sister Lizzie, bold and thoughtless, flushed with the passion of youth, bestowed herself on the tempter, and brought home a nameless child. Josie shivered and worked on, with the vision of schooldays all fled, with a face wan and tired,—worked until, on a summer's day, some one married another; then Josie crept to her mother like a hurt child, and slept—and sleeps.

. . .

My journey was done, and behind me lay hill and dale, and Life and Death. How shall man measure Progress there where the dark-faced Josie lies? How many heartfuls of sorrow shall balance a bushel of wheat? How hard a thing is life to the lowly, and yet how human and real! And all this life and love and strife and failure,—is it the twilight of nightfall or the flush of some faint-dawning day?

Thus sadly musing, I rode to Nashville in the Jim Crow car.

Discussion Questions

1. How willing are you to go to the "less lovely" places of your community and of the world to work and serve?
2. What role does service play in your education? What role do you think it should play?
3. Why do Josie and other young people in the reading have such a great longing for education? How is their thirst to learn similar to or different from the way you approach your own education?
4. What has changed since DuBois's time regarding race and relationships between blacks and whites? Is your education preparing you to think about and address racial inequalities in today's world?
5. What do you sense was DuBois's attitude toward Christian faith in the lives of the people he was working with? How was his way of thinking in line with or out of step with Christ's message that the gospel is good news for the poor?

CHAPTER 32
Virginia Woolf

Introduction to *A Room of One's Own*
BETHANY WILLIAMSON

Virginia Woolf (1882–1941), a modernist English writer known for her stream-of-consciousness narrative style, presented *A Room of One's Own* as a lecture before publishing the work in 1929. Tasked with examining the topic of "women and fiction," Woolf claimed that "a woman must have money and a room of her own if she is to write fiction."[1] She develops her argument not with a logical series of points but with an *essay*—literally, an *attempt*—that follows imaginative tangents of thought to understand why, and with what consequences, women have been denied these resources for centuries. In the process, Woolf offers a reminder that we humans think not in vacuums or ivory towers but as embodied individuals. Our lived experience gives us eyes to see and voices to express truth.

Woolf begins her essay with an anecdote: During a moment of thought, while walking across the green turf of an Oxbridge college, she is rudely interrupted by a man saying she cannot walk on the grass. The interruption instantly recalls her from the life of her mind to the material reality of her body. Woolf goes on to describe thinking metaphorically, as a process of "fishing" for true ideas, and she laments that the man's interruption "sent my little fish into hiding." This experience leads Woolf down a path of meandering inquiry, as her mind jumps from one question to the next in pursuit of that fish: What distinguishes fact from fiction and truth from illusion? How do material conditions—from luncheons to labor—affect artistic creation? As a feminist writer, she focuses on women's experience: What would have happened to Shakespeare's genius sister, if he had had one? And what are the consequences—to society and literary history alike—of valuing stories about war and sport while devaluing stories about fashion, feeling, and "the accumulation of unrecorded life"?

Woolf's thoughts keep returning to the question of how our material—and gendered—reality shapes the way we think, write, and imagine the world. "The human frame being what it is, heart, body and brain all mixed together," Woolf contends, "one cannot think well, love well, sleep well, if one has not dined

---

1. http://gutenberg.net.au/ebooks02/0200791h.html.

well." In other words, creativity cannot flourish in conditions of physical and economic constraint. At the same time, Woolf uses her stream-of-consciousness style to illustrate how embodied limits and material constraints can actually sharpen perspective and fuel creativity. Interruptions are frustrating, but they can propel us to ask new questions and think in new directions; as a result, interruptions can lead us to see truths about history, institutions, and ourselves.

Woolf suggests that we should live unashamedly in our bodies—telling the truth about the reality we know—while also striving to imagine a world beyond our own experience. And she reminds us that, even as we work to repair broken systems and recover missing voices, we should also ask ourselves what experiences and perspectives we truly value. As you read the excerpted passages, focus particularly on how Woolf invites us to embrace our own embodied (and interrupted!) experiences, as we envision and pursue a more just and equitable world.

From *A Room of One's Own*

When you asked me to speak about women and fiction I sat down on the banks of a river and began to wonder what the words meant. They might mean simply a few remarks about Fanny Burney; a few more about Jane Austen; a tribute to the Brontës and a sketch of Haworth Parsonage under snow; some witticisms if possible about Miss Mitford; a respectful allusion to George Eliot; a reference to Mrs Gaskell and one would have done. But at second sight the words seemed not so simple. The title women and fiction might mean, and you may have meant it to mean, women and what they are like; or it might mean women and the fiction that they write; or it might mean women and the fiction that is written about them; or it might mean that somehow all three are inextricably mixed together and you want me to consider them in that light. But when I began to consider the subject in this last way, which seemed the most interesting, I soon saw that it had one fatal drawback. I should never be able to come to a conclusion. I should never be able to fulfil what is, I understand, the first duty of a lecturer—to hand you after an hour's discourse a nugget of pure truth to wrap up between the pages of your notebooks and keep on the mantelpiece for ever. All I could do was to offer you an opinion upon one minor point—a woman must have money and a room of her own if she is to write fiction; and that, as you will see, leaves the great problem of the true nature of woman and the true nature of fiction unsolved. I have shirked the duty of coming to a conclusion upon these two questions—women and fiction remain, so far as I am concerned, unsolved problems. But in order to make some amends I am going to do what I can to show you how I arrived at this opinion about the room and the money. I am going to develop in your presence as fully and freely as I can the train of thought which led me to think this. Perhaps if I lay bare the ideas, the prejudices, that lie behind this statement you will find that they have some bearing upon women and some upon fiction. At any rate, when a subject is highly controversial—and any question about sex is that—one cannot hope to tell the truth. One can only show how one came to hold whatever opinion one does hold. One can only give one's audience the chance of drawing their own conclusions as they observe the limitations, the prejudices, the idiosyncrasies of the speaker. Fiction here is likely to contain more truth than fact . . .

Here then was I (call me Mary Beton, Mary Seton, Mary Carmichael or by any name you please—it is not a matter of any importance) sitting on the banks of a river a week or two ago in fine October weather, lost in thought. That collar I have spoken of, women and fiction, the need of coming to some conclusion on a subject that raises all sorts of prejudices and passions, bowed my head to the ground. To the right and left bushes of some sort, golden and crimson, glowed with the colour, even it seemed burnt with the heat, of fire. On the further bank the willows wept in perpetual lamentation, their hair about their shoulders. The river reflected whatever it chose of sky and bridge and burning tree, and when the undergraduate had oared his boat through the reflections they closed again, completely, as if he had never been. There one might have sat the clock round lost in thought. Thought—to call it by a prouder name than it deserved—had let its line down into the stream. It swayed, minute after minute, hither and thither among the reflections and the weeds, letting the water lift it and sink it, until—you know the little tug—the sudden conglomeration of an idea at the end of one's line: and then the cautious hauling of it in, and the careful laying of it out? Alas, laid on the grass how small, how insignificant this thought of mine looked; the sort of fish that a good fisherman puts back into the water so that it may grow fatter and be one day worth cooking and eating. I will not trouble you with that thought now, though if you look carefully you may find it for yourselves in the course of what I am going to say.

But however small it was, it had, nevertheless, the mysterious property of its kind—put back into the mind, it became at once very exciting, and important; and as it darted and sank, and flashed hither and thither, set up such a wash and tumult of ideas that it was impossible to sit still. It was thus that I found myself walking with extreme rapidity across a grass plot. Instantly a man's figure rose to intercept me. Nor did I at first understand that the gesticulations of a curious-looking object, in a cut-away coat and evening shirt, were aimed at me. His face expressed horror and indignation. Instinct rather than reason came to my help; he was a Beadle; I was a woman. This was the turf; there was the path.

Only the Fellows and Scholars are allowed here; the gravel is the place for me. Such thoughts were the work of a moment. As I regained the path the arms of the Beadle sank, his face assumed its usual repose, and though turf is better walking than gravel, no very great harm was done. The only charge I could bring against the Fellows and Scholars of whatever the college might happen to be was that in protection of their turf, which has been rolled for 300 years in succession, they had sent my little fish into hiding. What idea it had been that had sent me so audaciously trespassing I could not now remember.

―――――――

If one is a woman one is often surprised by a sudden splitting off of consciousness, say in walking down Whitehall, when from being the natural inheritor of that civilization, she becomes, on the contrary, outside of it, alien and critical. Clearly the mind is always altering its focus, and bringing the world into different perspectives. But some of these states of mind seem, even if adopted spontaneously, to be less comfortable than others. In order to keep oneself continuing in them one is unconsciously holding something back, and gradually the repression becomes an effort. But there may be some state of mind in which one could continue without effort because nothing is required to be held back. And this perhaps, I thought, coming in from the window, is one of them. For certainly when I saw the couple get into the taxicab the mind felt as if, after being divided, it had come together again in a natural fusion. The obvious reason would be that it is natural for the sexes to co-operate. One has a profound, if irrational, instinct in favour of the theory that the union of man and woman makes for the greatest satisfaction, the most complete happiness. But the sight of the two people getting into the taxi and the satisfaction it gave me made me also ask whether there are two sexes in the mind corresponding to the two sexes in the body, and whether they also require to be united in order to get complete satisfaction and happiness? And I went on amateurishly to sketch a plan of the soul so that in each of us two powers preside, one male, one female; and in the man's brain the man predominates over the woman, and in the woman's brain the woman predominates over the man. The normal and comfortable state of being is that when the two live in harmony together, spiritually co-operating. If one is a man, still the woman part of his brain must have effect; and a woman also must have intercourse with the man in her. Coleridge perhaps meant this when he said that a great mind is androgynous. It is when this fusion takes place that the mind is fully fertilized and uses all its faculties. Perhaps a mind that is purely masculine cannot create, any more than a mind that is purely feminine, I thought.

It was delightful to read a man's writing again. It was so direct, so straightforward after the writing of women. It indicated such freedom of mind, such liberty
of person, such confidence in himself. One had a sense of physical well-being in
the presence of this well-nourished, well-educated, free mind, which had never
been thwarted or opposed, but had had full liberty from birth to stretch itself
in whatever way it liked. All this was admirable. But after reading a chapter or
two a shadow seemed to lie across the page. It was a straight dark bar, a shadow
shaped something like the letter 'I'. One began dodging this way and that to
catch a glimpse of the landscape behind it. Whether that was indeed a tree or
a woman walking I was not quite sure. Back one was always hailed to the letter
'I'. One began to be tired of 'I'. Not but what this 'I' was a most respectable 'I';
honest and logical; as hard as a nut, and polished for centuries by good teaching
and good feeding. I respect and admire that 'I' from the bottom of my heart.
But—here I turned a page or two, looking for something or other—the worst
of it is that in the shadow of the letter 'I' all is shapeless as mist. Is that a tree?
No, it is a woman. But . . . she has not a bone in her body, I thought, watching
Phoebe, for that was her name, coming across the beach. Then Alan got up and
the shadow of Alan at once obliterated Phoebe. For Alan had views and Phoebe
was quenched in the flood of his views. . . . But why was I bored? Partly because
of the dominance of the letter 'I' and the aridity, which, like the giant beech tree,
it casts within its shade. Nothing will grow there. And partly for some more
obscure reason. There seemed to be some obstacle, some impediment in Mr A's
mind which blocked the fountain of creative energy and shored it within narrow limits.

It is the power of suggestion that one most misses, I thought, taking Mr B the
critic in my hand and reading, very carefully and very dutifully, his remarks upon
the art of poetry. Very able they were, acute and full of learning; but the trouble
was that his feelings no longer communicated; his mind seemed separated into
different chambers; not a sound carried from one to the other. . . . When a book
lacks suggestive power, however hard it hits the surface of the mind it cannot
penetrate within.

It is fatal to be a man or woman pure and simple; one must be woman-manly
or man-womanly. It is fatal for a woman to lay the least stress on any grievance;

to plead even with justice any cause; in any way to speak consciously as a woman. And fatal is no figure of speech; for anything written with that conscious bias is doomed to death. It ceases to be fertilized. Brilliant and effective, powerful and masterly, as it may appear for a day or two, it must wither at nightfall; it cannot grow in the minds of others. Some collaboration has to take place in the mind between the woman and the man before the art of creation can be accomplished. Some marriage of opposites has to be consummated. The whole of the mind must lie wide open if we are to get the sense that the writer is communicating his experience with perfect fullness. There must be freedom and there must be peace.

———

Here, then, Mary Beton ceases to speak. She has told you how she reached the conclusion—the prosaic conclusion—that it is necessary to have five hundred a year and a room with a lock on the door if you are to write fiction or poetry. She has tried to lay bare the thoughts and impressions that led her to think this. She has asked you to follow her flying into the arms of a Beadle, lunching here, dining there, drawing pictures in the British Museum, taking books from the shelf, looking out of the window. While she has been doing all these things, you no doubt have been observing her failings and foibles and deciding what effect they have had on her opinions. You have been contradicting her and making whatever additions and deductions seem good to you. That is all as it should be, for in a question like this truth is only to be had by laying together many varieties of error.

———

You may object that in all this I have made too much of the importance of material things. Even allowing a generous margin for symbolism, that five hundred a year stands for the power to contemplate, that a lock on the door means the power to think for oneself, still you may say that the mind should rise above such things; and that great poets have often been poor men. Let me then quote to you the words of your own Professor of Literature, who knows better than I do what goes to the making of a poet. Sir Arthur Quiller-Couch writes: 'What are the great poetical names of the last hundred years or so? Coleridge, Wordsworth, Byron, Shelley, Landor, Keats, Tennyson, Browning, Arnold, Morris, Rossetti, Swinburne—we may stop there. Of these, all but Keats, Browning, Rossetti were University men, and of these three, Keats, who died young, cut off in his prime, was the only one not fairly well to do. It may seem a brutal thing to say, and it is a sad thing to say: but, as a matter of hard fact, the theory that poetical genius bloweth where it listeth, and equally in poor and rich, holds little truth. . . . These are dreadful facts, but let us face them. It is—however dishonouring to us as a nation—certain that, by some fault in our commonwealth, the poor poet has not in these days, nor has had for two hundred years, a dog's chance. . . .'

Nobody could put the point more plainly. . . . Intellectual freedom depends upon material things. Poetry depends upon intellectual freedom. And women have always been poor, not for two hundred years merely, but from the beginning of time. Women have had less intellectual freedom than the sons of Athenian slaves. Women, then, have not had a dog's chance of writing poetry. That is why I have laid so much stress on money and a room of one's own. However, thanks to the toils of those obscure women in the past, of whom I wish we knew more, thanks, curiously enough to two wars, the Crimean which let Florence Nightingale out of her drawing-room, and the European War which opened the doors to the average woman some sixty years later, these evils are in the way to be bettered. Otherwise you would not be here tonight, and your chance of earning five hundred pounds a year, precarious as I am afraid that it still is, would be minute in the extreme.

————

Like most uneducated Englishwomen, I like reading—I like reading books in the bulk. Lately my diet has become a trifle monotonous; history is too much about wars; biography too much about great men; poetry has shown, I think, a tendency to sterility, and fiction but I have sufficiently exposed my disabilities as a critic of modern fiction and will say no more about it. Therefore I would ask you to write all kinds of books, hesitating at no subject however trivial or however vast. By hook or by crook, I hope that you will possess yourselves of money enough to travel and to idle, to contemplate the future or the past of the world, to dream over books and loiter at street corners and let the line of thought dip deep into the stream.

————

What is meant by 'reality'? It would seem to be something very erratic, very undependable—now to be found in a dusty road, now in a scrap of newspaper in the street, now a daffodil in the sun. It lights up a group in a room and stamps some casual saying. It overwhelms one walking home beneath the stars and makes the silent world more real than the world of speech—and then there it is again in an omnibus in the uproar of Piccadilly. Sometimes, too, it seems to dwell in shapes too far away for us to discern what their nature is. But whatever it touches, it fixes and makes permanent. That is what remains over when the skin of the day has been cast into the hedge; that is what is left of past time and of our loves and hates. Now the writer, as I think, has the chance to live more than other people in the presence of this reality. It is his business to find it and collect it and communicate it to the rest of us. So at least I infer from reading LEAR or EMMA or LA RECHERCHE DU TEMPS PERDU. For the reading of these books seems to perform a curious couching operation on the senses; one sees more intensely afterwards; the world seems bared of its covering and given an intenser life. Those are the enviable people who live at enmity with unreality; and those are the pitiable who are knocked on the head by the thing done without knowing or caring. So that when I ask you to earn money and have a room of your own, I am asking you to live in the presence of reality, an invigorating life, it would appear, whether one can impart it or not.

———

When I rummage in my own mind I find no noble sentiments about being companions and equals and influencing the world to higher ends. I find myself saying briefly and prosaically that it is much more important to be oneself than anything else. Do not dream of influencing other people, I would say, if I knew how to make it sound exalted. Think of things in themselves.

———

For my belief is that if we live another century or so—I am talking of the common life which is the real life and not of the little separate lives which we live as individuals—and have five hundred a year each of us and rooms of our own; if we have the habit of freedom and the courage to write exactly what we think; if we escape a little from the common sitting-room and see human beings not always in their relation to each other but in relation to reality; and the sky, too, and the trees or whatever it may be in themselves; if we look past Milton's bogey, for no human being should shut out the view; if we face the fact, for it is a fact, that there is no arm to cling to, but that we go alone and that our relation is to the world of reality and not only to the world of men and women, then the opportunity will come and the dead poet who was Shakespeare's sister will put on the body which she has so often laid down. Drawing her life from the lives of the unknown who were her forerunners, as her brother did before her, she will be born. As for her coming without that preparation, without that effort on our part, without that determination that when she is born again she shall find it possible to live and write her poetry, that we cannot expect, for that would be impossible. But I maintain that she would come if we worked for her, and that so to work, even in poverty and obscurity, is worth while.

Discussion Questions

1. What do you think Woolf means when she writes, "when a subject is highly controversial . . . one cannot hope to tell the truth"? What has been your own experience of discussing "controversial" ideas with people in your community, whether friends or family members, coworkers or classmates? Does Woolf's observation ring true?

2. How does the stream-of-consciousness form of Woolf's essay illustrate her argument about seeking and telling the truth? In other words, what kind of thought process lends itself best to a pursuit of truth?

3. Throughout her life Woolf wrestled with significant mental health challenges, which in turn informed her art. What specific challenges or "interruptions" have you faced? How have these challenges given you a unique story and perspective, enhancing your creativity and empathy?

CHAPTER 33

G. K. Chesterton

Introduction to "Modern Elfland"

J. CAMERON MOORE

G. K. Chesterton (1874–1936) was an English journalist, novelist, poet, biographer, social critic, and Christian apologist. Chesterton consistently argued that we undervalue our own possessions, our own homes, and our own lives. Instead of seeing ourselves as fantastic and remarkable creatures inhabiting a world of wonders, we tend toward a bored dissatisfaction with our environments, especially our homes and our families. Chesterton believed the root of this problem was a lack of imagination; we fail to see our own lives accurately because we do not properly imagine them.

He wrote in his *Autobiography* that the whole of his work (more than a hundred books, five thousand articles, and a thousand poems) grew out of the problem of how we "could be made to realise the wonder and splendour of being alive, in environments which [our] own daily criticism treated as dead-alive, and which [our] imagination had left for dead."[1] The solution to our tendency toward contempt for our own lives lies in an imaginative shock which can restore us to ourselves. "At the back of our brains, so to speak, there was a forgotten blaze or bust of astonishment at our own existence. The object of the artistic and spiritual life was to dig for this submerged sunrise of wonder; so that a man sitting in a chair might suddenly understand that he was actually alive, and be happy."[2] Chesterton's favorite place to begin such rehabilitation of our imaginations is the home.

However, in our modern world of suburbs and SUVs, our homes often appear prosaic and dull. Adventure is located somewhere and somewhen else. We are drawn to fantastic novels, movies, shows, and video games in part because they offer the excitement that our own neighborhoods seem to lack. Yet Chesterton suggested that even in those places that appear inimical to imagination and adventure, we might find what we seek. "Modern Elfland" is a meditation on this possibility by imagining what the traditional fairy-tale journey might look like in the modern world.

---

1. G. K. Chesterton, *Autobiography* (San Francisco: Ignatius, 1936), 134.
2. Chesterton, *Autobiography*, 99.

The poem invites us to reimagine our education. The speaker of the poem sets out with excitement for a new destination. We can certainly imagine such excitement before a journey—perhaps we set out for our own educations with similar feelings. Yet fairyland is not what we expect in the poem, and often our studies seem to be the opposite of an adventure. College writing and introduction to biology courses don't often fill us with anticipation and wonder. Yet the poem suggests that what we need are not new subjects but new eyes with which to see them.

The first step toward restoring our vision is to approach these subjects from fresh new perspectives and with great expectation. Although the speaker of the poem is shocked to find the groves and glades of fairyland replaced by an industrial city, the old enchantment is still at work: "The word that witched the wood and hills / Spoke in the iron and the stone." Not only does the speaker discover fairyland in the middle of the city, but he can finally see his own home for what it truly is: a place of wonder and magic. Whether in the sciences, the arts, business, or the humanities, most of us have experienced the thrill of learning, the "eureka" moment of intellectual discovery. "Modern Elfland" offers a model for how we might approach the areas of our studies that our imaginations have left for dead.

Modern Elfland

I cut a staff in a churchyard copse,
I clad myself in ragged things,
I set a feather in my cap
That fell out of an angel's wings.

I filled my wallet with white stones,
I took three foxgloves in my hand,
I slung my shoes across my back,
And so I went to fairyland.

But lo, within that ancient place
Science had reared her iron crown,
And the great cloud of steam went up
That telleth where she takes a town.

But cowled with smoke and starred with lamps,
That strange land's light was still its own;
The word that witched the woods and hills
Spoke in the iron and the stone.

Not Nature's hand had ever curved
That mute unearthly porter's spine.
Like sleeping dragon's sudden eyes
The signals leered along the line.

The chimneys thronging crooked or straight
Were fingers signalling the sky;
The dog that strayed across the street
Seemed four-legged by monstrosity.

'In vain,' I cried, 'though you too touch
The new time's desecrating hand,
Through all the noises of a town
I hear the heart of fairyland.'

I read the name above a door,
Then through my spirit pealed and passed:
'This is the town of thine own home,
And thou hast looked on it at last.'

Discussion Questions

1. What elements of the traditional fairy tale are present in the first two stanzas of the poem? How do they shape our expectations of what is to follow?
2. What has happened to fairyland when the speaker arrives? Despite its current state, what is still true of fairyland?
3. How does the poem make the familiar aspects of modern life (trains, chimneys, and dogs) strange and mysterious?
4. How might this poem help us to reimagine our own homes? What practical guides does it offer for such a project?
5. What areas of your education, especially those outside of your major or focus, has your imagination left for dead? How might you begin reimagining those areas?

CHAPTER 34

T. S. Eliot

Introduction to "Preludes"

JOY MOORE

Do you look around at the mundanity of human life and wonder whether this is all there is? Do you hear these fears and hopeless musings from others? How are we to reckon with the deprivation evident everywhere? What do we do with our yearnings for something more to be true?

The poem below, "Preludes," reveals a speaker confronting this very tension. Reading it, we find ourselves in a city, moving through night and day, our senses overwhelmed by undesirable smells, sights, and sounds. Far from a romanticized view of urban life, this poem takes us into the gritty reality a city dweller endures. These are "the burnt-out ends of smoky days" and mornings filled with "faint stale smells of beer" and "muddy feet that press / To early coffee-stands." It's a world of restless nights in which "you tossed a blanket from bed . . . and waited . . . dozed," unable to avoid the "sordid images / of which your soul was constituted," only to wake and return to another day of "insistent feet" and "a blackened street / Impatient to assume the world." A bleak, despairing depiction of human life, this poem catalogs the yellowing scraps of the day and the haunting shadows of night.

Yet something else haunts the poem, too, and the speaker cannot restrain it entirely. In section IV, speaking directly, at last, the speaker confesses a suspicion that something more is here: "I am moved by fancies that are curled / Around these images, and cling: / The notion of some infinitely gentle / Infinitely suffering thing." This sudden admission of spiritual yearning is quickly dismissed, though, for the speaker finds the impulse embarrassing and tells the reader to "Wipe your hand across your mouth, and laugh" for the world is as "vacant" as it appears.

But is it? The poem's title, "Preludes," demands that we ask, *prelude to what*? Is it possible that the "dingy shades" and morning stench have something more to say to us? Is it possible that despair itself tells us there's something beyond the banality we see around? Why are we even capable of hope? Is it illusion, or is it the grace to recognize that more is present than we have eyes to see? What "curl[s] / Around these images" of our lives? What truths glint in the periphery? How might the longings of our lives, even those laced with loneliness or despair, be preludes to something truer, trying to break in?

This poem was written by T.S. Eliot (1888, USA–1965, England), considered one of the foremost writers and critics of the twentieth century, who had a keen intelligence and a distrust of religion during much of his early life. He wrote major works, including "The Waste Land" (1921), that critiqued the modern condition and were hailed for their astute perceptions. Yet, Eliot's own spiritual concerns surfaced continually over his life, and "Preludes" indicates one such time. Though he dismissed, in the poem, belief as laughable, those "fancies" persisted, and he converted to Christianity in 1927. During those same years between "The Waste Land" and his conversion, Eliot found his writing career stalled and, to challenge himself, accepted his publisher's invitation to write a series of Christmas poems, the "Ariel" poems. Doing so, he said, "released the stream," and he went on to write other significant poems, including, "Ash Wednesday" and "The Four Quartets," which reflect his transformed vision of hope despite present despair.[1]

"Preludes," which evinces early signs of Eliot's transformation, helps us remember that what we see is not all that is. As Christian learners, we devote ourselves to seeking truth, attending to the realities manifest in this world and the deep and invisible yearnings within us for such goods as wholeness, beauty, meaning, and joy. Doing so invites us to see that our struggles and difficulties, whether external in the world or internal in ourselves, become avenues through which we transform; without them—without challenges or dissatisfactions—we would not be beckoned onward toward greater truth and meaning.

Preludes

I

The winter evening settles down
With smell of steaks in passageways.
Six o'clock.
The burnt-out ends of smoky days.
And now a gusty shower wraps
The grimy scraps
Of withered leaves about your feet
And newspapers from vacant lots;
The showers beat
On broken blinds and chimney-pots,
And at the corner of the street
A lonely cab-horse steams and stamps.

---

1. John Lehmann, "T. S. Eliot Talks about Himself and the Drive to Create," *New York Times Book Review*, November 9, 1953, https://archive.nytimes.com/www.nytimes.com/books/97/04/20/reviews/eliot-lehmann.html.

And then the lighting of the lamps.

II

The morning comes to consciousness
Of faint stale smells of beer
From the sawdust-trampled street
With all its muddy feet that press
To early coffee-stands.
With the other masquerades
That time resumes,
One thinks of all the hands
That are raising dingy shades
In a thousand furnished rooms.

III

You tossed a blanket from the bed,
You lay upon your back, and waited;
You dozed, and watched the night revealing
The thousand sordid images
Of which your soul was constituted;
They flickered against the ceiling.
And when all the world came back
And the light crept up between the shutters
And you heard the sparrows in the gutters,
You had such a vision of the street
As the street hardly understands;
Sitting along the bed's edge, where
You curled the papers from your hair,
Or clasped the yellow soles of feet
In the palms of both soiled hands.

IV

His soul stretched tight across the skies
That fade behind a city block,
Or trampled by insistent feet
At four and five and six o'clock;
And short square fingers stuffing pipes,
And evening newspapers, and eyes
Assured of certain certainties,

The conscience of a blackened street
Impatient to assume the world.

I am moved by fancies that are curled
Around these images, and cling:
The notion of some infinitely gentle
Infinitely suffering thing.

Wipe your hand across your mouth, and laugh;
The worlds revolve like ancient women
Gathering fuel in vacant lots.

Discussion Questions

1. List the images you find in the poem (anything you can imagine with your senses—see, hear, smell, touch, taste). What makes them suggest the speaker has a bleak outlook?
2. How do you think these images compel the speaker to sense something more is going on than what he sees?
3. Why do you think he uses the word "fancies"? What does that reveal about the speaker's own attitude toward religious belief?
4. Have you ever considered the experience of dissatisfaction as an invitation forward into something larger? How might our experience of lacking and of longing for better—whether in school, in personal life, in the world, etc.—be a prelude to some truer reality?

CHAPTER 35

C. S. Lewis

Introduction to "Learning in War-Time"

J. CAMERON MOORE

C. S. Lewis (1898–1963) was a Christian apologist and novelist. He is perhaps best known for his fantasy novel series, the Chronicles of Narnia, and for *Mere Christianity*, an introduction to the Christian faith adapted from BBC radio talks he gave in the 1940s. Although the Chronicles of Narnia are fantasy stories and *Mere Christianity* is a work of apologetics, both attempt to present the basic truths of Christianity in popular forms easily accessible to the general public. By trade, however, Lewis was a professor and taught English literature first at Oxford and later at Cambridge.

The essay below comes from his time at Oxford where, in addition to teaching, he occasionally preached. Lewis delivered this sermon to Oxford students at the University Church of St. Mary the Virgin in October 1939, less than two months after England's declaration of war on Nazi Germany. With Germany's rapid conquest of Poland having occurred just a few weeks earlier, Lewis recognized that the fate of Europe was at stake. Widespread military conscription had gone into effect in the previous month, and in less than a year, German aircraft would be routinely bombing London and other major cities across Great Britain.

In light of such considerations, Lewis asked a question that many of his students were surely asking: Given the precipice from which the world appears to be falling, why continue to study algebra, zoology, and grammar? His answer to that question falls back upon first principles about the kind of world we live in and what God calls Christians to do in such a world. After defending *why* students should still attend classes and turn in their homework during a war, Lewis turned to *how* his audience might go about that work with the sounds of Europe collapsing in the distance.

At the heart of Lewis's argument lies a definition of what it means to be a Christian learner. In college we often talk about faith and learning, but we tend to keep them separate. Required Bible classes and weekly chapel services advance our faith while learning is relegated to Economics 101 and Spanish 204. To suggest that an economics course might have something to do with our faith sounds strange. However, Lewis argued that what makes learning Christian is not the content of the material but the end to which study is directed: the glory of God.

Lewis made it clear that our work in Economics 101, New Testament Theology, and on the custodial staff "become spiritual on precisely the same condition, that of being offered to God." Thus, all of our learning, regardless of the subject, can be a kind of worship where we offer back to God our talents and our labor.

Moreover, Lewis declared that the immediacy of war and potentiality of death differ little from our normal, mundane reality. For Christians, we should always think of what we do in light of our impending death; war just brings this reality closer to the surface. No one is guaranteed to live to graduation or much beyond it. Then again, you may live a hundred years. What comprises a good life remains the same whether you have a year or a century left on earth. If learning is important to the woman who will die an octogenarian, it should also be important to the young man who may be drafted to the front lines.

Learning in War-Time
A sermon preached in the Church of St. Mary the Virgin, Oxford, Autumn 1939

A University is a society for the pursuit of learning. As students, you will be expected to make yourselves, or to start making yourselves, into what the Middle Ages called clerks: into philosophers, scientists, scholars, critics, or historians. And at first sight this seems to be an odd thing to do during a great war. What is the use of beginning a task which we have so little chance of finishing? Or, even if we ourselves should happen not to be interrupted by death or military service, why should we—indeed how can we—continue to take an interest in these placid occupations when the lives of our friends and the liberties of Europe are in the balance? Is it not like fiddling while Rome burns? Now it seems to me that we shall not be able to answer these questions until we have put them by the side of certain other questions which every Christian ought to have asked himself in peace-time. I spoke just now of fiddling while Rome burns. But to a Christian the true tragedy of Nero must be not that he fiddles while the city was on fire but that he fiddles on the brink of hell. You must forgive me for the crude monosyllable. I know that many wiser and better Christians than I in these days do not like to mention heaven and hell even in a pulpit. I know, too, that nearly all the references to this subject in the New Testament come from a single source. But then that source is Our Lord Himself. People will tell you it is St. Paul, but that is untrue. These overwhelming doctrines are dominical. They are not really removable from the teaching of Christ or of His Church. If we do not believe them, our presence in this church is great tomfoolery. If we do, we must sometime overcome our spiritual prudery and mention them. The moment we do so we can see that every Christian who comes to a university must at all times face a question compared with which the questions raised by the war are relatively unimportant. He must ask himself how it is right, or even psychologically possible, for creatures who are every moment advancing either to heaven or to hell, to spend any fraction of the little time allowed them in this world on such comparative trivialities as literature or art, mathematics or biology. If human culture can stand up to that, it can stand up to anything. To admit that we can retain our interest in learning under the shadow of these eternal issues, but not under the shadow of a European war, would be to admit that our ears are closed to the voice of reason and very wide open to the voice of our nerves and our mass emotions.

This indeed is the case with most of us: certainly with me. For that reason I think it important to try to see the present calamity in a true perspective, the war creates no absolutely new situation: it simply aggravates the permanent human situation so that we can no longer ignore it. Human life has always been lived on the edge of a precipice. Human culture has always had to exist under the shadow of something infinitely more important than itself. If men had postponed the search for knowledge and beauty until they were secure the search would never have begun. We are mistaken when we compare war with "normal life." Life has never been normal. Even those periods which we think most tranquil, like the nineteenth century, turn out, on closer inspection, to be full of cries, alarms, difficulties, emergencies. Plausible reasons have never been lacking for putting off all merely cultural activities until some imminent danger has been averted or some crying injustice put right. But humanity long ago chose to neglect those plausible reasons. They wanted knowledge and beauty now, and would not wait for the suitable moment that never comes. Periclean Athens leaves us not only the Parthenon but, significantly, the Funeral Oration. The insects have chosen a different line: they have sought first the material welfare and security of the hive, and presumably they have their reward. Men are different. They propound mathematical theorems in beleaguered cities, conduct metaphysical arguments in condemned cells, make jokes on scaffold, discuss the last new poem while advancing to the walls of Quebec, and comb their hair at Thermopylae. This is not panache; it is our nature.

But since we are fallen creatures, the fact that this is now our nature would not, by itself, prove that it is rational or right. We have to inquire whether there is really any legitimate place for the activities of the scholar in a world such as this. That is, we have always to answer the question: "How can you be so frivolous and selfish as to think about anything but the salvation of human souls?" and we have, at the moment, to answer the additional question, "How can you be so frivolous and selfish as to think of anything but the war?" Now part of our answer will be the same for both questions. The one implies that our life can, and ought, to become exclusively and explicitly religious: the other, that it can and ought to become exclusively national. I believe that our whole life can, and indeed must, become religious in a sense to be explained later. But if it is meant that all our activities are to be of the kind that can be recognized as "sacred" and ties are to be of the kind that can be recognized as "sacred" and opposed to "secular," then I would give a single reply to both my imaginary assailants. I would say, "Whether it ought to happen or not, the thing you are recommending is not going to happen." Before I became a Christian I do not think I fully realized that one's life, after conversion, would inevitably consist in doing most of the same things one had been doing before: one hopes, in a new spirit, but still the same things. Before I went to the last war I certainly expected that my life in the trenches would, in some mysterious sense, be all war. In fact, I found that the nearer you got to the front line the less everyone spoke and thought of the allied cause and the progress of the campaign; and I am pleased to find that Tolstoy, in the greatest war book ever written, records the same thing—and so, in its own way, does the Iliad. Neither conversion nor enlistment in the army is really going to obliterate our human life. Christians and soldiers are still men: the infidel's idea of a religious life, and the civilian's idea of active service, are fantastic. If you attempted, in either case, to suspend your whole intellectual and aesthetic activity, you would only succeed in substituting a worse cultural life for a better. You are not, in fact, going to read nothing, either in the Church or in the line: if you don't read good books you will read bad ones. If you don't go on thinking rationally, you will think irrationally. If you reject aesthetic satisfactions, you will fall into sensual satisfactions. There is therefore this analogy between the claims of our religion and the claims of the war: neither of them for most of us, will simply cancel or remove from the slate the merely human life which we were leading before we entered them. But they will operate in this way for different reasons. The war will fail to absorb our whole attention because it is a finite object, and therefore intrinsically unfitted to support the whole attention of a human soul. In order to avoid misunderstanding I must here make a few distinctions. I believe our cause to be, as human causes go, very righteous, and I therefore believe it to be a duty to participate in this war. And every duty is a religious duty, and our obligation to perform every duty is therefore absolute. Thus we may have a duty to rescue a drowning man, and perhaps, if we live on a dangerous coast, to learn life-saving so as to be ready for any drowning man when he turns up. It may be our duty to lose our own lives in saving him. But if anyone devoted himself to life-saving in the sense of giving it his total attention—so that he thought and spoke of nothing else and demanded the cessation of all other human activities until everyone had learned to swim—he would be a monomaniac. The rescue of drowning men is, then, a duty worth dying for, but not worth living for. It seems to me that all political duties (among which I include military duties) are of this kind. A man may have to die for our country: but no man must, in any exclusive sense, live for his country. He who surrenders himself without reservation to the temporal claims of a nation, or a party, or a class is rendering to Caesar that which, of all things, most emphatically belongs to God: himself. It is for a very different reason that religion cannot occupy the whole of life in the sense of excluding all our natural activities. For, of course, in some sense, it must occupy the whole of life. There is no question of a compromise between the claims of God and the claims of culture, or politics, or anything else. God's claim is infinite and inexorable. You can refuse it: or you can begin to try to grant it. There is no middle way. Yet in spite of this it is clear that Christianity does not exclude any of the ordinary human activities. St. Paul tells people to get on with their jobs. He even assumes that Christians may go to dinner parties, and, what is more, dinner parties given by pagans. Our Lord attends a wedding and provides miraculous wine. Under the aegis of His Church, and in the most Christian ages, learning and the arts flourish. The solution of this paradox is, of course, well known to you. "Whether ye eat or drink or whatsoever ye do, do all to the glory of God." All our merely natural activities will be accepted, if they are offered to God, even the humblest: and all of them, even the noblest, will be sinful if they are not. Christianity does not simply replace our natural life and substitute a new one: it is rather a new organization which exploits, to its own supernatural ends, these natural materials. No doubt, in a given situation, it demands the surrender of some, or all, our merely human pursuits: it is better to be saved with one eye, than, having two, to be cast into Gehenna. But it does this, in a sense, *per accidens*—because, in those special circumstances, it has ceased to be possible to practice this or that activity to the glory of God. There is no essential quarrel between the spiritual life and the human activities as such. Thus the omnipresence of obedience to God in a Christian's life is, in a way, analogous to the omnipresence of God in space. God does not fill space as a body fills it, in the sense that parts of Him are in different parts of space, excluding other objects from them. Yet He is everywhere—totally present at every point of space—according to good theologians.

We are now in a position to answer the view that human culture is an inexcusable frivolity on the part of creatures loaded with such awful responsibilities as we. I reject at once an idea which lingers in the mind of some modern people that cultural activities are in their own right spiritual and meritorious—as though scholars and poets were intrinsically more pleasing to God than scavengers and bootblacks. I think it was Matthew Arnold who first used the

English word *spiritual* in the sense of the German *geistlich*, and so inaugurated this most dangerous and most anti-Christian error. Let us clear it forever from our minds. The work of a Beethoven, and the work of a charwoman, become spiritual on precisely the same condition, that of being offered to God, of being done humbly "as to the Lord." This does not, of course, mean that it is for anyone a mere toss-up whether he should sweep rooms or compose symphonies. A mole must dig to the glory of God and a cock must crow. We are members of one body, but differentiated members, each with his own vocation. A man's upbringing, his talents, his circumstances, are usually a tolerable index of his vocation. If our parents have sent us to Oxford, if our country allows us to remain there, this is prima facie evidence that the life which we, at any rate, can best lead to the glory of God at present is the learned life.

By leading that life to the glory of God I do not, of course, mean any attempt to make our intellectual inquiries work out to edifying conclusions. That would be, as Bacon says, to offer to the author of truth the unclean sacrifice of a lie. I mean the pursuit of knowledge and beauty, in a sense, for their own sake, but in a sense which does not exclude their being for God's sake. An appetite for these things exists in the human mind, and God makes no appetite in vain. We can therefore pursue knowledge as such, and beauty, as such, in the sure confidence that by so doing we are either advancing to the vision of God ourselves or indirectly helping others to do so. Humility, no less than the appetite, encourages us to concentrate simply on the knowledge or the beauty, not too much concerning ourselves with their ultimate relevance to the vision of God. That relevance may not be intended for us but for our betters—for men who come after and find the spiritual significance of what we dug out in blind and humble obedience to our vocation. This is the teleological argument that the existence of the impulse and the faculty prove that they must have a proper function in God's scheme—the argument by which Thomas Aquinas probes that sexuality would have existed even without the Fall. The soundness of the argument, as regards culture, is proved by experience. The intellectual life is not the only road to God, nor the safest, but we find it to be a road, and it may be the appointed road for us. Of course, it will be so only so long as we keep the impulse pure and disinterested. That is the great difficulty. As the author of the *Theologia Germanica* says, we may come to love knowledge—our knowing—more than the thing known: to delight not in the exercise of our talents but in the fact that they are ours, or even in the reputation they bring us. Every success in the scholar's life increases this danger. If it becomes irresistible, he must give up his scholarly work. The time for plucking out the right eye has arrived.

That is the essential nature of the learned life as I see it. But it has indirect values which are especially important today. If all the world were Christian, it might not matter if all the world were uneducated. But, as it is, a cultural life will exist outside the Church whether it exists inside or not. To be ignorant and simple now—not to be able to meet the enemies on their own ground—would be to throw down our weapons, and betray our uneducated brethren who have, under God, no defense but us against the intellectual attacks of the heathen. Good philosophy must exist, if for no other reason, because bad philosophy needs to be answered. The cool intellect must work not only against cool intellect on the other side, but against the muddy heathen mysticisms which deny intellect altogether.

Most of all, perhaps we need intimate knowledge of the past. Not that the past has any magic about it, but because we cannot study the future, and yet need something to set against the present, to remind us that periods and that much which seems certain to the uneducated is merely temporary fashion. A man who has lived in many places is not likely to be deceived by the local errors of his native village: the scholar has lived in many times and is therefore in some degree immune from the great cataract of nonsense that pours from the press and the microphone of his own age.

The learned life then is, for some, a duty. At the moment it looks as if it were your duty. I am well aware that there may seem to be an almost comic discrepancy between the high issues we have been considering and the immediate task you may be set down to, such as Anglo-Saxon sound laws or chemical formulae. But there is a similar shock awaiting us in every vocation—a young priest finds himself involved in choir treats and a young subaltern in accounting for pots of jam. It is well that it should be so. It weeds out the vain, windy people and keeps in those who are both humble and tough. On that kind of difficulty we need waste no sympathy.

But the peculiar difficulty imposed on you by the war is another matter: and of it I would again repeat, what I have been saying in one form or another ever since I started—do not let your nerves and emotions lead you into thinking your present predicament more abnormal than it really is. Perhaps it may be useful to mention the three mental exercises which may serve as defenses against the three enemies which war raises up against the scholar. The first enemy is excitement—the tendency to think and feel about the war when we had intended to think about our work. The best defense is a recognition that in this, as in everything else, the war has not really raised up a new enemy but only aggravated an old one. There are always plenty of rivals to our work. We are always falling in love or quarreling, looking for jobs or fearing to lose them, getting ill and recovering, following public affairs. If we let ourselves, we shall always be waiting for some distraction or other to end before we can really get down to our work. The only people who achieve much are those who want knowledge so badly that they seek it while the conditions are still unfavorable. Favorable conditions never come. There are, of course, moments when the pressure of the excitement is so great that any superhuman self-control could not resist it. They come both in war and peace. We must do the best we can.

The second enemy is frustration—the feeling that we shall not have time to finish. If I say to you that no one has time to finish, that the longest human life leaves a man, in any branch of learning, a beginner, I shall seem to you to be saying something quite academic and theoretical. You would be surprised if you knew how soon one begins to feel the shortness of the tether: of how many things, even in middle life, we have to say "No time for that," "Too late now," and "Not for me." But Nature herself forbids you to share that experience. A more Christian attitude, which can be attained at any age, is that of leaving futurity in God's hands. We may as well, for God will certainly retain it whether we leave it to Him or not. Never, in peace or war, commit your virtue or your happiness to the future. Happy work is best done by the man who takes his long-term plans somewhat lightly and works from moment to moment "as to the Lord." It is only our daily bread that we are encouraged to ask for. The present is the only time in which any duty can be done or any grace received.

The third enemy is fear. War threatens us with death and pain. No man—and specially no Christian who remembers Gethsemane—need try to attain a stoic indifference about these things: but we can guard against the illusions of the imagination. We think of the streets of Warsaw and contrast the deaths there suffered with an abstraction called Life. But there is no question of death or life for any of us; only a question of this death or of that—of a machine gun bullet now or a cancer forty years later. What does war do to death? It certainly does not make it more frequent; 100 per cent of us die, and the percentage cannot be increased. It puts several deaths earlier; but I hardly suppose that that is what we fear. Certainly when the moment comes, it will make little difference how many years we have behind us. Does it increase our chance of a painful death? I doubt it. As far as I can find out, what we call natural death is usually preceded by suffering; and a battlefield is one of the very few places where one has a reasonable prospect of dying with no pain at all. Does it decrease our chances of dying at peace with God? I cannot believe it. If active service does not persuade a man to prepare for death, what conceivable concatenation of circumstance would? Yet war does do something to death. It forces us to remember it. The only reason why the cancer at sixty or the paralysis at seventy-five do not bother us is that we forget them. War makes death real to us: and that would have been regarded as one of its blessings by most of the great Christians of the past. They thought it good for us to be always aware of our mortality. I am inclined to think they were right.

All the animal life in us, all schemes of happiness that centered in this world, were always doomed to a final frustration. In ordinary times only a wise man can realize it. Now the stupidest of us know. We see unmistakable the sort of universe in which we have all along been living, and must come to terms with it. If we had foolish un-Christian hopes about human culture, they are now shattered. If we thought we were building up a heaven on earth, if we looked for something that would turn the present world from a place of pilgrimage into a permanent city satisfying the soul of man, we are disillusioned, and not a moment too soon. But if we thought that for some souls, and at some times, the life of learning, humbly offered to God, was, in its own small way, one of the appointed approaches to the Divine reality and the Divine beauty which we hope to enjoy hereafter, we can think so still.

Discussion Questions

1. At the beginning of the essay, Lewis broadened the context from college students in wartime to all Christians at all times. What arguments did he use to support that widening of focus?
2. How might our particular work in college be done "as to the Lord," according to Lewis? What qualities ought to define the Christian scholar?
3. How might this essay change the way you approach your own classes, especially those you don't particularly like?
4. Lewis identified excitement, frustration, and fear as three enemies of study that his audience must resist. What did Lewis mean by each of those terms? Are they still relevant for college students in the twenty-first century? If so, how?
5. What other distractions must contemporary students confront in their learning?

CHAPTER 36

Dietrich Bonhoeffer

Introduction to *Life Together*

DAVID I. SMITH

You open a slim volume by a German theologian who died opposing Hitler in 1945. It's a classic. It's about community and learning. The author is one of the most important thinkers of the twentieth century, but this book starts with a Bible verse—not a particularly philosophical Bible verse, at that. It's one of those verses that rolls easily off the tongue. "Behold, how good and how pleasant it is for brethren to dwell together in unity!" (Ps. 133:1 KJV). Your mind starts fishing for familiar maps to orient you. Perhaps it's one of those sermons about how important community is, about getting along and experiencing warm fellowship, about being nice. Perhaps you glow faintly in anticipation or roll your eyes in reflexive cynicism.

By the fourth sentence—if you are reading closely, following the author's thoughts instead of just overlaying your own—he has headed in a surprising direction. If you persevere with the book, this will not be the last time he raises a familiar topic and then catches you dancing to the wrong beat. Living among other Christians is a privilege, not a right. Jesus lived among enemies and died alone for the sake of their peace. Christians should follow. (Soon after writing this, Bonhoeffer will be in prison, in solitary confinement. He'll die there. Alone.) We're not ten lines in, and this book is already sterner than it looked, despite the jolly opening line.

In the time between the cross and the end, Bonhoeffer continues, grace allows Christians to live in community with other Christians. They get to take joy and comfort from one another. The presence of another Christian is a "physical sign of the gracious presence of the triune God." Okay, that's a big thought (file it for class discussion), but at least we're back to counting our blessings. You relax a little. Too soon.

"Christian community means community through Jesus Christ and in Jesus Christ. There is no Christian community that is more than this and none that is less than this." Bonhoeffer being Bonhoeffer, he offers you a dense thought and keeps needling you to think it through. If this is true, then Christian community is not based on liking the same things, sharing the same politics, being from the same ethnic background, living in the same place, liking one

233

another, or feeling a sense of fellowship. Those are other kinds of community. Christian community is through and in Christ. Nothing more, nothing less. It's not about hanging out with those you like. It's not about attraction. It's not about your tribe.

You start to realize that this is not an easy word. The other in whom you are to take joy and comfort, who is a gracious sign of God's presence to you, may not be the one you enjoy. Perhaps it's the student next to you in class with the wrong politics. Or the professor you don't quite agree with. Maybe it's the stern German theologian you were made to read. You realize that Bonhoeffer is not asking you to rejoice in warm feelings of fellowship. He is calling you to discipline yourself in thankfulness so you can live with those whom God called when you wouldn't have. He wants you to read closely and think in unfamiliar ways about familiar ideas. He wants you to join him in living Christian community as a demanding practice, not a warm ideal, within the very process of your studies.

From *Life Together*[1]

"Behold, how good and how pleasant it is for brethren to dwell together in unity!" (Ps. 133:1). In the following we shall consider a number of directions and precepts that the Scriptures provide us for our life together under the Word.

It is not simply to be taken for granted that the Christian has the privilege of living among other Christians. Jesus Christ lived in the midst of his enemies. At the end all his disciples deserted him. On the Cross he was utterly alone, surrounded by evildoers and mockers. For this cause he had come, to bring peace to the enemies of God. So the Christian, too, belongs not in the seclusion of a cloistered life but in the thick of foes. There is his commission, his work. "The Kingdom is to be in the midst of your enemies. And he who will not suffer this does not want to be of the Kingdom of Christ; he wants to be among friends, to sit among roses and lilies, not with the bad people but the devout people. O you blasphemers and betrayers of Christ! If Christ had done what you are doing who would ever have been spared?" (Luther).

"I will sow them among the people: and they shall remember me in far countries" (Zech. 10:9). According to God's will Christendom is a scattered people, scattered like seed "into all the kingdoms of the earth" (Deut. 28:25). That is its curse and its promise. God's people must dwell in far countries among the unbelievers, but it will be the seed of the Kingdom of God in all the world.

"I will . . . gather them; for I have redeemed them: . . . and they shall return" (Zech. 10:8, 9). When will that happen? It has happened in Jesus Christ, who

---

1. Dietrich Bonhoeffer, *Life Together*, trans. John W. Doberstein (New York: Harper & Row, 1954).

died "that he should gather together in one the children of God that were scattered abroad" (John 11:52), and it will finally occur visibly at the end of time when the angels of God "shall gather together his elect from the four winds, from one end of heaven to the other" (Matt. 24:31). Until then, God's people remain scattered, held together solely in Jesus Christ, having become one in the fact that, dispersed among unbelievers, they remember Him in the far countries.

So between the death of Christ and the Last Day it is only by a gracious anticipation of the last things that Christians are privileged to live in visible fellowship with other Christians. It is by the grace of God that a congregation is permitted to gather visibly in this world to share God's Word and sacrament. Not all Christians receive this blessing. The imprisoned, the sick, the scattered lonely, the proclaimers of the Gospel in heathen lands stand alone. They know that visible fellowship is a blessing. They remember, as the Psalmist did, how they went "with the multitude . . . to the house of God, with the voice of joy and praise, with a multitude that kept holyday" (Ps. 42:4). But they remain alone in far countries, a scattered seed according to God's will. Yet what is denied them as an actual experience they seize upon more fervently in faith. Thus the exiled disciple of the Lord, John the Apocalyptist, celebrates in the loneliness of Patmos the heavenly worship with his congregations "in the Spirit on the Lord's day" (Rev. 1:10). He sees the seven candlesticks, his congregations, the seven stars, the angels of the congregations, and in the midst and above it all the Son of Man, Jesus Christ, in all the splendor of the resurrection. He strengthens and fortifies him by His Word. This is the heavenly fellowship, shared by the exile on the day of his Lord's resurrection.

The physical presence of other Christians is a source of incomparable joy and strength to the believer. Longingly, the imprisoned apostle Paul calls his "dearly beloved son in the faith," Timothy, to come to him in prison in the last days of his life; he would see him again and have him near. Paul has not forgotten the tears Timothy shed when last they parted (II Tim. 1:4). Remembering the congregation in Thessalonica, Paul prays "night and day . . . exceedingly that we might see your face" (I Thess. 3:10). The aged John knows that his joy will not be full until he can come to his own people and speak face to face instead of writing with ink (II John 12).

The believer feels no shame, as though he were still living too much in the flesh, when he yearns for the physical presence of other Christians. Man was created a body, the Son of God appeared on earth in the body, he was raised in the body, in the sacrament the believer receives the Lord Christ in the body, and the resurrection of the dead will bring about the perfected fellowship of God's spiritual physical creatures. The believer therefore lauds the Creator, the Redeemer, God, Father, Son and Holy Spirit, for the bodily presence of a brother. The prisoner, the sick person, the Christian in exile sees in the companionship of a fellow Christian a physical sign of the gracious presence of the triune God. Visitor and visited in loneliness recognize in each other the Christ who is present in the body; they receive and meet each other as one meets the Lord, in reverence, humility, and joy. They receive each other's benedictions as the benediction of the Lord Jesus Christ. But if there is so much blessing and joy even in a single encounter of brother with brother, how inexhaustible are the riches that open up for those who by God's will are privileged to live in the daily fellowship of life with other Christians!

It is true, of course, that what is an unspeakable gift of God for the lonely individual is easily disregarded and trodden under foot by those who have the gift every day. It is easily forgotten that the fellowship of Christian brethren is a gift of grace, a gift of the Kingdom of God that any day may be taken from us, that the time that still separates us from utter loneliness may be brief indeed. Therefore, let him who until now has had the privilege of living a common Christian life with other Christians praise God's grace from the bottom of his heart. Let him thank God on his knees and declare: It is grace, nothing but grace, that we are allowed to live in community with Christian brethren.

The measure with which God bestows the gift of visible community is varied. The Christian in exile is comforted by a brief visit of a Christian brother, a prayer together and a brother's blessing; indeed, he is strengthened by a letter written by the hand of a Christian. The greetings in the letters written with Paul's own hand were doubtless tokens of such community. Others are given the gift of common worship on Sundays. Still others have the privilege of living a Christian life in the fellowship of their families. Seminarians before their ordination receive the gift of common life with their brethren for a definite period. Among earnest Christians in the Church today there is a growing desire to meet together with other Christians in the rest periods of their work for common life under the Word. Communal life is again being recognized by Christians today as the grace that it is, as the extraordinary, the "roses and lilies" of the Christian life.

Through and in Jesus Christ

Christianity means community through Jesus Christ and in Jesus Christ. No Christian community is more or less than this. Whether it be a brief, single encounter or the daily fellowship of years, Christian community is only this. We belong to one another only through and in Jesus Christ. What does this mean? It means, first, that a Christian needs others because of Jesus Christ. It means, second, that a Christian comes to others only through Jesus Christ. It means, third, that in Jesus Christ we have been chosen from eternity, accepted in time, and united for eternity.

Discussion Questions

1. How might you have started a book about Christian community? What does your answer reveal about how you think about community?
2. Why might a theologian writing in Germany in 1939 be thinking about how Christian community is not based on things like ethnicity? How is this thought still relevant?
3. Do you think of the people around you in your classes as members of a community for whom you are called to care? How does this work itself out in your learning practices?
4. What happens to how you read a text like this if you think of its author as your neighbor?

CHAPTER 37

Simone Weil

Introduction to "Reflections on the Right Use of School Studies with a View to the Love of God"

PAUL J. CONTINO

Many of us live tethered to an iPhone. To the extent that the device provides easy access to information and connection to others, it is a blessing. But as an easy portal to instant gratification and infinite distraction, it is also a curse. In recent years, numerous studies point up our diminishing capacity to pay attention. Even longtime readers confess that they are less likely to read long, complex works. People are less rooted in religious traditions and communal practices, and report being lonelier and more anxious and depressed. In 1942 French religious and social thinker Simone Weil wrote an essay in which both students and teachers can find a beacon of hope, a spur toward renewing their practice of attention through their quotidian "school studies."

Weil argued that individuals' silent, solitary attention to their schoolwork and scholarship can foster their capacity to fulfill Christ's twofold commandment: to love God fully and to love our neighbor as we love ourselves (Luke 10:27). Provocatively, she claimed that becoming more attentive to God and others "forms the real object and almost the sole interest of studies." Yes, we must strive to do each academic task well, as a good in itself. But our "deep purpose" must be to sustain our attentive work "with a view to prayer." Such purposeful practice will intensify our love for the subject for, as Weil insisted, the "joy of learning is as indispensable in study as breathing is in running."

Even those subjects that don't *immediately* interest us can become occasions to practice attention and offer a path toward the human *telos*—our ultimate objective—to love God and love neighbor. This transcendent *telos* need not eclipse a rapt, receptive focus on the subject itself. But such focus can never be greedily instrumental. Rather, as Weil emphasized, attention is marked by nonattachment: students empty themselves of the desire for high grades, recognition, or success. Attention to a task itself—be it a geometry problem, chemistry experiment, or analysis of a Shakespeare sonnet—entails "waiting, not seeking anything, . . . ready to receive in its naked truth the object [or, we might say, the *subject*] that is to penetrate it." The "negative effort" entailed in attention bears an affinity to the Taoist notion of *wu wei*: action that is nonaction, or put another way, action that is patient, committed, and willing, never rushed nor willful.

Weil had a deep affinity to Asian religions and was herself raised in a Jewish family. But her vision remained deeply Christian. When she described that final fruit of attentive study—our capacity to fully attend to another person—she claimed that "the soul empties itself of all its own contents in order to receive into itself the being it is looking at, just as he is, in all his truth." "Make your mind like that of Christ," Saint Paul exhorted the Philippians, for in Christ's incarnation, his acceptance of death on the cross, he "emptied himself" (2:2–8). Our study can bear fruit in charity, by which we may participate in Christ's *kenosis*, his self-emptying.

Written about a year before Weil's death, her essay is the fruit of her own arduous efforts as both teacher and student. In her words and actions, she could be extreme. In 1943, while relatively safe in England, she stood in stubborn solidarity with her fellow French who had little food. Refusing to eat, she fell mortally ill. Simone Weil may not herself have modeled what we call a "balanced" life. But in her single-minded, persevering focus on the cruciform reality of God's love, many have found in her "a saint for our time." Her essay makes a compelling case that in our daily practice of studious attention, we may find a pearl of great price.

From "Reflections on the Right Use of School Studies with a View to the Love of God"

This was probably written by Simone Weil in April 1942 and sent to Father Perrin when he was superior of the Dominicans of Montpellier, in order to help the Catholic students with whom he was in contact.

The key to a Christian conception of studies is the realisation that prayer consists of attention. It is the orientation of all the attention of which the soul is capable towards God. The quality of attention counts for much in the quality of the prayer. Warmth of heart cannot make up for it.

It is the highest part of the attention only which makes contact with God, when prayer is intense and pure enough for such a contact to be established; but the whole attention is turned towards God.

Of course school exercises only develop a lower kind of attention. Nevertheless they are extremely effective in increasing the power of attention which will be available at the time of prayer, on condition that they are carried out with a view to this purpose and this purpose alone.

Although people seem to be unaware of it to-day, the development of the faculty of attention forms the real object and almost the sole interest of studies. Most school tasks have a certain intrinsic interest as well, but such an interest is secondary. All tasks which really call upon the power of attention are interesting for the same reason and to an almost equal degree.

School children and students who love God should never say: "For my part I like mathematics"; "I like French"; "I like Greek." They should learn to like all these subjects, because all of them develop that faculty of attention which, directed towards God, is the very substance of prayer.

If we have no aptitude or natural taste for geometry, this does not mean that our faculty for attention will not be developed by wrestling with a problem or studying a theorem. On the contrary, it is almost an advantage.

It does not even matter much whether we succeed in finding the solution or understanding the proof, although it is important to try really hard to do so. Never in any case whatever is a genuine effort of the attention wasted. It always has its effect on the spiritual plane and in consequence on the lower one of the intelligence, for all spiritual light lightens the mind.

If we concentrate our attention on trying to solve a problem of geometry, and if at the end of an hour we are no nearer to doing so than at the beginning, we have nevertheless been making progress each minute of that hour in another more mysterious dimension. Without our knowing or feeling it, this apparently barren effort has brought more light into the soul. The result will one day be discovered in prayer. Moreover it may very likely be felt besides in some department of the intelligence in no way connected with mathematics. Perhaps he who made the unsuccessful effort will one day be able to grasp the beauty of a line of *Racine* more vividly on account of it. But it is certain that this effort will bear its fruit in prayer. There is no doubt whatever about that.

Students must therefore work without any wish to gain good marks, to pass examinations, to win school successes; without any reference to their natural abilities and tastes; applying themselves equally to all their tasks, with the idea that each one will help to form in them the habit of that attention which is the substance of prayer. When we set out to do a piece of work, it is necessary to wish to do it correctly, because such a wish is indispensable if there is to be true effort. Underlying this immediate objective, however, our deep purpose should aim solely at increasing the power of attention with a view to prayer; as, when we write, we draw the shape of the letter on paper, not with a view to the shape, but with a view to the idea we want to express. To make this the sole and exclusive purpose of our studies is the first condition to be observed if we are to put them to the right use.

The second condition is to take great pains to examine squarely and to contemplate attentively and slowly each school task in which we have failed, seeing how unpleasing and second-rate it is, without seeking any excuse or overlooking any mistake or any of our tutor's corrections, trying to get down to the origin of each fault. There is a great temptation to do the opposite, to give a sideways glance at the corrected exercise if it is bad, and to hide it forthwith. Most of us do this nearly always. We have to withstand this temptation. Incidentally, moreover, nothing is more necessary for academic success, because, despite all our efforts, we work without making much progress when we refuse to give our attention to the faults we have made and our tutor's corrections.

This way of looking is first of all attentive. The soul empties itself of all its own contents in order to receive into itself the being it is looking at, just as he is, in all his truth.

Only he who is capable of attention can do this.

So it comes about that, paradoxical as it may seem, a Latin prose or a geometry problem, even though they are done wrong, may be of great service one day, provided we devote the right kind of effort to them. Should the occasion arise, they can one day make us better able to give someone in affliction exactly the help required to save him, at the supreme moment of his need.

For an adolescent, capable of grasping this truth and generous enough to desire this fruit above all others, studies could have their fullest spiritual effect, quite apart from any particular religious belief.

Academic work is one of those fields which contain a pearl so precious that it is worth while to sell all our possessions, keeping nothing for ourselves, in order to be able to acquire it.

Discussion Questions

1. Weil insisted that school studies be "carried out with a view to this purpose and to this purpose alone": the love of God in prayer and the love of the afflicted neighbor. But how can we focus fully on a particular task of study if we're "viewing" ahead to this transcendent goal?

2. When you examine the mistakes you've made in an exam, or your teacher's comments in an essay, how do you respond? How might Weil invite an alternative response?

3. Studious attention is marked by willing receptivity, not willful "muscular effort" or "frowning application." Can you recall moments in which you felt a sense of complete, seemingly effortless immersion while engaged in an artistic or athletic activity—a state of "flow" or being "in the zone."

Describe this experience, and then ask, *Have I experienced this in my studies? Could I?*

4. How is the "faithful waiting" that Weil insisted is integral to genuine study different from simple procrastination? Reflect on an example from your experience.

5. To give another person full attention, Weil says that our soul must empty "itself of all its own contents in order" to be fully receptive to the other person. What, specifically, must we empty ourselves of? How does such self-emptying make us fully present and attentive?

CHAPTER 38

Dorothy L. Sayers

Introduction to "The Lost Tools of Learning"
GINA DALFONZO

For Dorothy L. Sayers, Christianity was first and foremost a religion of the mind. This was the highest compliment she could have paid to Christianity. Sayers wrote to one correspondent, "I am quite incapable of 'religious emotion,'" and went on to explain, "Since I cannot come at God through intuition, or through my emotions, or through my 'inner light' (except in the unendearing form of judgement and conviction of sin) there is only the intellect left.... I do not know whether we can be saved by the intellect, but I do know that I can be saved by nothing else."[1]

Sayers wasn't arguing for a faith based solely on logic and reason. Nor was she trying to advocate some elite version of the faith that could be understood by only a few geniuses. Rather, she was making the case that to genuinely appreciate and grasp, or at least begin to grasp, the beauty and profundity of the Christian faith, one must bring the intellect into play.

Sayers battled her whole life against propaganda, muddled thinking, subpar educational methods, and all else that threatened to distort the mind's perception of God and faith. Although best known for her Lord Peter Wimsey mystery novels, Sayers also had a significant career as an apologist, producing books, essays, and plays designed to elucidate the truths of the faith for people who lived in a supposedly Christian culture but had never learned the basics of Christianity.

Although she found it annoying and time-consuming, Sayers corresponded with and debated critics of Christianity because she could not resist the urge to straighten out their misunderstandings of the faith. In a letter to her good friend C. S. Lewis, she lamented, "God is simply taking advantage of the fact that I can't stand intellectual chaos, and it isn't fair."[2]

This is the context in which Sayers wrote and delivered her essay "The Lost Tools of Learning" at Oxford University in 1947. She wanted to get to the root of the problems she saw in her culture: people being far too easily misled,

---

1. Dorothy L. Sayers, *The Letters of Dorothy Sayers*, ed. Barbara Reynolds, vol. 4 (Bloomington: Indiana University Press, 1995), 137.
2. Sayers, *Letters*, 2:413.

unable to formulate a rational argument, or even write a coherent sentence. And she thought that the way to do that was to go back to the educational system, where the trouble began, and make some major changes. Actually, she wanted to tear it up and start over again, but she knew that would never happen! Still, she seized the opportunity to lay out her desired model, based on educational practices of the Middle Ages, in which students were taught the methods for learning new subjects before being taught the subjects themselves. Once children were given the tools to learn, Sayers explained, the world of learning would open up to them and they would possess the ability to grapple with subjects of all kinds.

Wishful thinking? Perhaps. But Sayers's essay has remained popular ever since, suggesting that she was not the only one who felt this way. In fact, the ideas she expressed were so influential that many schools and educators use versions of her model today and point to her essay as their inspiration. For anyone who loves to learn—and for anyone who wants to learn to love God with all their mind—her talk is valuable reading.

From "The Lost Tools of Learning"

That I, whose experience of teaching is extremely limited, and whose life of recent years has been almost wholly out of touch with educational circles, should presume to discuss education is a matter, surely, that calls for no apology. It is a kind of behaviour to which the present climate of opinion is wholly favourable. Bishops air their opinions about economics; biologists, about metaphysics; celibates, about matrimony; inorganic chemists about theology; the most irrelevant people are appointed to highly-technical ministries; and plain, blunt men write to the papers to say that Epstein and Picasso do not know how to draw. Up to a certain point, and provided that the criticisms are made with a reasonable modesty, these activities are commendable. Too much specialisation is not a good thing. There is also one excellent reason why the veriest amateur may feel entitled to have an opinion about education. For if we are not all professional teachers, we have all, at some time or other, been taught. Even if we learnt nothing—perhaps in particular if we learnt nothing—our contribution to the discussion may have a potential value.

If we are to produce a society of educated people, fitted to preserve their intellectual freedom amid the complex pressures of our modern society, we must turn back the wheel of progress some four or five hundred years, to the point at which education began to lose sight of its true object, towards the end of the Middle Ages.

Has it ever struck you as odd, or unfortunate, that to-day, when the proportion of literacy throughout Western Europe is higher than it has ever been, people should have become susceptible to the influence of advertisement and mass-propaganda to an extent hitherto unheard-of and unimagined? . . . do you some-times have an uneasy suspicion that the product of modern educational methods is less good than he or she might be at disentangling fact from opinion and the proven from the plausible?

Have you ever, in listening to a debate among adult and presumably responsible people, been fretted by the extraordinary inability of the average debater to speak to the question, or to meet and refute the arguments of speakers on the other side? . . .

Have you ever followed a discussion in the newspapers or elsewhere and noticed how frequently writers fail to define the terms they use? . . .

Have you ever been faintly troubled by the amount of slipshod syntax going about? . . . Do you ever find that young people, when they have left school, not only forget most of what they have learnt (that is only to be expected) but forget also, or betray that they have never really known, how to tackle a new subject for themselves?

Are you often bothered by coming across grown-up men and women who seem unable to distinguish between a book that is sound, scholarly and prop-erly documented, and one that is to any trained eye, very conspicuously none of these things?

Now the first thing we notice [in the education of the Middle Ages] is that . . . the whole of the Trivium was in fact intended to teach the pupil the proper use of the tools of learning, before he began to apply them to "subjects" at all. First, he learned a language: not just how to order a meal in a foreign language, but the structure of language—a language–and hence of language itself—what it was, how it was put together and how it worked. Secondly, he learned how to use language: how to define his terms and make accurate statements; how to con-struct an argument and how to detect fallacies in argument (his own arguments and other people's). Dialectic, that is to say, embraced Logic and Disputation. Thirdly, he learned to express himself in language: how to say what he had to say elegantly and persuasively. At this point, any tendency to express himself windily or to use his eloquence so as to make the worse appear the better reason would, no doubt, be restrained by his previous teaching in Dialectic. If not, his teacher and his fellow-pupils, trained along the same lines, would be quick to point out where he was wrong; for it was they whom he had to seek to persuade. At the end of his course, he was required to compose a thesis upon some theme set by his masters or chosen by himself, and afterwards to defend his thesis against the criticism of the faculty. By this time he would have learned—or woe betide him—not merely to write an essay on paper, but to speak audibly and intelligibly from a platform, and to use his wits quickly when heckled. The heckling, moreover, would not consist solely of offensive personalities or of irrelevant queries about what Julius Cæsar said in 55 B.C.—though no doubt mediæval dialectic was enlivened in practice by plenty of such primitive repartee. But there would also be questions, cogent and shrewd, from those who had already run the gauntlet of debate, or were making ready to run it.

The truth is that for the last 300 years or so we have been living upon our educational capital. . . . the scholastic tradition, though broken and maimed, still lingered in the public schools and universities. . . . Right down to the nineteenth century, our public affairs were mostly managed, and our books and journals were for the most part written, by people brought up in homes, and trained in places, where that tradition was still alive in the memory and almost in the blood. Just so, many people to-day who are atheist or agnostic in religion, are governed in their conduct by a code of Christian ethics which is so rooted in their unconscious assumptions that it never occurs to them to question it. But one cannot live on capital forever.

A tradition, however firmly rooted, if it is never watered, though it dies hard, yet in the end it dies. And to-day a great number—perhaps the majority—of the men and women who handle our affairs, write our books and our newspapers, carry out research, present our plays and our films, speak from our platforms and pulpits—yes, and who educate our young people, have never, even in a lingering traditional memory, undergone the scholastic discipline. Less and less do the children who come to be educated bring any of that tradition with them. We have lost the tools of learning—the axe and the wedge, the hammer and the saw, the chisel and the plane—that were so adaptable to all tasks. Instead of them, we have merely a set of complicated jigs, each of which will do but one task and no more, and in using which eye and hand receive no training, so that no man ever sees the work as a whole or "looks to the end of the work." What use is it to pile task on task and prolong the days of labour, if at the close the chief object is left unattained? It is not the fault of the teachers—they work only too hard already. The combined folly of a civilisation that has forgotten its own roots is forcing them to shore up the tottering weight of an educational structure that is built upon sand. They are doing for their pupils the work which the pupils themselves ought to do. For the sole true end of education is simply this: to teach men how to learn for themselves; and whatever instruction fails to do this is effort spent in vain.

Discussion Questions

1. Sayers gives two reasons why she, who is not a professional educator, should express her thoughts on education: because "too much specialisation is not a good thing" and because she has experienced being taught. Do you agree that these things qualify her to write and speak on the subject? Why or why not?

2. Can you think of some modern examples of the "unfortunate" phenomena Sayers points out: people falling for propaganda, unskilled debaters, and writers failing to define their terms or using bad grammar and syntax?

3. Do you agree with Sayers that, when it comes to educational methods, it might be possible to go back to the Middle Ages? What objections might be raised to the idea?

4. Sayers starts discussing grammar as necessarily attached to languages, but then she goes on to discuss the grammar of history, mathematics, and other subjects. How would you say she is defining *grammar* here?

5. Do you agree with Sayers that the purpose of education is to learn how to learn? If so, why? If not, what is education for?

CHAPTER 39

Flannery O'Connor

Introduction to "The Enduring Chill"

JULIANNA LEACHMAN

Seeking to reenergize her work on her second novel, *The Violent Bear It Away*, Flannery O'Connor set the longer work aside during the fall of 1957 to focus her attention on "The Enduring Chill." In this story, O'Connor drew on her own experiences of falling ill and being forced to leave her New England community of artists to return home to her mother's care. Yet this story isn't autobiographical. Whereas O'Connor learned to appreciate the limitations such a return imposed on her life and her work, her character Asbury rages against the perceived injustice of his autonomy being stripped from him.

Asbury Fox is unwilling to learn from those around him because he believes they have nothing to teach him. He's a New York intellectual, after all, and a suffering artist. What could he possibly learn from a couple of country women, two submissive and thoughtless farmhands, an idiot doctor, and a Jesuit priest who has never even heard of James Joyce? If only they could appreciate his intelligence and art, he could teach them so much, he thinks.

The way Asbury treats the other characters in the story reveals that he views them only through the lens of his art. Each interaction with another person becomes for Asbury an opportunity to manipulate them for his own purposes. He weighs their value on the scale of how intelligent they are or how useful they may be for his intellectual and vocational pursuits, and then he dismisses them when his interactions don't lead to artistic production.

It seems that Asbury's self-importance has skewed his understanding of vocation, which he boils down to education and aspiration. He is unwilling to consider anything except his own desires, and he refuses to take responsibility for himself. Asbury thinks of himself as an artist, but as his sister Mary George points out, he has never published so much as a poem, much less a novel or a play. The only thing he's written that he hasn't burned afterward is a long letter blaming his mother for his failures in life. This letter is his only artistic legacy. He wants to be an artist without actually making art.

Full of self-pity, pride, and indignation, Asbury fails to see that humility and love are necessary components for any vocational pursuit, which for him is detached from any higher purpose. He has positioned himself as his ultimate goal, and he treats God the same way he treats other people: as fodder for his artistic pursuits. For him, God is an intellectual question to discuss, a symbol to portray, not the Creator and Savior of the world. "The artist prays by creating," Asbury self-righteously tells Father Finn.

The truth that he isn't actually dying comes as a shock to Asbury, ruining the tragic portrait he has painted of himself. Still more shocking is the realization that he will be forced to rely on his mother's care for the rest of his life. No longer self-sufficient, Asbury must face the truth that he was never actually self-sufficient; none of us really are.

Finally, Asbury's pride is broken. When Asbury catches his reflection in the mirror, he begins to see himself for who he is: "a lazy ignorant conceited youth." Humility becomes step one for an education from an old life of pride to a new life of dependence.

From "The Enduring Chill"

Asbury's train stopped so that he would get off exactly where his mother was standing waiting to meet him. Her thin spectacled face below him was bright with a wide smile that disappeared as she caught sight of him bracing himself behind the conductor. The smile vanished so suddenly, the shocked look that replaced it was so complete, that he realized for the first time that he must look as ill as he was. . . .

He was pleased that she should see death in his face at once. His mother, at the age of sixty, was going to be introduced to reality and he supposed that if the experience didn't kill her, it would assist her in the process of growing up. He stepped down and greeted her. . . .

"I don't feel like talking," he said at once. "I've had a bad trip." . . .

He had felt the end coming on for nearly four months. Alone in his freezing flat, huddled under his two blankets and his overcoat and with three thicknesses of the New York Times between, he had had a chill one night, followed by a violent sweat that left the sheets soaking and removed all doubt from his mind about his true condition. . . .

He could not, as his friend Goetz had recommended, prepare to see it all as illusion, either what had gone before or the few weeks that were left to him. Goetz was certain that death was nothing at all.

However, out of some feeling for his welfare, Goetz had put forth $4.50 to take him to a lecture on Vedanta. It had been a waste of his money. While Goetz had listened enthralled to the dark little man on the platform, Asbury's bored gaze had roved among the audience.

Finally, at end of the row, it had rested on a lean spectacled figure in black, a priest.

When the lecture was over a few students met in Goetz's flat, the priest among them, but he was equally reserved. He listened with a marked politeness to the discussion of Asbury's approaching death, but he said little. A girl in a sari remarked that self-fulfillment was out of the question since it meant salvation and the word was meaningless. "Salvation," quoted Goetz, "is the destruction of a simple prejudice, and no one is saved."

"And what do you say to that?" Asbury asked the priest and returned his reserved smile over the heads of the others. The borders of this smile seemed to touch on some icy clarity.

"There is," the priest said, "a real probability of the New Man, assisted, of course," he added brittlely, "by the Third Person of the Trinity."

When he got up to leave, he silently handed Asbury a small card on which he had written his name, Ignatius Vogle, S.J., and an address. Perhaps, Asbury thought now, he should have used it for the priest appealed to him as a man of the world, someone who would have understood the unique tragedy of his death, a death whose meaning had been far beyond the twittering group around them.

His mother knew at once what he meant: he meant he was going to have a nervous breakdown. She did not say a word. She did not say that this was precisely what she could have told him would happen. When people think they are smart—even when they are smart—there is nothing anybody else can say to make them see things straight, and with Asbury, the trouble was that in addition to being smart, he had an artistic temperament. She did not know where he had got it from because his father, who was a lawyer and businessman and farmer and politician all rolled into one, had certainly had his feet on the ground; and she had certainly always had hers on it.

She could have told Asbury what would help him. She could have said, "If you would get out in the sunshine, or if you would work for a month in the dairy, you'd be a different person!" but she knew exactly how that suggestion would be received. He would be a nuisance in the dairy but she would let him work in there if he wanted to.

She knew that if he would get in there now, or get out and fix fences, or do any kind of work—real work, not writing—that he might avoid this nervous breakdown.

She supposed the truth was that she simply didn't understand how it felt to be sensitive or how peculiar you were when you were an artist. His sister said he was not an artist and that he had no talent and that that was the trouble with him . . . Mary George had said that if Asbury had had any talent, he would by now have published something. What had he ever published, she wanted to know, and for that matter, what had he ever written? Mrs. Fox had pointed out that he was only twenty-five years old and Mary George had said that the age most people published something at was twenty-one, which made him exactly four years overdue. Mrs. Fox was not up on things like that but she suggested that he might be writing a very long book. Very long book, her eye, Mary George said, he would do well if he came up with so much as a poem. Mrs. Fox hoped it wasn't going to be just a poem.

While he was still in New York, he had written a letter to his mother which filled two notebooks. He did not mean it to be read until after his death. It was such a letter as Kafka had addressed to his father.

He knew, of course, that his mother would not understand the letter at once. Her literal mind would require some time to discover the significance of it, but he thought she would be able to see that he forgave her for all she had done to him. For that matter, he supposed that she would realize what she had done to him only through the letter. He didn't think she was conscious of it at all. Her self-satisfaction itself was barely conscious, but because of the letter, she might experience a painful realization and this would be the only thing of value he had to leave her.

If reading it would be painful to her, writing it had sometimes been unbearable to him—for in order to face her, he had had to face himself. "I came here to escape the slave's atmosphere of home," he had written, "to find freedom, to liberate my imagination, to take it like a hawk from its cage and set it 'whirling off into the widening gyre' (Yeats) and what did I find? It was incapable of flight. It was some bird you had domesticated, sitting huffy in its pen, refusing to come out!" The next words were underscored twice. "I have no imagination. I have no talent. I can't create. I have nothing but the desire for these things. Why didn't you kill that too? Woman, why did you pinion me?"

Writing this, he had reached the pit of despair and he thought that reading it, she would at least begin to sense his tragedy and her part in it.

He felt that even if she didn't understand at once, the letter would leave her with an enduring chill and perhaps in time lead her to see herself as she was.

He had destroyed everything else he had ever written—his two lifeless novels, his half-dozen stationary plays, his prosy poems, his sketchy short stories—and kept only the two notebooks that contained the letter. They were in the black suitcase that his sister, huffing and blowing, was now dragging up the second flight of stairs. His mother was carrying the smaller bag and came on ahead. He turned over as she entered the room.

"Close the blinds and let me sleep," he said.

When she was gone, he lay for some time staring at the water stains on the gray walls. Descending from the top molding, long icicle shapes had been etched by leaks and, directly over his bed on the ceiling, another leak had made a fierce bird with spread wings. It had an icicle crosswise in its beak and there were smaller icicles depending from its wings and tail. It had been there since his childhood and had always irritated him and sometimes had frightened him. He had often had the illusion that it was in motion and about to descend mysteriously and set the icicle on his head. He closed his eyes and thought: I won't have to look at it for many more days. And presently he went to sleep.

When he woke up in the afternoon, there was a pink open-mouthed face hanging over him and from two large familiar ears on either side of it the black tubes of Block's stethoscope extended down to his exposed chest. The doctor, seeing he was awake, made a face like a Chinaman, rolled his eyes almost out of his head and cried, "Say AHHHH!" . . .

Asbury sat up and thrust his thudding head forward and said, "I didn't send for you. I'm not answering any questions. You're not my doctor. What's wrong with me is way beyond you."

"Most things are beyond me," Block said. "I ain't found anything yet that I thoroughly understood," and he sighed and got up. His eyes seemed to glitter at Asbury as if from a great distance.

————

In the next few days, though he grew rapidly worse, his mind functioned with a terrible clarity. On the point of death, he found himself existing in a state of illumination that was totally out of keeping with the kind of talk he had to listen to from his mother.

He listened irritably while his mother detailed the faults of the help. "Those two are not stupid," she said. "They know how to look out for themselves."

"They need to," he muttered, but there was no use to argue with her. Last year he had been writing a play about the Negro and he had wanted to be around them for a while to see how they really felt about their condition, but the two who worked for her had lost all their initiative over the years. They didn't talk. The one called Morgan was light brown, part Indian; the other, older one, Randall, was very black and fat. When they said anything to him, it was as if they were speaking to an invisible body located to the right or left of where he actually was, and after two days working side by side with them, he felt he had not established rapport. He decided to try something bolder than talk and one afternoon as he was standing near Randall, watching him adjust a milker, he had quietly taken out his cigarettes and lit one. The Negro had stopped what he was doing and watched him. He waited until Asbury had taken two draws and then he said, "She don't 'low no smoking in here."

The other one approached and stood there, grinning.

"I know it," Asbury said and after a deliberate pause, he shook the package and held it out, first to Randall, who took one, and then to Morgan, who took one.

It was one of those moments of communion when the difference between black and white is absorbed into nothing.

The next day two cans of milk had been returned from the creamery because it had absorbed the odor of tobacco. He took the blame and told his mother that it was he and not the Negroes who had been smoking. "If you were doing it, they were doing it," she had said. "Don't you think I know those two?" She was incapable of thinking them innocent; but the experience had so exhilarated him that he had been determined to repeat it in some other way.

The next afternoon when he and Randall were in the milk house pouring the fresh milk into the cans, he had picked up the jelly glass the Negroes drank out of and, inspired, had poured himself a glassful of the warm milk and drained it down. Randall had stopped pouring and had remained, half-bent, over the can, watching him. "She don't 'low that," he said. "That the thing she don't 'low."

Asbury poured out another glassful and handed it to him.

"She don't 'low it," he repeated.

Asbury continued to hold the glass out to him. "You took the cigarette," he said. "Take the milk. It's not going to hurt my mother to lose two or three glasses of milk a day. We've got to think free if we want to live free!"

Asbury despised milk. The first warm glassful had turned his stomach. He drank half of what he was holding and handed the rest to the Negro, who took it and gazed down inside the glass as if it contained some great mystery; then he set it on the floor by the cooler.

He had tried the same thing the next day and the next and the next but he could not get them to drink the milk. A few afternoons later when he was standing outside the milk house about to go in, he heard Morgan ask, "Howcome you let him drink that milk every day?"

"What he do is him," Randall said. "What I do is me."

The insufferableness of life at home had overcome him and he had returned to New York two days early. So far as he was concerned he had died there, and the question now was how long he could stand to linger here. He could have hastened his end but suicide would not have been a victory. Death was coming to him legitimately, as a justification, as a gift from life. That was his greatest triumph. Then too, to the fine minds of the neighborhood, a suicide son would indicate a mother who had been a failure, and while this was the case, he felt that it was a public embarrassment he could spare her. What she would learn from the letter would be a private revelation.

He had sealed the notebooks in a manila envelope and had written on it: "To be opened only after the death of Asbury Porter Fox." He had put the envelope in the desk drawer in his room and locked it and the key was in his pajama pocket until he could decide on a place to leave it.

When they sat on the porch in the morning, his mother felt that some of the time she should talk about subjects that were of interest to him. The third morning she started in on his writing. "When you get well," she said, "I think it would be nice if you wrote a book about down here. We need another good book like Gone with the Wind."

He could feel the muscles in his stomach begin to tighten.

"Put the war in it," she advised. "That always makes a long book."

He put his head back gently as if he were afraid it would crack. After a moment he said, "I am not going to write any book."

"Well," she said, "if you don't feel like writing a book, you could just write poems. They're nice."

She realized that what he needed was someone intellectual to talk to, but Mary George was the only intellectual she knew and he would not talk to her.

For a time they sat there in silence. Then his mother looked up. He was sitting forward again and smiling at her. His face was brightening more and more as if he had just had an idea that was brilliant. She stared at him. "I'll tell you who I want to come," he said. For the first time since he had come home, his expression was pleasant; though there was also, she thought, a kind of crafty look about him.

"Who do you want to come?" she asked suspiciously.

"I want a priest," he announced.

"A priest?" his mother said in an uncomprehending voice.

"Preferably a Jesuit," he said, brightening more and more. "Yes, by all means a Jesuit. They have them in the city. You can call up and get me one."

"What is the matter with you?" his mother asked.

"Most of them are very well-educated," he said, "but Jesuits are foolproof. A Jesuit would be able to discuss something besides the weather." Already, remembering Ignatius Vogle, S.J., he could picture the priest. This one would be a trifle more worldly perhaps, a trifle more cynical. Protected by their ancient institution, priests could afford to be cynical, to play both ends against the middle. He would talk to a man of culture before he died—even in this desert! Furthermore, nothing would irritate his mother so much. He could not understand why he had not thought of this sooner.

He continued to grow worse. In the next few days he became so much weaker and badgered her so constantly about the Jesuit that finally in desperation she decided to humor his foolishness. She made the call, explaining in a chilly voice that her son was ill, perhaps a little out of his head, and wished to speak to a priest.

He could tell by the fact that she made the call that her assurance was beginning to shatter. Whenever she let Block in or out, there was much whispering in the downstairs hall. That evening, he heard her and Mary George talking in low voices in the parlor. He thought he heard his name and he got up and tiptoed into the hall and down the first three steps until he could hear the voices distinctly.

"I had to call that priest," his mother was saying. "I'm afraid this is serious. I thought it was just a nervous breakdown but now I think it's something real. Doctor Block thinks it's something real too and whatever it is is worse because he's so run-down."

"Block is an idiot," Mary George said. "You've got to face the facts: Asbury can't write so he gets sick. He's going to be an invalid instead of an artist. Do you know what he needs?"

"No," his mother said.

"Two or three shock treatments," Mary George said. "Get that artist business out of his head once and for all."

His mother gave a little cry and he grasped the banister.

He went back to bed. In a sense she was right. He had failed his god, Art, but he had been a faithful servant and Art was sending him Death.

The moon came up and Asbury was aware of a presence bending over him and a gentle warmth on his cold face. He knew that this was Art come to wake him and he sat up and opened his eyes. Across the hill all the lights were on in his mother's house.

The next day his mother noted something almost ethereal about his ravaged face.

All morning he waited, looking irritably up at the ceiling where the bird with the icicle in its beak seemed poised and waiting too; but the priest did not arrive until late in the afternoon. As soon as his mother opened the door, a loud unintelligible voice began to boom in the downstairs hall. Asbury's heart beat wildly. In a second there was a heavy creaking on the stairs. Then almost at once his mother, her expression constrained, came in followed by a massive old man who plowed straight across the room, picked up a chair by the side of the bed and put it under himself.

"I'm Father Finn—from Purrgatory," he said in a hearty voice. He had a large red face, a stiff brush of gray hair and was blind in one eye, but the good eye, blue and clear, was focused sharply on Asbury.

"It's so nice to have you come," Asbury said. "This place is incredibly dreary. There's no one here an intelligent person can talk to. I wonder what you think of Joyce, Father?"

The priest lifted his chair and pushed closer. "You'll have to shout," he said. "Blind in one eye and deaf in one ear."

"What do you think of Joyce?" Asbury said louder.

"Joyce? Joyce who?" asked the priest.

"James Joyce," Asbury said and laughed.

The priest brushed his huge hand in the air as if he were bothered by gnats. "I haven't met him," he said. "Now. Do you say your morning and night prayers?" Asbury appeared confused. "Joyce was a great writer," he murmured, forgetting to shout.

"You don't eh?" said the priest. "Well you will never learn to be good unless you pray regularly. You cannot love Jesus unless you speak to Him."

"The artist prays by creating," Asbury ventured.

"Not enough!" snapped the priest. "If you do not pray daily, you are neglecting your immortal soul. Do you know your catechism?"

Asbury saw he had made a mistake and that it was time to get rid of the old fool. "Listen," he said, "I'm not a Roman."

"A poor excuse for not saying your prayers!" the old man snorted.

Asbury slumped slightly in the bed. "I'm dying," he shouted.

"But you're not dead yet!" said the priest, "and how do you expect to meet God face to face when you've never spoken to Him? How do you expect to get what you don't ask for? God does not send the Holy Ghost to those who don't ask for Him. Ask Him to send the Holy Ghost."

"The Holy Ghost?" Asbury said.

"Are you so ignorant you've never heard of the Holy Ghost?" the priest asked.

"Certainly I've heard of the Holy Ghost," Asbury said furiously, "and the Holy Ghost is the last thing I'm looking for!"

"And He may be the last thing you get," the priest said, his one fierce eye inflamed.

"How can the Holy Ghost fill your soul when it's full of trash?" the priest roared. "The Holy Ghost will not come until you see yourself as you are—a lazy ignorant conceited youth!" he said, pounding his fist on the little bedside table.

Mrs. Fox burst in. "Enough of this!" she cried. "How dare you talk that way to a poor sick boy? You're upsetting him. You'll have to go."

"The poor lad doesn't even know his catechism," the priest said, rising.

"I should think you would have taught him to say his daily prayers. You have neglected your duty as his mother." He turned back to the bed and said affably, "I'll give you my blessing and after this you must say your daily prayers without fail," whereupon he put his hand on Asbury's head and rumbled something in Latin. "Call me any time," he said, "and we can have another little chat," and then he followed Mrs. Fox's rigid back out. The last thing Asbury heard him say was, "He's a good lad at heart but very ignorant."

The next morning he was so weak that she made up her mind he must go to the hospital.

He was convinced that the end was approaching, that it would be today, and he was tormented now thinking of his useless life. He felt as if he were a shell that had to be filled with something but he did not know what. He began to take note of everything in the room as if for the last time—the ridiculous antique furniture, the pattern in the rug, the silly picture his mother had replaced. He even looked at the fierce bird with the icicle in its beak and felt that it was there for some purpose that he could not divine.

There was something he was searching for, something that he felt he must have, some last significant culminating experience that he must make for himself before he died—make for himself out of his own intelligence. He had always relied on himself and had never been a sniveler after the ineffable.

As the day wore on, he grew more and more frantic for fear he would die without making some last meaningful experience for himself.

Suddenly he thought of that experience of communion that he had had in the dairy with the Negroes when they had smoked together, and at once he began to tremble with excitement. They would smoke together one last time.

After a moment, turning his head on the pillow, he said, "Mother, I want to tell the Negroes good-bye."

His mother paled. For an instant her face seemed about to fly apart. Then the line of her mouth hardened; her brows drew together. "Good-bye?" she said in a flat voice. "Where are you going?"

For a few seconds he only looked at her. Then he said, "I think you know. Get them. I don't have long."

"This is absurd," she muttered but she got up and hurried out.

Presently he heard their steps on the stair.

"Here's Randall and Morgan," his mother said, ushering them in. "They've come to tell you hello."

The two of them came in grinning and shuffled to the side of the bed. They stood there, Randall in front and Morgan behind. "You sho do look well," Randall said. "You looks very well."

"You looks well," the other one said. "Yessuh, you looks fine."

"Mother," Asbury said in a forced voice. "I'd like to talk to them alone." His mother stiffened; then she marched out. She walked across the hall and into the room on the other side and sat down. Through the open doors he could see her begin to rock in little short jerks. The two Negroes looked as if their last protection had dropped away.

Asbury's head was so heavy he could not think what he had been going to do. "I'm dying," he said.

Both their grins became gelid. "You looks fine," Randall said.

"I'm going to die," Asbury repeated. Then with relief he remembered that they were going to smoke together. He reached for the package on the table and held it out to Randall, forgetting to shake out the cigarettes.

The Negro took the package and put it in his pocket. "I thank you," he said. "I certainly do prechate it."

Asbury stared as if he had forgotten again. After a second he became aware that the other Negro's face had turned infinitely sad; then he realized that it was not sad but sullen. He fumbled in the drawer of the table and pulled out an unopened package and thrust it at Morgan.

"I thanks you, Mist Asbury," Morgan said, brightening. "You certly does look well."

"Mother!" Asbury called in a shaking voice. His mother stood up. "Mister Asbury has had company long enough now," she called. "You all can come back tomorrow."

He knew now there would be no significant experience before he died. There was nothing more to do but give her the key to the drawer where the letter was, and wait for the end.

He awoke a little after six to hear Block's car stop below in the driveway. The sound was like a summons, bringing him rapidly and with a clear head out of his sleep. He had a sudden terrible foreboding that the fate await-ing him was going to be more shattering than any he could have reckoned on. He lay absolutely motionless, as still as an animal the instant before an earthquake.

Block and his mother talked as they came up the stairs but he did not dis-tinguish their words. The doctor came in making faces; his mother was smiling. "Guess what you've got, Sugarpie!" she cried. Her voice broke in on him with the force of a gunshot.

Block leaned over him and smiled. "You ain't going to die," he said, with deep satisfaction.

Block's gaze seemed to reach down like a steel pin and hold whatever it was until the life was out of it. "Undulant fever ain't so bad, Azzberry," he murmured. "It's the same as Bang's in a cow."

The boy gave a low moan and then was quiet.

"He must have drunk some unpasteurized milk up there," his mother said softly and then the two of them tiptoed out as if they thought he were about to go to sleep. When the sound of their footsteps had faded on the stairs, Asbury sat up again.

He glanced across the room into the small oval-framed dresser mirror. The eyes that stared back at him were the same that had returned his gaze every day from that mirror but it seemed to him that they were paler. They looked shocked clean as if they had been prepared for some awful vision about to come down on him.

The old life in him was exhausted. He awaited the coming of new. It was then that he felt the beginning of a chill, a chill so peculiar, so light, that it was like a warm ripple across a deeper sea of cold. His breath came short. The fierce bird which through the years of his childhood and the days of his illness had been poised over his head, waiting mysteriously, appeared all at once to be in motion. Asbury blanched and the last film of illusion was torn as if by a whirlwind from his eyes. He saw that for the rest of his days, frail, racked, but enduring, he would live in the face of a purifying terror. A feeble cry, a last impossible protest escaped him. But the Holy Ghost, emblazoned in ice instead of fire, continued, implacable, to descend.

Discussion Questions

1. O'Connor focused specifically on the Holy Ghost in this story. From what you read here, what role does the Holy Ghost play in artistic creation, vocational discernment, or illumination?

2. In his letter to his mother, Asbury complains, "I have no imagination. I have no talent. I can't create. I have nothing but the desire for these things." Why is desire for imagination, talent, and creation not enough for Asbury to pursue his vocation? What else does Asbury need?

3. Asbury's view of education is centered on the mind, and his view of success is strictly cosmopolitan. His mother's view of education, on the other hand, is centered on the body, and her view of success is distinctly rural. Where do you see these bifurcated views promulgated in our culture today?

4. After reading this story, what would you say is the purpose of education according to Flannery O'Connor? What, ultimately, serves to educate Asbury?

CHAPTER 40

Josef Pieper

Introduction to *Leisure: The Basis of Culture* and "Learning How to See Again"

JAY BEAVERS

The excerpts below, from the German philosopher Josef Pieper, are defenses of leisure and contemplation. They advocate for right being and right seeing at a time of remarkable busyness and upheaval. Pieper lived and wrote when West Germany was rapidly rebuilding after the destruction of World War II. It was a busy time. Yet Pieper understood the need for resistance to the culture of "total labor" that threatened to shove aside any appreciation for contemplation or the liberal arts and remove the possibility of the leisure that enables them.

To be at leisure is to adopt a posture of festive gratefulness toward the good gifts of creation. Pieper differentiated leisure from the sins of sloth and idleness with which it is erroneously associated. Leisure not only spares us from the deadening effects of work for work's sake but also orients us rightly in the world, providing space for the exercise of those parts of ourselves that make us truly human and that put us in contact with the divine.

Pieper's works remind us of the wisdom of the ancient Greeks for whom the word *school* was derived from a word that meant "leisure." It was once commonplace to regard the liberal arts as a necessary corollary to what were called the *artes serviles* or servile work. The liberal arts are, therefore, the freeing arts. They are pursued freely as good in themselves and not as bound to some other end, but more importantly, the liberal arts are conceived in leisure for the purpose of leisure. They require and inspire contemplation. The liberal arts teach us that knowledge is not a fungible good to be purchased for money and expended toward practical ends but the free gift of past generations, which we are to receive gratefully and in a spirit of celebration.

Leisure, therefore, is not a luxury; it is a necessity far more foundational than work. We were created on a Saturday to share in God's eternal Sunday. Even after the fall, it is leisure that places us in the way of grace, gives meaning to our lives, and advances culture toward its noblest purposes. A culture that undervalues leisure is in danger of losing itself and reducing its people to servitors and functionaries. Pieper here reminded us to retain what is most precious in human life by turning from our labors to the leisure for which we were created.

The second excerpt, from Pieper's "Learning How to See Again," advocates for the necessity of seeing thoroughly and with discernment in an age when so much competes for our passive attention. Pieper began with the startling statement that none of us have fully seen everything that is visible to us. I suspect most of us have experienced the mesmerizing effect of watching a wood fire burn or a fast-flowing creek run. These simple and mundane phenomena can so entrance us because no matter how long we look, we will never come to the end of our seeing.

Pieper asserted that this is the case with everything we look upon, and that we must train our eyes to see as artists do. For Pieper, the creation of tangible art both required and enabled this right kind of seeing. For art to be successful at all, the artist must have learned to see more of what is there than the casual observer, like the way light suffuses a person's skin or the way the muscles of a face interact when a person smiles. Without this deeper seeing, we risk losing our mental grip on reality.

From *Leisure: The Basis of Culture*

Idleness, in the old sense of the word, so far from being synonymous with leisure, is more nearly the inner prerequisite which renders leisure impossible: it might be described as the utter absence of leisure, or the very opposite of leisure. Leisure is only possible when a man is at one with himself, when he acquiesces in his own being, whereas the essence of *acedia* is the refusal to acquiesce in one's own being. Idleness and the incapacity for leisure correspond with one another. Leisure is the contrary of both.

Compared with the exclusive ideal of work as activity leisure implies (in the first place) an attitude of nonactivity, of inward calm, of silence; it means not being "busy" but letting things happen.

Leisure is not the attitude of mind of those who actively intervene, but of those who are open to everything, not of those who grab and grab hold, but of those who leave the reins loose and who are free and easy themselves. . . . When we really let our minds rest contemplatively on a rose in bud, on a child at play, on a divine mystery, we are rested and quickened as though by a dreamless sleep. Or as the Book of Job says, "God giveth songs in the night" (Job 35:10).

Compared with the exclusive ideal of work as toil, leisure appears (secondly) in its character as an attitude of contemplative "celebration," a word that, properly understood, goes to the very heart of what we mean by leisure. Leisure is possible only on the premise that man consents to his own true nature and abides in concord with the meaning of the universe (whereas idleness, as we have said, is the refusal of such consent). Leisure draws its vitality from affirmation.

The festival is the origin of leisure, and the inward and ever-present meaning of leisure. And because leisure is thus by its nature a celebration, it is more than effortless; it is the direct opposite of effort.

Thirdly . . . leisure does not exist for the sake of work—however much strength it may give a man to work; the point of leisure is not to be a restorative, a pick-me-up, whether mental or physical; and though it gives new strength, mentally and physically, and spiritually too, that is not the point.

The point and the justification of leisure are not that the functionary should function faultlessly and without a breakdown, but that the functionary should continue to be a man—and that means that he should not be wholly absorbed in the clear-cut milieu of his strictly limited function; the point is also that he should retain the faculty of grasping the world as a whole and realizing his full potentialities as an entity meant to reach Wholeness.

Because Wholeness is what man strives for, the power to achieve leisure is one of the fundamental powers of the human soul. Like the gift for contemplative absorption in the things that are, and like the capacity of the spirit to soar in festive celebration, the power to know leisure is the power to overstep the boundaries of the workaday world and reach out to superhuman, life-giving existential forces that refresh and renew us before we turn back to our daily work. Only in genuine leisure does a "gate to freedom" open. Through that gate man may escape from the "restricted area" of that "latent anxiety" which a keen observer has perceived to be the mark of the world of work, where "work and unemployment are the two inescapable poles of existence."

In leisure—not of course exclusively in leisure, but always in leisure—the truly human values are saved and preserved because leisure is the means whereby the sphere of the "specifically human" can, over and again, be left behind—not as a result of any violent effort to reach out, but as in an ecstasy (the ecstasy is indeed more "difficult" than the most violent exertion, more "difficult" because not invariably at our beck and call; a state of extreme tension is more easily induced than a state of relaxation and case *although* the latter is effortless); the full enjoyment of leisure is hedged in by paradoxes of this kind, and it is itself a state at once very human and superhuman. Aristotle says of leisure, "A man will live thus, not to the extent that he is a man, but to the extent that a divine principle dwells within him."

From "Learning How to See Again" in
Only the Lover Sings: Art and Contemplation

Man's ability to *see* is in decline. Those who nowadays concern themselves with culture and education will experience this fact again and again. We do not mean here, of course, the physiological sensitivity of the human eye. We mean the spiritual capacity to perceive the visible reality as it truly is.

To be sure, no human being has ever really *seen* everything that lies visibly in front of his eyes. The world, including its tangible side, is unfathomable. Who would ever have perfectly perceived the countless shapes and shades of just one wave swelling and ebbing in the ocean! And yet, there are degrees of perception. Going below a certain bottom line quite obviously will endanger the integrity of man as a spiritual being. It seems that nowadays we have arrived at this bottom line.

At stake here is this: How can man be saved from becoming a totally passive consumer of mass-produced goods and a subservient follower beholden to every slogan the managers may proclaim? The question really is: How can man preserve and safeguard the foundation of his spiritual dimension and an uncorrupted relationship to reality?

The capacity to perceive the visible world "with our own eyes" is indeed an essential constituent of human nature. We are talking here about man's essential inner richness—or, should the threat prevail, man's most abject inner poverty. And why so? To *see* things is the first step toward that primordial and basic mental grasping of reality, which constitutes the essence of a man as a spiritual being.

A better and more immediately effective remedy is this: *to be active oneself in artistic creation, producing shapes and forms for the eye to see.*

Nobody has to observe and study the visible mystery of a human face more than the one who sets out to sculpt it in a tangible medium. And this holds true not only for a manually formed image. The verbal "image" as well can thrive only when it springs from a higher level of visual perception. We sense the intensity of observation required simply to say, "The girl's eyes were gleaming like wet currants" (Tolstoy).

Before you can express anything in tangible form, you first need eyes to see. The mere attempt, therefore, to create an artistic form compels the artist to take a fresh look at the visible reality; it requires authentic and personal observation. Long before a creation is completed, the artist has gained for himself another and more intimate achievement: a deeper and more receptive vision, a more intense awareness, a sharper and more discerning understanding, a more patient openness for all things quiet and inconspicuous, an eye for things previously overlooked. In short: the artist will be able to perceive with new eyes the abundant wealth of all visible reality, and, thus challenged, additionally acquires the inner capacity to absorb into his mind such an exceedingly rich harvest. The capacity to *see* increases.

Discussion Questions

1. Do you tend to work to live or live to work? How would Pieper justify a life of contemplation in the midst of so much busyness and where there is so much practical work to be done?
2. What are some key qualities of leisure according to Pieper? When have you experienced true leisure as Pieper described it?
3. Do you tend to mistrust things that come easily? If so, how might an appreciation of leisure reorient the way you ascribe value to the things, people, and tasks in your life?
4. How does Pieper's admonition to pursue leisure enable us to live our faith more fully?
5. What practical steps can you take to help establish your life around leisure?

CHAPTER 41

David Foster Wallace

Introduction to "This Is Water"

RICK OSTRANDER

The scene is easy to imagine: It's a warm, sunny morning in Kenyon, Ohio, in 2005. You're a Kenyon College graduating senior, dressed in your cap and gown and sitting in a folding chair on the football field. Soon you will walk across the stage, shake the president's hand, receive your diploma, and wave excitedly to your family members sitting in the stands. But first you must endure the obligatory commencement speech by some dignitary who has been invited to fill up twenty minutes of the ceremony with inspiring platitudes.

Instead, a young white guy ambles to the podium—an author you've never heard of named David Foster Wallace. His long hair is unkempt, he's clearly uncomfortable wearing academic regalia, and he's already perspiring from nervousness as he pulls out a prepared text to read. But he has a captivating intensity about him as he launches into his speech. He uses unexpected terms such as *bullshitty*; he asserts, "The plain fact is that you graduating seniors do not yet have any clue what daily life really means"; and he concludes with what he calls "the capital *T* Truth, with a whole lot of rhetorical niceties stripped away." At the end of twenty-two minutes, the somewhat stunned audience applauds politely, then gets on with the diplomas.

David Foster Wallace's talk has achieved a reputation as one of the best commencement speeches ever. Amazingly, the only reason we have it today is because a visiting student recorded it, and the transcription eventually went viral on the internet. Why is Wallace's speech so memorable? Perhaps it's because he burrowed beneath the usual clichés about the value of critical thinking to get at a deeper truth: that education is really about becoming aware of our own limited perspective and more open to interpreting our experience in different ways.

Like any wise non-Christian thinker, Wallace provided important insights for the Christian learner but is only partially correct. His brilliant speech fell short in one important way. As creatures made in God's image and embedded in his creation, we don't simply get to construct meaning out of thin air. Rather, we think best when we are attuned to and aware of the God-infused world around us. This is, I think, part of what Paul meant in Romans when he said to be "transformed by the renewing of your mind" (12:2).

The problem is, we inhabit a culture of busyness and technology, of devices and multitasking, that undermines these important qualities of attention and deep reflection. That is why, as philosopher James K. A. Smith and others suggest, we need to develop disciplines of mind and body and daily habits that enable us to truly pay attention in a culture of distraction. And that is why Christian learning happens in community. We need fellow students and faculty mentors to help us develop these habits.

Like fish swimming in water, oblivious to the fact they are *in* water, we can either drift through our lives unthinkingly, immersed in our daily activities and distractions, or we can move toward awareness, attention, and depth. Christian education is an invitation into that journey.

From "This Is Water"

Greetings and congratulations to Kenyon's graduating class of 2005.

There are these two young fish swimming along and they happen to meet an older fish swimming the other way, who nods at them and says "Morning, boys. How's the water?" And the two young fish swim on for a bit, and then eventually one of them looks over at the other and goes "What the hell is water?"

This is a standard requirement of U.S. commencement speeches, the deployment of didactic little parable-ish stories. The story turns out to be one of the better, less bullshitty conventions of the genre, but if you're worried that I plan to present myself here as the wise, older fish explaining what water is to you younger fish, please don't be. I am not the wise old fish. The point of the fish story is merely that the most obvious, important realities are often the ones that are hardest to see and talk about. Stated as an English sentence, of course, this is just a banal platitude, but the fact is that in the day-to-day trenches of adult existence, banal platitudes can have a life or death importance, or so I wish to suggest to you on this dry and lovely morning.

Of course, the main requirement of speeches like this is that I'm supposed to talk about your liberal arts education's meaning, to try to explain why the degree you are about to receive has actual human value instead of just a material payoff. So let's talk about the single most pervasive cliché in the commencement speech genre, which is that a liberal arts education is not so much about filling you up with knowledge as it is about "teaching you how to think."

Twenty years after my own graduation, I have come gradually to understand that the liberal arts cliché about teaching you how to think is actually shorthand for a much deeper, more serious idea: learning how to think really means learning how to exercise some control over how and what you think. It means being conscious and aware enough to choose what you pay attention to and to choose how you construct meaning from experience. Because if you cannot exercise this kind of choice in adult life, you will be totally hosed.

By way of example, let's say it's an average adult day, and you get up in the morning, go to your challenging, white-collar, college-graduate job, and you work hard for eight or ten hours, and at the end of the day you're tired and somewhat stressed and all you want is to go home and have a good supper and maybe unwind for an hour, and then hit the sack early. You haven't had time to shop this week because of your challenging job, and so now after work you have to get in your car and drive to the supermarket. It's the end of the work day and the traffic is apt to be very bad.

And the store is hideously lit and infused with soul-killing muzak or corporate pop and it's pretty much the last place you want to be but you can't just get in and quickly out; you have to wander all over the huge, over-lit store's confusing aisles to find the stuff you want and you have to maneuver your junky cart through all these other tired, hurried people with carts. You finally get to the checkout line's front, and you pay for your food, and you get told to "Have a nice day" in a voice that is the absolute voice of death.

Everyone here has done this, of course. But it hasn't yet been part of you graduates' actual life routine, day after week after month after year. But it will be. And many more dreary, annoying, seemingly meaningless routines besides. But that is not the point. The point is that petty, frustrating crap like this is exactly where the work of choosing is going to come in. Because my natural default setting is the certainty that situations like this are really all about me. About *my* hungriness and *my* fatigue and *my* desire to just get home, and it's going to seem for all the world like everybody else is just in my way.

The thing is that, of course, there are totally different ways to think about these kinds of situations. In this traffic, all these vehicles stopped and idling in my way, it's not impossible that some of these people in SUV's have been in horrible auto accidents in the past, and now find driving so terrifying that their therapist has all but ordered them to get a huge, heavy SUV so they can feel safe enough to drive. Or I can choose to force myself to consider the likelihood that everyone else in the supermarket's checkout line is just as bored and frustrated as I am, and that some of these people probably have harder, more tedious and painful lives than I do.

That is real freedom. That is being educated, and understanding how to think. The alternative is unconsciousness, the default setting, the rat race, the constant gnawing sense of having had, and lost, some infinite thing. I know that this stuff probably doesn't sound fun and breezy or grandly inspirational the way a commencement speech is supposed to sound. What it is, as far as I can see, is the capital-T Truth, with a whole lot of rhetorical niceties stripped away. The real value of a real education has almost nothing to do with knowledge and everything to do with simple awareness; awareness of what is so real and essential, so hidden in plain sight all around us, all the time, that we have to keep reminding ourselves over and over: "This is water."

"This is water." It is unimaginably hard to do this, to stay conscious and alive in the adult world day in and day out. Which means yet another grand *cliché* turns out to be true: your education really *is* the job of a lifetime. And it commences *now*. I wish you way more than luck.

Discussion Questions

1. Foster said that one purpose of education is to teach us to be a little less arrogant. How does arrogance get in the way of real learning?
2. If a Christian university were to take Foster's insights seriously, in what ways would it be different?
3. What is it in your life that works against the ability to reflect more deeply and intentionally about your existence and surroundings? What could you do to change that?
4. Envisioning yourself at the Kenyon ceremony in person, what sort of reception do you think Wallace's speech received? Why?

CHAPTER 42

Marilynne Robinson

Introduction to "Reclaiming a Sense of the Sacred"
BRENT NEWSOM

Some thinkers in our postmodern age presume a fundamental opposition exists between science and religion. Influential voices among the "New Atheists" such as Richard Dawkins come to mind as examples, but it is equally true that many Christians, clinging to scriptural revelation as the sole (or at least primary) avenue to truth, view science as antithetical to faith in a number of ways.

Such stark dichotomies, viewed from the Christian perspective, echo an ancient debate from the early centuries of church history, known as the patristic age. Back then the question was what place, if any, the study of secular, pagan philosophies should have in the life of the Christian. On one side, thinkers like Tertullian argued that Greek philosophy could only lead the believer astray, asking, "What has Jerusalem to do with Athens, the Church with [Plato's] Academy, the Christian with the heretic?"[1] Other theologians, however, like Clement of Alexandria and St. Augustine of Hippo, believed that reason, rightly applied to the study of philosophy, would lead one toward truth and, ultimately, toward knowledge of God.

Similarly, contemporary author Marilynne Robinson refutes the dichotomy between science and religion. Robinson is best known for her novels: *Housekeeping* (1980) and the quartet *Gilead* (2004), *Home* (2008), *Lila* (2014), and *Jack* (2020). *Gilead* was awarded the Pulitzer Prize; it and much of her other work engages with the theological legacy of John Calvin. She is also a prolific and widely respected essayist, however.

In "Reclaiming a Sense of the Sacred,"[2] Robinson challenges the simplistic scientific rejection of religious understanding while also calling the faithful to embrace the sense of wonder and beauty in the created order that scientific knowledge helps to illuminate. In that sense, she follows in the footsteps of Clement and Augustine, not to mention the many Christian thinkers in the

---

1. *Early Latin Theology*, trans. and ed. S. L. Greenslade (Philadelphia: Westminster, 1956), 35–36. Reprinted in *Sources of the Western Tradition*, ed. Marvin Perry, vol. 1, *From Ancient Times to the Enlightenment*, 9th ed. (Boston: Wadsworth Cengage, 2014), 171–72.

2. The essay excerpted here appears as "Freedom of Thought" in her essay collection *When I Was a Child I Read Books* (New York: Farrar, Straus and Giroux, 2012).

intervening centuries who have also resisted overly narrow or compartmental-
ized approaches to truth. What Robinson emphasizes from her contemporary
vantage point is that a scientifically informed society nonetheless needs religious
thinking, needs art and literature, needs music—for the arts and humanities
are able to frame our knowledge of the world in terms of human significance, to
illuminate the mysterious and complex realities of the soul.

One step toward reconciling scientific and religious forms of knowledge
and reclaiming our sense of sacred reality, Robinson suggests, is to encourage
"systematic doubt"—that is, a principled scrutiny of ideas presented as scientific truth, for scientific inquiry, like all other human pursuits, is shaped by "the
universal variable, human nature." On the other hand, we ought not conceive
of ancient religious literature as explanatory in a scientific sense but instead as a
gateway to timeless and essential truths about the beautiful and terrible mystery
of human existence. To put it succinctly, in response to the question, "How are
we called to think?" Robinson seems to answer, "Freely."

"Reclaiming a Sense of the Sacred"

Over the years of writing and teaching, I have tried to free myself of constraints I felt, limits to the range of exploration I could make, to the kind of
intuition I could credit. I realized gradually that my own religion, and religion
in general, could and should disrupt these constraints, which amount to a small
and narrow definition of what human beings are and how human life is to be
understood. And I have often wished my students would find religious standards present in the culture that would express a real love for human life and
encourage them also to break out of these same constraints.

For the educated among us, moldy theories we learned as sophomores, mem-
orized for the test and never consciously thought of again, exert an authority
that would embarrass us if we stopped to consider them. I was educated at a center of behaviorist psychology and spent a certain amount of time pestering rats.
There was some sort of maze-learning experiment involved in my final grade,
and since I remember the rat who was my colleague as uncooperative, or perhaps
merely incompetent at being a rat, or tired of the whole thing, I don't remember
how I passed. I'm sure coercion was not involved, since this rodent and I avoided
contact. Bribery was, of course, central to the experiment and no black mark
against either of us, though I must say, mine was an Eliot Ness among rats for its
resistance to the lure of, say, Cheerios.

I should probably have tried raising the stakes. The idea was, in any case,
that behavior was conditioned by reward or its absence, and that one could
extrapolate meaningfully from the straightforward demonstration of rattish

self-interest promised in the literature, to the admittedly more complex question of human motivation. I have read subsequently that a female rat is so gratified at having an infant rat come down the reward chute that she will do whatever is demanded of her until she has filled her cage with them. This seems to me to complicate the definition of self-interest considerably, but complexity was not a concern of the behaviorism of my youth, which was reductionist in every sense of the word.

It wasn't all behaviorism. We also pondered Freud's argument that primordial persons, male, internalized the father as superego by actually eating the poor fellow. Since then we have all felt bad—well, the male among us, at least. Whence human complexity, whence civilization. I did better on that exam. The plot was catchy.

The situation of the undergraduate rarely encourages systematic doubt. What Freud thought was important because it was Freud who thought it, and so with B. F. Skinner and whomever else the curriculum held up for our admiration. There must be something to all this, even if it has only opened the door a degree or two on a fuller understanding. So I thought at the time. And I also thought it was a very bleak light that shone through that door, and I shouldered my share of the supposedly inevitable gloom that came with being a modern.

In English class we studied a poem by Robert Frost, "The Oven Bird." The poem asks "what to make of a diminished thing." That diminished thing, said the teacher, was human experience in the modern world. Oh dear. Modern aesthetics. We must learn from this poem "in singing not to sing." To my undergraduate self I thought, "But what if I like to sing?" And then my philosophy professor assigned us Jonathan Edwards's *Doctrine of Original Sin Defended*, in which Edwards argues for "the arbitrary constitution of the universe," illustrating his point with a gorgeous footnote about moonlight that even then began to dispel the dreary determinisms I was learning elsewhere. Improbable as that may sound to those who have not read the footnote.

At a certain point I decided that everything I took from studying and reading anthropology, psychology, economics, cultural history, and so on did not square at all with my sense of things, and that the tendency of much of it was to posit or assume a human simplicity within a simple reality and to marginalize the sense of the sacred, the beautiful, everything in any way lofty. I do not mean to suggest, and I underline this, that there was any sort of plot against religion, since religion in many instances abetted these tendencies and does still, not least by retreating from the cultivation and celebration of learning and of beauty, by dumbing down, as if people were less than God made them and in need of nothing so much as condescension. Who among us wishes the songs we sing, the sermons we hear, were just a little dumber? People today—television—video games—diminished things. This is always the pretext.

Simultaneously, and in a time of supposed religious revival, and among those especially inclined to feel religiously revived, we have a society increasingly defined by economics and an economics increasingly reminiscent of my experience with that rat, so-called rational-choice economics, which assumes that we will all find the shortest way to the reward, and that this is basically what we should ask of ourselves and—this is at the center of it all—of one another. After all these years of rational choice, brother rat might like to take a look at the packaging just to see if there might be a little melamine in the inducements he was being offered, hoping, of course, that the vendor considered it rational to provide that kind of information. We do not deal with one another as soul to soul, and the churches are as answerable for this as anyone.

If we think we have done this voiding of content for the sake of other people, those to whom we suspect God may have given a somewhat lesser brilliance than our own, we are presumptuous and also irreverent. William Tyndale, who was burned at the stake for his translation of the Bible, who provided much of the most beautiful language in what is called by us the King James Bible, wrote, he said, in the language a plowboy could understand. He wrote to the comprehension of the profoundly poor, those who would be, and would have lived among, the utterly unlettered. And he created one of the undoubted masterpieces of the English language. Now we seem to feel beauty is an affectation of some sort. And this notion is as influential in the churches as it is anywhere. The Bible, Christianity, should have inoculated us against this kind of disrespect for ourselves and one another. Clearly it has not.

For me, at least, writing consists very largely of exploring intuition. A character is really the sense of a character, embodied, attired, and given voice as he or she seems to require. Where does this creature come from? From watching, I suppose. From reading emotional significance in gestures and inflections, as we all do all the time. These moments of intuitive recognition float free from their particular occasions and recombine themselves into nonexistent people the writer and, if all goes well, the reader feel they know.

There is a great difference, in fiction and in life, between knowing someone and knowing *about* someone. When a writer knows *about* his character, he is writing for plot. When he *knows* his character, he is writing to explore, to feel reality on a set of nerves somehow not quite his own. Words like "sympathy," "empathy" and "compassion" are overworked and overcharged—there is no word for the experience of seeing an embrace at a subway stop or hearing an argument at the next table in a restaurant. Every such instant has its own emotional coloration, which memory retains or heightens, and so the most sidelong, unintended moment becomes a part of what we have seen of the world. Then, I suppose, these moments, as they have seemed to us, constellate themselves into something a little like a spirit, a little like a human presence in its mystery and distinctiveness.

Two questions I can't really answer about fiction are (1) where it comes from, and (2) why we need it. But that we do create it and also crave it is beyond dispute. There is a tendency, considered highly rational, to reason from a narrow set of interests, say survival and procreation, which are supposed to govern our lives, and then to treat everything that does not fit this model as anomalous clutter, extraneous to what we are and probably best done without. But all we really know about what we are is what we do. There is a tendency to fit a tight and awkward carapace of definition over humankind, and to try to trim the living creature to fit the dead shell.

The advice I give my students is the same advice I give myself—forget definition, forget assumption, watch. We inhabit, we are part of, a reality for which explanation is much too poor and small. No physicist would dispute this, though he or she might be less ready than I am to have recourse to the old language and call reality miraculous. By my lights, fiction that does not acknowledge this at least tacitly is not true. Why is it possible to speak of fiction as true or false? I have no idea. But if a time comes when I seem not to be making the distinction with some degree of reliability in my own work, I hope someone will be kind enough to let me know.

When I write fiction, I suppose my attempt is to simulate the integrative work of a mind perceiving and reflecting, drawing upon culture, memory, conscience, belief or assumption, circumstance, fear and desire—a mind shaping the moment of experience and response and then reshaping them both as narrative, holding one thought against another for the effect of affinity or contrast, evaluating and rationalizing, feeling compassion, taking offense. These things do happen simultaneously, after all. None of them is active by itself, and none of them is determinative, because there is that mysterious thing the cognitive scientists call self-awareness, the human ability to consider and appraise one's own thoughts. I suspect this self-awareness is what people used to call the soul.

Modern discourse is not really comfortable with the word "soul," and in my opinion the loss of the word has been disabling, not only to religion but to literature and political thought and to every humane pursuit. In contemporary religious circles, souls, if they are mentioned at all, tend to be spoken of as saved or lost, having answered some set of divine expectations or failed to answer them, having arrived at some crucial realization or failed to arrive at it. So the soul, the masterpiece of creation, is more or less reduced to a token signifying cosmic acceptance or rejection, having little or nothing to do with that miraculous thing, the felt experience of life, except insofar as life offers distractions or temptations.

Having read recently that there are more neurons in the human brain than there are stars in the Milky Way, and having read any number of times that the human brain is the most complex object known to exist in the universe, and that the mind is not identical with the brain but is more mysterious still, it seems to me this astonishing nexus of the self, so uniquely elegant and capable, merits a name that would indicate a difference in kind from the ontological run of things, and for my purposes "soul" would do nicely.

Perhaps I should pause here to clarify my meaning, since there are those who feel that the spiritual is diminished or denied when it is associated with the physical. I am not among them. In his Letter to the Romans, Paul says, "Ever since the creation of the world [God's] invisible nature, namely, his eternal power and deity, has been clearly perceived in the things that have been made." If we are to consider the heavens, how much more are we to consider the magnificent energies of consciousness that make whomever we pass on the street a far grander marvel than our galaxy? At this point of dynamic convergence, call it self or call it soul, questions of right and wrong are weighed, love is felt, guilt and loss are suffered. And, over time, formation occurs, for weal or woe, governed in large part by that unaccountable capacity for self-awareness.

The locus of the human mystery is perception of this world. From it proceeds every thought, every art. I like Calvin's metaphor—nature is a shining garment in which God is revealed and concealed. As we perceive we interpret, and we make hypotheses. Something is happening, it has a certain character or meaning which we usually feel we understand at least tentatively, though experience is almost always available to reinterpretations based on subsequent experience or reflection. Here occurs the weighing of moral and ethical choice. Behavior proceeds from all this, and is interesting, to my mind, in the degree that it can be understood to proceed from it.

We are much afflicted now by tedious, fruitless controversy. Very often, perhaps typically, the most important aspect of a controversy is not the area of disagreement but the hardening of agreement, the tacit granting on all sides of assumptions that ought not to be granted on any side. The treatment of the physical as a distinct category antithetical to the spiritual is one example. There is a deeply rooted notion that the material exists in opposition to the spiritual, precludes or repels or trumps the sacred as an idea. This dichotomy goes back at least to the dualism of the Manichees, who believed the physical world was the creation of an evil god in perpetual conflict with a good god, and to related teachings within Christianity that encouraged mortification of the flesh, renunciation of the world and so on.

For almost as long as there has been science in the West, there has been a significant strain in scientific thought which assumed that the physical and material preclude the spiritual. The assumption persists among us still, vigorous as ever, that if a thing can be "explained," associated with a physical process, it has been excluded from the category of the spiritual. But the "physical" in this sense is only a disappearingly thin slice of being, selected, for our purposes, out of the totality of being by the fact that we perceive it as solid, substantial. We all know that if we were the size of atoms, chairs and tables would appear to us as loose clouds of energy. It seems to me very amazing that the arbitrarily selected "physical" world we inhabit is coherent and lawful. An older vocabulary would offer the word "miraculous." Knowing what we know now, an earlier generation might see divine providence in the fact of a world coherent enough to be experienced by us as complete in itself, and as a basis upon which all claims to reality can be tested. A truly theological age would see in this divine Providence intent on making a human habitation within the wild roar of the cosmos.

But almost everyone, for generations now, has insisted on a sharp distinction between the physical and the spiritual. So we have had theologies that really proposed a "God of the gaps," as if God were not manifest in the creation, as the Bible is so inclined to insist, but instead survives in those dark places, those black boxes, where the light of science has not yet shone. And we have atheisms and agnosticisms that make precisely the same argument, only assuming that at some time the light of science will indeed dispel the last shadow in which the holy might have been thought to linger.

Religious experience is said to be associated with activity in a particular part of the brain. For some reason this is supposed to imply that it is delusional. But all thought and experience can be located in some part of the brain, that brain more replete than the starry heaven God showed to Abraham, and we are not in the habit of assuming that it is all delusional on these grounds. Nothing could justify this reasoning, which many religious people take as seriously as any atheist could do, except the idea that the physical and the spiritual cannot abide together, that they cannot be one dispensation.

We live in a time when many religious people feel fiercely threatened by science. O ye of little faith. Let them subscribe to *Scientific American* for a year and then tell me if their sense of the grandeur of God is not greatly enlarged by what they have learned from it. Of course many of the articles reflect the assumption at the root of many problems, that an account, however tentative, of some structure of the cosmos or some transaction of the nervous system successfully claims that part of reality for secularism. Those who encourage a fear of science are actually saying the same thing. If the old, untenable dualism is put aside, we are instructed in the endless brilliance of creation. Surely to do this is a privilege of modern life for which we should all be grateful.

For years I have been interested in ancient literature and religion. If they are not one and the same, certainly neither is imaginable without the other. Indeed, literature and religion seem to have come into being together, if by literature I can be understood to include pre-literature, narrative whose purpose is to put human life, causality and meaning in relation, to make each of them in some degree intelligible in terms of the other two. I was taught, more or less, that we moderns had discovered other religions with narratives resembling our own, and that this discovery had brought all religion down to the level of anthropology. Sky gods and earth gods presiding over survival and procreation. Humankind pushing a lever in the hope of aperiodic reward in the form of rain or victory in the next tribal skirmish. From a very simple understanding of what religion has been we can extrapolate to what religion is now and is intrinsically, so the theory goes. This pattern, of proceeding from presumed simplicity to a degree of elaboration that never loses the primary character of simplicity, is strongly recurrent in modern thought.

I think much religious thought has also been intimidated by this supposed discovery, which is odd, since it certainly was not news to Paul, or Augustine, or Thomas Aquinas, or Calvin. All of them quote the pagans with admiration. Perhaps only in Europe was one form of religion ever so dominant that the fact of other forms could constitute any sort of problem. There has been an influential modern tendency to make a sort of slurry of religious narratives, asserting the discovery of universals that don't actually exist among them. Mircea Eliade is a prominent example. And there is Joseph Campbell. My primary criticism of this kind of scholarship is that it does not bear scrutiny. A secondary criticism I would offer is that it erases all evidence that religion has, anywhere and in any form, expressed or stimulated thought. In any case, the anthropological bias among these writers, which may make it seem free of all parochialism, is in fact absolutely Western, since it regards all religion as human beings acting out their nature and no more than that, though I admit there is a gauziness about this worldview to which I will not attempt to do justice here.

This is the anthropologists' answer to the question, why are people almost always, almost everywhere, religious. Another answer, favored by those who claim to be defenders of science, is that religion formed around the desire to explain what prescientific humankind could not account for. Again, this notion does not bear scrutiny. The literatures of antiquity are clearly about other business.

Some of these narratives are so ancient that they clearly existed before writing, though no doubt in the forms we have them they were modified in being written down. Their importance in the development of human culture cannot be overstated. In antiquity people lived in complex city-states, carried out the work and planning required by primitive agriculture, built ships and navigated at great distances, traded, made law, waged war, and kept the records of their dynasties. But the one thing that seems to have predominated, to have laid out their cities and filled them with temples and monuments, to have established their identities and their cultural boundaries, to have governed their calendars and enthroned their kings, were the vivid, atemporal stories they told themselves about the gods, the gods in relation to humankind, to their city, to themselves.

I suppose it was in the 18th century of our era that the notion became solidly fixed in the Western mind that all this narrative was an attempt at explaining what science would one day explain truly and finally. Phoebus drives his chariot across the sky, and so the sun rises and sets. Marduk slays the sea monster Tiamat, who weeps, whence the Tigris and the Euphrates. It is true that in some cases physical reality is accounted for, or at least described, in the terms of these myths. But the beauty of the myths is not accounted for by this theory, nor is the fact that, in literary forms, they had a hold on the imaginations of the populations that embraced them which expressed itself again as beauty. Over time these narratives had at least as profound an effect on architecture and the visual arts as they did on literature. Anecdotes from them were painted and sculpted everywhere, even on house hold goods, vases and drinking cups.

This kind of imaginative engagement bears no resemblance whatever to an assimilation of explanatory models by these civilizations. Perhaps the tendency to think of classical religion as an effort at explaining a world otherwise incomprehensible to them encourages us to forget how sophisticated ancient people really were. They were inevitably as immersed in the realm of the practical as we are. It is strangely easy to forget that they were capable of complex engineering, though so many of their monuments still stand. The Babylonians used quadratic equations.

Yet in many instances ancient people seem to have obscured highly available real-world accounts of things. A sculptor would take an oath that the gods had made an idol, after he himself had made it. The gods were credited with walls and ziggurats, when cities themselves built them. Structures of enormous shaped stones went up in broad daylight in ancient cities, the walls built around the Temple by Herod in Roman-occupied Jerusalem being one example.

The ancients knew, though we don't know, how this was done, obviously. But they left no account of it. This very remarkable evasion of the law of gravity was seemingly not of great interest to them. It was the gods themselves who walled in Troy.

In Virgil's *Aeneid*, in which the poet in effect interprets the ancient Greek epic tradition by attempting to renew it in the Latin language and for Roman purposes, there is one especially famous moment. The hero, Aeneas, a Trojan who has escaped the destruction of his city, sees a painting in Carthage of the war at Troy and is deeply moved by it and by what it evokes, the *lacrimae rerum*, the tears in things. This moment certainly refers to the place in classical civilization of art that pondered and interpreted the Homeric narratives, which were the basis of Greek and Roman religion. My point here is simply that pagan myth, which the Bible in various ways acknowledges as analogous to biblical narrative despite grave defects, is not a naive attempt at science.

It is true that almost a millennium separated Homer and Virgil. It is also true that through those centuries the classical civilizations had explored and interpreted their myths continuously. Aeschylus, Sophocles, and Euripides would surely have agreed with Virgil's Aeneas that the epics and the stories that surround them and flow from them are indeed about *lacrimae rerum*, about a great sadness that pervades human life. The Babylonian *Epic of Gilgamesh* is about the inevitability of death and loss. This is not the kind of language, nor is it the kind of preoccupation, one would find in a tradition of narrative that had any significant interest in explaining how the leopard got his spots.

The notion that religion is intrinsically a crude explanatory strategy that should be dispelled and supplanted by science is based on a highly selective or tendentious reading of the literatures of religion. In some cases it is certainly fair to conclude that it is based on no reading of them at all. Be that as it may, the effect of this idea, which is very broadly assumed to be true, is again to reinforce the notion that science and religion are struggling for possession of a single piece of turf, and science holds the high ground and gets to choose the weapons.

In fact there is no moment in which, no perspective from which, science as science can regard human life and say that there is a beautiful, terrible mystery in it all, a great pathos. Art, music and religion tell us that. And what they tell us is true, not after the fashion of a magisterium that is legitimate only so long as it does not overlap the autonomous republic of science. It is true because it takes account of the universal variable, human nature, which shapes everything it touches, science as surely and profoundly as anything else. And it is true in the tentative, suggestive, ambivalent, self-contradictory style of the testimony of a hundred thousand witnesses, who might, taken all together, agree on no more than the shared sense that something of great moment has happened, is happening, will happen, here and among us.

I hasten to add that science is a great contributor to what is beautiful and also terrible in human existence. For example, I am deeply grateful to have lived in the era of cosmic exploration. I am thrilled by those photographs of deep space, as many of us are. Still, if it is true, as they are saying now, that bacteria return from space a great deal more virulent than they were when they entered it, it is not difficult to imagine that some regrettable consequence might follow our sending people to tinker around up there. One article noted that a human being is full of bacteria, and there is nothing to be done about it.

Science might note with great care and precision how a new pathology emerged through this wholly unforeseen impact of space on our biosphere, but it could not, scientifically, absorb the fact of it and the origin of it into any larger frame of meaning. Scientists might mention the law of unintended consequences—mention it softly, because that would sound a little flippant in the circumstances. But religion would recognize in it what religion has always known, that there is a mystery in human nature and in human assertions of brilliance and intention, a recoil the Greeks would have called irony and attributed to some angry whim of the gods, to be interpreted as a rebuke of human pride if it could be interpreted at all. Christian theology has spoken of human limitation, fallen-ness, an individually and collectively disastrous bias toward error. I think we all know that the earth might be reaching the end of its tolerance for our presumptions. We all know we might at any time feel the force of unintended consequences, many times compounded. Science has no language to account for the fact that it may well overwhelm itself, and more and more stand helpless before its own effects.

Of course science must not be judged by the claims certain of its proponents have made for it. It is not in fact a standard of reasonableness or truth or objectivity. It is human, and has always been one strategy among others in the more general project of human self-awareness and self-assertion. Our problem with ourselves, which is much larger and vastly older than science, has by no means gone into abeyance since we learned to make penicillin or to split the atom. If antibiotics have been used without sufficient care and have pushed the evolution of bacteria beyond the reach of their own effectiveness, if nuclear fission has become a threat to us all in the insidious form of a disgruntled stranger with a suitcase, a rebuke to every illusion of safety we entertained under fine names like Strategic Defense Initiative, old Homer might say, "the will of Zeus was moving toward its end." Shakespeare might say, "There is a destiny that shapes our ends, rough-hew them how we will."

The tendency of the schools of thought that have claimed to be most impressed by science has been to deny the legitimacy of the kind of statement it cannot make, the kind of exploration it cannot make. And yet science itself has been profoundly shaped by that larger bias toward irony, toward error, which has been the subject of religious thought since the emergence of the stories in Genesis that tell us we were given a lavishly beautiful world and are somehow, by our nature, complicit in its decline, its ruin. Science cannot think analogically, though this kind of thinking is very useful for making sense and meaning out of the tumult of human affairs.

We have given ourselves many lessons in the perils of being half right, yet I doubt we have learned a thing. Sophocles could tell us about this, or the book of Job. We all know about hubris. We know that pride goeth before a fall. The problem is that we don't recognize pride or hubris in ourselves, any more than Oedipus did, any more than Job's so-called comforters. It can be so innocuous-seeming a thing as confidence that one is right, is competent, is clear-sighted, or confidence that one is pious or pure in one's motives.

As the disciples said, "Who then can be saved?" Jesus replied, "With men this is impossible, but with God all things are possible," in this case speaking of the salvation of the pious rich. It is his consistent teaching that the comfortable, the confident, the pious stand in special need of the intervention of grace. Perhaps this is true because they are most vulnerable to error—like the young rich man who makes the astonishing decision to turn his back on Jesus's invitation to follow him, therefore on the salvation he sought—although there is another turn in the story, and we learn that Jesus will not condemn him. I suspect Jesus should be thought of as smiling at the irony of the young man's self-defeat—from which, since he is Jesus, he is also ready to rescue him ultimately.

The Christian narrative tells us that we individually and we as a world turn our backs on what is true, essential, wholly to be desired. And it tells us that we can both know this about ourselves and forgive it in ourselves and one another, within the limits of our mortal capacities. To recognize our bias toward error should teach us modesty and reflection, and to forgive it should help us avoid the inhumanity of thinking we ourselves are not as fallible as those who, in any instance, seem most at fault. Science can give us knowledge, but it cannot give us wisdom. Nor can religion, until it puts aside nonsense and distraction and becomes itself again.

Discussion Questions

1. How might Robinson's anecdote about the rat in her laboratory experiments relate to her essay's broader concerns about how we think?

2. What do you think Robinson meant when she said, "The situation of the undergraduate rarely encourages systematic doubt"? Why did she suggest such doubt is necessary?

3. Try to construct Venn diagrams illustrating the relationships, as Robinson sees them, between the physical and the spiritual, between religion and science, between religion and narrative, and between science, religion, and "the beautiful, terrible mystery" of human existence. What do you learn by visualizing these relationships in this way?

4. What are the implications of Robinson's essay for how we might think about science? About religion? About literature or other arts?

5. Think of a narrative (perhaps a parable, a biblical narrative, a short story, a novel, or a film) that has given you wisdom about human experience. What did it teach you? Could you have learned this from a different format (for example, a lecture, straightforward explanation, or personal experience)?

CHAPTER 43

Wendell Berry

Introduction to "Manifesto: The Mad Farmer Liberation Front"

JEFFREY BILBRO

Wendell Berry (1934–) is a Kentucky farmer as well as a poet, essayist, and novelist. This poem—as well as several others—is written in the voice of the Mad Farmer, a character that Berry finds useful for probing the insanities of his culture. The poem's first word sounds its central note: love. What do you love? This is the fundamental question that a Christian learner must ask. The answer you give will guide the questions you pursue and the kinds of knowledge you consider to be valid. As the title of one of Berry's essays has it, in a phrase borrowed from the novelist E. M. Forster, "It all turns on affection."[1]

If your affections center on profit and personal comfort, you will be happy to become a good cog in an industrial machine. Or, as the Mad Farmer puts it, "Your mind will be punched in a card / and shut away in a little drawer." Such a mind will ask merely what it needs to know to pass the test, to improve its company's bottom line, to advance its career. Questions that don't relate to these limited concerns will be uninteresting and simply ignored.

Berry's Mad Farmer, however, enjoins you to love the Lord and the world, which as John 3:16 declares is also beloved by God. If you allow these twin loves to orient your imagination, you will begin to ask an incredibly wide-ranging, challenging set of questions—questions that he admits "have no answers." For instance, What undeserving person am I called to love today? What do I need to know to love her well? What can I do today to build topsoil for the next millennium? What do the dead have to say to me? How can I practice resurrection? As one of Berry's fictional characters notes, these are the kinds of questions to which you cannot be given answers; you must live them out, perhaps a little at a time.

The Mad Farmer's loves and questions lead him to seamlessly link ecological cycles with theological patterns. He advises us to listen to carrion because, after all, the earth composts death and decay into fertile topsoil that will host new life. In this regard, the dirt might be able to teach us a thing or two about practicing resurrection—as Berry writes in another poem, "Christmas / night

---

1. E. M. Forster and Alfred Kazin, *Howards End*, repr. ed. (New York: Everyman's Library, 1991), 304.

and Easter morning are this soil's only laws."[2] These are the surprising connections that a foxlike mind, a mind that "makes more tracks than necessary," can intuit.

And although the industrial mind is happy to abide by the strict divisions that the modern university has built between different academic disciplines, a Christian imagination, an imagination striving to love the world, can exclude nothing. Berry elaborates on this notion in his essay "Two Economies," claiming, "The first principle of the Kingdom of God is that it includes everything; in it, the fall of every sparrow is a significant event. . . . Another principle . . . is that everything in the Kingdom of God is joined both to it and to everything else that is in it." If you think this kingdom sounds confusing, it gets worse: "A third principle is that humans do not and can never know either all the creatures that the Kingdom of God contains or the whole pattern or order by which it contains them."[3] The kingdom of God and its order are always beyond our comprehension, which is why the Mad Farmer tells us to "Praise ignorance." Yet if we love this kingdom and its creatures, we will find ourselves fascinated by its patterns and will spend our lives seeking to understand it as best we can. Such knowledge, gained in the service to love, is itself a doxology.

"Manifesto: The Mad Farmer Liberation Front"

Love the quick profit, the annual raise,
vacation with pay. Want more
of everything ready-made. Be afraid
to know your neighbors and to die.
And you will have a window in your head.
Not even your future will be a mystery
any more. Your mind will be punched in a card
and shut away in a little drawer.
When they want you to buy something
they will call you. When they want you
to die for profit they will let you know.
So, friends, every day do something
that won't compute. Love the Lord.
Love the world. Work for nothing.
Take all that you have and be poor.

---

2. Wendell Berry, *This Day: Collected and New Sabbath Poems 1979–2012* (Berkeley, CA: Counterpoint, 2013), 321.

3. Wendell Berry, "Two Economies," in *Home Economics* (San Francisco: North Point, 1987), 54–75.

Love someone who does not deserve it.
Denounce the government and embrace
the flag. Hope to live in that free
republic for which it stands.
Give your approval to all you cannot
understand. Praise ignorance, for what man
has not encountered he has not destroyed.
Ask the questions that have no answers.
Invest in the millennium. Plant sequoias.
Say that your main crop is the forest
that you did not plant,
that you will not live to harvest.
Say that the leaves are harvested
when they have rotted into the mold.
Call that profit. Prophesy such returns.
Put your faith in the two inches of humus
that will build under the trees
every thousand years.
Listen to carrion—put your ear
close, and hear the faint chattering
of the songs that are to come.
Expect the end of the world. Laugh.
Laughter is immeasurable. Be joyful
though you have considered all the facts.
So long as women do not go cheap
for power, please women more than men.
Ask yourself: Will this satisfy
a woman satisfied to bear a child?
Will this disturb the sleep
of a woman near to giving birth?
Go with your love to the fields.
Lie easy in the shade. Rest your head
in her lap. Swear allegiance
to what is nighest your thoughts.
As soon as the generals and the politicos
can predict the motions of your mind,
lose it. Leave it as a sign
to mark the false trail, the way
you didn't go. Be like the fox

who makes more tracks than necessary,
some in the wrong direction.
Practice resurrection.

Discussion Questions

1. List some of your loves. How do you imagine a good or successful life?
2. What might you need to know to pursue the good life you imagine? What questions arise from your loves?
3. What is lost when we maintain a strict division between different classes and academic disciplines?
4. What disparate disciplines might you be able to bring together in your own life and thinking? What do you suppose you could learn from their interplay?

Appendix
Prayers and Liturgies for Students

Introduction
JACOB STRATMAN

How do we read the texts in this book? How do we approach learning? Are there virtues important to cultivate as readers and as learners? Is there a Christian way of learning? I've spent most of my career thinking about and writing about these questions. And I've come to the conclusion that the moments just before you begin to read (commence studying and learning) can be the most formational moments of your learning. How can asking God for love and humility and wisdom, and a host of other fruits of the Spirit, allow us to read rightly—to study and learn with a heart and head oriented toward the Creator of all knowledge?

A couple of years ago, I started learning tai chi. This ancient martial art has helped me find balance and control of my body and my mind, especially during stressful periods and times when I feel distracted. Before I begin the 103-movement long form (a lot to learn and memorize, I assure you), I begin with a particular approach that I have been taught. I breathe and center myself before I begin the routine. In this way, I take just a few minutes to recognize that what I'm about to do is difficult, taxing, and important; this moment allows me to focus not only on the task at hand but on the reasons, purposes, and motivations for the task. It's quite freeing.

What would it look like, I wonder, if you spent a few moments in the morning, at the beginning of each class session, or before you began studying in the evening (or all of these times), seeking to center yourself and focus on the reasons for this learning? What would it look like if you approached your learning moments with prayer? Whether you are reading Holy Scripture, memorizing mathematical formulas, studying the human anatomy, or learning about the best marketing plans for cheese, all of this learning belongs to God. Why not acknowledge this truth with prayer—a liturgy to recognize God's sovereignty over the learning and your position as the guest (receiver of all that is good)? Additionally, prayer can invite you to see your studies as a part of a spiritual rhythm—a practice that is as much a part of studying as reading and writing. There's no more need to integrate faith and learning, you might come to believe, because it's all the same thing. The "and" isn't necessary anymore; it's just *faithful learning*.

Over the years, Paul J. Griffiths has helped me consider how I approach my learning. In a lecture titled "Studiousness: How (and What) Christians Should Want to Know," he made the following claim: "There must then be a properly-ordered intellectual appetite, a desire to know that seeks the right knowledge for the right purposes and in the right ways."[1] No one told me this as a kid. I just thought you learned so you could do new things or because it's good to know stuff. Only as an adult have I come to believe, as Griffiths reminds me, "It is true that to the extent that any knowable object exists it may (and should) be known iconically, as a participant in God's excessive glory."[2] This is quite amazing. God speaks to us, directing our thoughts, giving us wisdom and discernment, expanding our capacity to love and empathize, and all the while brings us closer to his love. Engaging in prayer before we read, study, and learn trains and invites us to believe these truths.

Below are a few prayers and liturgies that I recommend to you before you begin any studying. These prayers won't baptize what you're reading. They aren't magic jujus to help you read better, learn more, or score better on your exams. These prayers, I hope and pray, anoint the reading practice. They invite the reader, you and me, into a holy place where God speaks and directs.

Prayers and Liturgies for Students

Samuel Johnson's "Before Any New Study" (found in his prayer journal after his death)

Almighty God, in whose hands are all the powers of man, who givest understanding, and takest it away; who, as it seemeth good unto Thee, enlightenest the thoughts of the simple, and darkenest the meditations of the wise, be present with me in my studies and enquiries. Grant, O Lord, that I may not lavish away the life which Thou hast given me on useless trifles, nor waste it in vain searches after things which Thou hast hidden from me. Enable me, by thy Holy Spirit so to shun sloth and negligence, that every day may discharge part of the task which Thou hast allotted me; and so further with thy help that labour which, without thy help, must be ineffectual, that I may obtain, in all my undertakings, such success as will most promote Thy glory, and the salvation of my own soul, for the sake of Jesus Christ. Amen.

---

1. Paul J. Griffiths, *The Vice of Curiosity: An Essay on Intellectual Appetite* (Winnipeg, MB: CMU Press, 2006), 63–64.
2. Griffiths, *The Vice of Curiosity*, 69.

Samuel Johnson's "After Time Negligently and Unprofitably Spent," Otherwise Known as "Something I Have to Say Every Day"

O Lord, in whose hands are life and death, by whose power I am sustained, by whose mercy I am spared, look down upon me with pity. Forgive me, that I have this day neglected the duty which Thou hast assigned to it, and suffered the hours, of which I must give account, to pass away without any endeavor to accomplish Thy will, or to promote my own salvation. Make me to remember, O God, that every day is Thy gift, and ought to be used according to Thy command. Grant me, therefore, so to repent of my negligence, that I may obtain mercy from Thee, and pass the time which Thou shalt yet allow me in diligent performance of Thy commands, through Jesus Christ. Amen.

"Prayer before Study" by Thomas Aquinas

Creator of all things, true source of light and wisdom, origin of all being, graciously let a ray of Your light penetrate the darkness of my understanding.

Take from me the double darkness in which I have been born, an obscurity of sin and ignorance.

Give me a keen understanding, a retentive memory, and the ability to grasp things correctly and fundamentally.

Grant me the talent of being exact in my explanations and the ability to express myself with thoroughness and charm.

Point out the beginning, direct the progress, and help in the completion. I ask this through Jesus Christ our Lord. Amen.

"Prayer before Study," from the Orthodox Prayer Book

Most blessed LORD, send the grace of Your Holy Spirit on me to strengthen me that I may learn well the subject I am about to study and by it become a better person for Your glory, the comfort of my family and for the benefit of Your Church and our nation. Amen.

St. Anthony's "Prayer for Wisdom"

Oh Light of the World, Infinite God, Father of Eternity, giver of Wisdom and Knowledge, and ineffable dispenser of every Spiritual Grace; who knowest all things before they are made, who makest the darkness and the light; put forth Thy hand and touch my mouth, and make it as a sharp sword to utter eloquently Thy Words.

Make my tongue, Oh Lord, as a chosen arrow, to declare faithfully Thy Wonders.

Put Thy Spirit, Oh Lord, in my heart, that I may perceive; in my soul, that I may retain; and in my conscience, that I may meditate.

Do Thou lovingly, holily, mercifully, clemently and gently inspire me with Thy Grace.

Do Thou teach, guide, and strengthen the comings in and goings out of my senses and my thoughts.

And let Thy discipline instruct me even to the end, and the Counsel of the Most High help me through Thy Infinite Wisdom and Mercy,

Amen.

A Prayer of Augustine of Hippo

O Thou who art the Light of the minds that know Thee,
the Life of the souls that love Thee,
the Strength of the wills that serve Thee.
Help us to know Thee that we may truly love Thee.
So to love Thee that we may fully serve Thee
Whose service is perfect freedom.

A Christian Litany of Humility by Rafael Cardinal Merry del Val

O Jesus! meek and humble of heart, *Hear me.*
From the desire of being esteemed, *Deliver me, Jesus.*
From the desire of being loved, *Deliver me, Jesus.*
From the desire of being extolled, *Deliver me, Jesus.*
From the desire of being honored, *Deliver me, Jesus.*
From the desire of being praised, *Deliver me, Jesus.*
From the desire of being preferred, *Deliver me, Jesus.*
From the desire of being consulted, *Deliver me, Jesus.*
From the fear of being humiliated, *Deliver me, Jesus.*
From the fear of being despised, *Deliver me, Jesus.*
From the fear of suffering rebukes, *Deliver me, Jesus.*
From the fear of being calumniated, *Deliver me, Jesus.*
From the fear of being forgotten, *Deliver me, Jesus.*
From the fear of being ridiculed, *Deliver me, Jesus.*
From the fear of being wronged, *Deliver me, Jesus.*
From the fear of being suspected, *Deliver me, Jesus.*
That others may be loved more than I, *Jesus, grant me the grace to desire it.*
That others may be esteemed more than I, *Jesus, grant me the grace to desire it.*
That, in the opinion of the world, others may increase and I may decrease,
       Jesus, grant me the grace to desire it.
That others may be chosen and I set aside, *Jesus, grant me the grace to desire it.*
That others may be praised and I unnoticed, *Jesus, grant me the grace to desire it.*

That others may be preferred to me in everything, *Jesus, grant me the grace to desire it*.

That others may become holier than I, provided that I may become as holy as I should, *Jesus, grant me the grace to desire it*.

From Irenaeus of Lyons (c. 130–202)

I appeal to you, Lord, God of Abraham, God of Isaac, God of Jacob and Israel, You the Father of our Lord Jesus Christ. Infinitely merciful as You are, it is Your will that we should learn to know You. You made heaven and earth; You rule supreme over all that is. You are the true, the only God; there is no other god above You. Through our Lord Jesus Christ . . . and the gifts of the Holy Spirit, grant that all who read what I have written here may know You, because You alone are God; let them draw strength from You; keep them from all teaching that is heretical, irreligious, or godless.

A Scholar's Prayer[3]

Bless, O Lord, us your servants,
Who are called to scholarly vocations.
Grant that what we apprehend with our minds
and profess through our words
May be grounded in truth
and offered confidently
with humility
to the greater good and well-being
of our students, our colleagues,
our academic communities
and the world at large,
through Jesus Christ, our Lord.

Amen

Prayer Attributed to John Henry Newman Said to Be Prayed on a Daily Basis by Mother Teresa

Dear Jesus, help me to spread Thy fragrance everywhere I go. Flood my soul with Thy Spirit and love. Penetrate and possess my whole being so utterly that all my life may only be a radiance of Thine. Shine through me and be so in me

---

3. Adam Omelianchuk, "A Scholar's Prayer," a university faculty prayer inspired by the Chorister's Prayer of the Royal College of Church Music, adapted by the C. S. Lewis Foundation, First Things, February 7, 2011, https://www.firstthings.com/blogs/firstthoughts/2011/02/a-scholars-prayer.

that every soul I come in contact with may feel Thy presence in my soul. Let them look up and see no longer me but only Jesus. Stay with me and then I shall begin to shine as you shine, so to shine as to be a light to others. Amen.

Liturgy for Students and Scholars by Douglas McKelvey

May I learn to love learning, O Lord, for the world is yours, and all things in it speak—each in their way—of you: of your mind, your designs, your artistry, your power, your unfolding purpose. All knowledge is your knowledge. All wisdom your wisdom. Therefore, as I apply myself to learning, may I be mindful that all created things are your creative expression, that all stories are held within your greater story, and that all disciplines of order and design are a chasing after your thoughts—so that greater mastery of these subjects will yield ever greater knowledge of the symmetry and wonder of your ways.

Along this journey, O Great Architect of Life and Beauty, bless me with teachers who are passionate about the subjects they teach, and with mentors who will take joy in awakening in me a fierce love for those parts of your creation and your story that they have already learned to love well. As I apply myself even to those subjects that I might at first find tedious, reward my efforts with new insights, fresh inspiration, small epiphanies, and with the firm conviction that you are at work in my heart in all circumstances, not only broadening my knowledge, but also shaping my heart by patience, endurance, and discipline that I might mature to more fitly and humbly serve the purposes of your great kingdom.

Give me a deepening knowledge of truth and a finer discernment of the ideas I encounter in my studies. Guard my mind always against error, and guard also my heart against the temptation to compare my own performance to the work of my peers, and so to fall into either of the twin traps of shame or pride. Grant instead that I might happily steward what scholarly gifts you have apportioned me, and that I might do so as means of preparing myself for service to you and to others, my identity drawn from your love and forgiveness, and not from my grades or accolades here. Open, O Lord, as you will, the paths of my life in the days yet to come. Use my studies to further shape my vision of what my place and call in this world might be. Begin to show me where my own deep gladness and the world's deep need might meet. And in that light, let me be mindful not only of my studies, but also mindful of the needs of my peers and even of my teachers. Let me respond with mercy to the failings of others. Let me be in this school, even in small ways, a bearer of love and light and reconciliation; which is to say, let me in humility be your child. God grant this child discernment and wisdom. Guard me from error. God grant this child knowledge and understanding. Lead me to truth. God bless the labors of this new season. Shape me for your service.

Prayers from Howard Thurman
I Need You

I need Your sense of time. Always I have an underlying anxiety about things. Sometimes I am in a hurry to achieve my ends and am completely without patience. It is hard for me to realize that some growth is slow, that not all processes are swift. I cannot discriminate between what takes time to develop and what can be rushed, because my sense of time is dulled. O to understand the meaning of perspective that I may do all things with a profound sense of leisure of time.

I need Your sense of order. The confusion of the details of living is sometimes overwhelming. The little things keep getting in my way, providing ready-made excuses for failure to do and be what I know I ought to do and be. Much time is spent on things that are not very important while significant things are put in an insignificant place in my scheme of order. I must unscramble my affairs so that my life will become order. O God, I need Your sense of order.

I need Your sense of the future. Teach me to know that life is ever on the side of the future. Keep alive in me the future look, the high hope. Let me not be frozen either by the past or the present. Grant me, O Patient One, Your sense of the future without which all life would sicken and die.

Our Little Lives

Our little lives, our big problems—these we place upon Your altar!
The quietness in Your temple of silence again and again rebuffs us:
For some there is no discipline to hold them steady in the waiting,
And the minds reject the noiseless invasion of Your spirit.
For some there is no will to offer what is central in the thoughts—
The confusion is so manifest, there is no starting place to take hold.
For some the evils of the world tear down all concentrations
And scatter the focus of the high resolves.
We do not know how to do what we know to do.
We do not know how to be what we know to be.
Our little lives, our big problems—these we place upon Your altar!
Pour out upon us whatever our spirits need of shock, of life, of release
That we may find strength for these days—
Courage and hope for tomorrow.
In confidence we rest in Your sustaining grace

Which makes possible triumph in defeat, gain in loss, and love in hate.
We rejoice this day to say:
Our little lives, our big problems—these we place upon Your altar!

A Prayer from Flannery O'Connor

Dear God, I cannot love Thee the way I want to. You are the slim crescent of a moon that I see and my self is the earth's shadow that keeps me from seeing all the moon. The crescent is very beautiful and perhaps that is all one like I am should or could see; but what I am afraid of, dear God, is that my self shadow will grow so large that it blocks the whole moon, and that I will judge myself by the shadow that is nothing.

I do not know you God because I am in the way. Please help me to push myself aside.

I want very much to succeed in the world with what I want to do. I have prayed to You about this with my mind and my nerves on it and strung my nerves into a tension over it and said, "oh God, please," and "I must," and "please, please." I have not asked You, I feel, in the right way. Let me henceforth ask You with resignation—that not being or meant to be a slacking up in prayer but a less frenzied kind, realizing that the frenzy is caused by an eagerness for what I want and not a spiritual trust. I do not wish to presume. I want to love.

Oh God, please make my mind clear.

Please make it clean.

I ask You for a greater love for my holy Mother and I ask her for a greater love for You.

Please help me to get down under things and find where You are.

Dietrich Bonhoeffer's Prayer

O God, early in the morning I cry to you.
Help me to pray
And to concentrate my thoughts on you;
I can't do this alone.
In me there's darkness,
But with you there's light;
I'm lonely, but you don't leave me;
I'm feeble in heart, but with you there's help;
I'm restless, but with you there's peace.
In me there's bitterness, but with you there's patience;
I don't understand your ways,
But you know the way for me.

O Heavenly Father,
I praise and thank you
For rest in the night;
I praise and thank you for this new day;
I praise and thank you for all your goodness
and faithfulness throughout my life.
You have granted me many blessings;
Now let me also accept what's hard from your hand.
You will lay on me no more than I can bear.
You make all things work together for good for your children.
Lord Jesus Christ,
You were poor and in distress, a captive and forsaken as I am.
You know all man's troubles;
You abide with me when all others fail me;
You remember and seek me;
It's your will that I should know you and turn to you.
Lord, I hear your call and follow;
Help me.
O Holy Spirit,
Give me faith that will protect me
from despair, from passions, and from vice;
Give me such love for God and human beings
as will blot out all hatred and bitterness;
Give me the hope that will deliver me
from fear and faint-heartedness.
Amen.

Contributors

J. L. Aijian (PhD, Baylor University) is a philosopher who focuses on Christian ethics and early modern epistemology, particularly the vice of acedia and the work of Blaise Pascal. She teaches great texts in the Torrey Honors College at Biola University.

Jason Baehr (PhD, University of Washington) is professor of philosophy at Loyola Marymount University in Los Angeles. He teaches and writes about intellectual virtues and their role in learning and living well.

Beth Allison Barr (PhD, University of North Carolina, Chapel Hill) is a Professor of History at Baylor University. She is the author of *The Making of Biblical Womanhood: How the Subjugation of Women Became Gospel Truth* and *The Pastoral Care of Women in Late Medieval England*, as well as a contributor to the popular Patheos blog *The Anxious Bench: The Relevance of Religious History for Today*.

Timothy E. G. Bartel (PhD, University of St. Andrews) serves as provost and professor of great texts and literature at the College at Saint Constantine. His poems and essays have appeared in *Christianity and Literature*, *The Hopkins Review*, *Notes & Queries*, and *Saint Katherine Review*. He is the author of *Glimpses of Her Father's Glory: Deification and Divine Light in Longfellow's Evangeline* and several volumes of poetry, most recently *Aflame but Unconsumed*.

Jason Baxter (PhD, University of Notre Dame) is associate professor of humanities and art history at Wyoming Catholic College. He is an author of many books, including *A Beginner's Guide to Dante's Divine Comedy*, *Falling Inward: Technology in the Age of Humanities*, and a new translation of the *Comedy*.

Jay Beavers (PhD, Baylor University) is assistant professor of English at Union University, where he teaches a wide range of courses as well as advising English secondary education students. He likes to spend his leisure in his garage woodshop making boxes and furniture with traditional hand tools.

Jeffrey Bilbro (PhD, Baylor University) is associate professor of English at Grove City College. His books include *Wendell Berry and Higher Education: Cultivating Virtues of Place* (written with Jack Baker), and *Virtues of Renewal: Wendell Berry's Sustainable Forms*.

Patricia Brown (PhD, University of Illinois) is professor of English at Azusa Pacific University. She specializes in African American literature.

Jonathan Callis (PhD, University of Notre Dame) is assistant professor of English at Oklahoma Baptist University, where he teaches about Jonathan Edwards and many other wonderful writers in the Western Civ and honors programs. When he's not reading or teaching, he enjoys playing basketball on campus and running after his five kids (including his identical triplet boys).

Paul Contino (PhD, University of Notre Dame) is professor of great books at Pepperdine University and the author of *Dostoevsky's Incarnational Realism: Finding Christ among the Karamazovs* as well as *Bakhtin and Religion: A Feeling for Faith*.

Jason Crawford (PhD, Harvard University) is associate professor of English at Union University, where he teaches courses both in literature and in the interdisciplinary Honors Community. He is the author of *Allegory and Enchantment: an Early Modern Poetics*.

Gina Dalfonzo (MA, George Mason University) is the author of *Dorothy and Jack: The Transforming Friendship of Dorothy L. Sayers and C. S. Lewis* and *One by One: Welcoming the Singles in Your Church* and the editor of *The Gospel in Dickens*. She is a columnist at Christ and Pop Culture and blogs at *Dickensblog* and at *Dear, Strange Things*.

Lanta Davis (PhD, Baylor University) is associate dean and associate professor of humanities and literature for the John Wesley Honors College at Indiana Wesleyan University. She teaches courses on the great texts and the sacramental imagination.

Tuan Hoang (PhD, University of Notre Dame) has taught in the great books and history programs at Pepperdine University since 2013.

Jennifer L. Holberg (PhD, University of Washington) has taught English at Calvin University since 1998. She also codirects the Calvin Center for Faith & Writing, home of the Festival of Faith and Writing. She is founding coeditor of the Duke University Press journal *Pedagogy: Critical Approaches to Teaching Literature, Language, Composition, and Culture.*

Scott Huelin (PhD, University of Chicago) has taught literature and theology at the secondary, undergraduate, and graduate levels for twenty-four years. He currently serves as professor of English and director for the Honors Community at Union University in Jackson, Tennessee.

Ravi Jain (MA, Reformed Theological Seminary) teaches The Scientific Revolution at the Geneva School. He coauthored the book *The Liberal Arts Tradition: A Philosophy of Christian Classical Education.* He has given over a hundred talks and workshops throughout the country and overseas on topics related to education, mathematics, and science.

Adam J. Johnson (PhD, Trinity Evangelical Divinity School) is associate professor of theology in the Torrey Honors College at Biola University. He has written and edited several books on the doctrine of the atonement, including *Atonement: A Guide for the Perplexed, T&T Clark Companion to Atonement,* and *The Reconciling Wisdom of God.*

Theresa Kenney (PhD, Stanford University) is professor of English at the University of Dallas and director of Christian Contemplative Studies and Medieval and Renaissance Studies. She has published on Middle English religious poetry as well as Austen, Brontë, Dante, Dickens, Donne, Southwell, and Suor Arcangela Tarabotti. Her books include *Women Are Not Human: An Anonymous Treatise and Responses, The Christ Child in Medieval Culture: Alpha es et O!* (coedited with Mary Dzon), and *"All Wonders in One Sight": The Christ Child among the Elizabethan and Stuart Poets.*

Julianna Leachman (PhD, University of Texas) is the upper school humanities teacher at St. Francis Episcopal School in Houston, Texas. Her research focuses on literature of Russia and the US South.

Louis Markos (PhD, University of Michigan) is professor of English and scholar in residence at Houston Baptist University and holds the Robert H. Ray Chair in Humanities. His eighteen books include *From Achilles to Christ: Why Christians Should Read the Pagan Classics, Heaven and Hell, Literature: A Student's Guide,* and three Christian Worldview Guides to *The Iliad, The Odyssey,* and *The Aeneid.*

H. Collin Messer (PhD, University of North Carolina, Chapel Hill) is a native of South Carolina and teaches American literature and humanities at Grove City College in Grove City, Pennsylvania.

Philip Irving Mitchell (PhD, Baylor University) is director of the honors program at Dallas Baptist University and teaches great books, as well as C. S. Lewis and J. R. R. Tolkien. He writes academically about twentieth-century Christianity and serves as the book review editor for the journal *Christianity and Literature*.

J. Cameron Moore (PhD, Baylor University) teaches English at Lumen Christi Catholic Highschool in Jackson, Michigan, and lectures in English at Hillsdale College. He teaches across the great tradition while focusing on twentieth-century British literature and G. K. Chesterton in particular.

Joy Moore (MFA, Pacific University) has taught creative writing, poetry, and interdisciplinary courses at the undergraduate level for the last decade and currently serves as the assistant director for the Honors Community at Union University in Jackson, Tennessee.

Scott H. Moore (PhD, Baylor University) associate professor of philosophy and great texts at Baylor University. He is the author of numerous essays and the books *How to Burn a Goat: Farming with the Philosophers* and *The Limits of Liberal Democracy: Religion and Politics at the End of Modernity* and the coeditor of *Finding a Common Thread: Reading Great Texts from Homer to O'Connor*.

Benjamin Myers (PhD, Washington University) is the Crouch-Mathis Professor of Literature at Oklahoma Baptist University and was the 2015–2016 Poet Laureate of the State of Oklahoma. He is the author of three books of poetry and of numerous essays and scholarly articles.

Brent Newsom (PhD, Texas Tech) is author of the poetry collection *Love's Labors* and librettist for the opera *A Porcelain Doll*, based on the life of Laura Bridgman. He is associate professor of English at Oklahoma Baptist University.

Rick Ostrander (PhD, University of Notre Dame) is an academic consultant, a former vice president at the Council for Christian Colleges & Universities, and the father of four Christian college graduates. His book *Why College Matters to God: An Introduction to Christian Learning* is currently in its third edition.

Angel Adams Parham (PhD, University of Wisconsin–Madison) is the Rev. Joseph H. Fichter, SJ, Distinguished Professor of Social Science and associate professor of sociology at Loyola University–New Orleans. Much of her work is in the area of comparative and historical sociology of race, assessing the many ways that the past continues to speak to the present.

Paul J. Pastor (MA, Western Seminary) is an editor, poet, and award-winning writer, whose books include *The Face of the Deep*, *The Listening Day*, *Palau: A Life on Fire* (with Luis Palau), and *Bower Lodge*. He lives in Oregon.

Anika T. Prather (PhD, University of Maryland) is the author of *Living in the Constellation of the Canon: The Lived Experiences of African American Students Reading Great Books Literature*. She teaches in the Classics Department of Howard University and is the founder of The Living Water School for independent learners, based on the educational philosophies of classical education and the Sudbury model.

Helen Rhee (PhD, Fuller Theological Seminary) is professor of religious studies at Westmont College, Santa Barbara, California. She specializes in early Christian history (second through fifth centuries) in its Greco-Roman context.

Julianne Sandberg (PhD, Southern Methodist University) is assistant professor of English at Samford University, where she teaches courses on Shakespeare, British literature, and first-year writing. Her work on early modern literature and religion has appeared in *Renaissance Studies*, *Philological Quarterly*, and *Studies in Philology*.

John Skillen (PhD, Duke University) taught medieval and Renaissance literature at Gordon College before launching the College's arts-oriented semester program in Orvieto (Italy), where he lived with his family for ten years. He now directs the Studio for Art, Faith and History and its program of seminars and locally engaged projects in visual art and theater, modeling how the work of the arts can enhance the work of the church and the academy. These themes are explored in his books *Putting Art (Back) in Its Place* and *Making School Beautiful*.

David I. Smith (PhD, University London) is professor of education and director of the Kuyers Institute for Christian Teaching and Learning at Calvin University in Grand Rapids, Michigan. He serves as editor of the *International Journal of Christianity and Education* and shares his writing at www.onchristianteaching.com.

Jacob Stratman (PhD, Marquette University) is dean of the College of Bible, Humanities, and Art at John Brown University. His first book of poems, *What I Have I Offer with Two Hands*, is a part of the Poiema Poetry Series (Cascade Books).

Bethany Williamson (PhD, Southern Methodist University) is associate professor of English at Biola University, where she teaches courses in British and world literatures, critical theory, and first-year writing. Her work has been published in journals such as *Eighteenth-Century Fiction, The Journal for Early Modern Cultural Studies, ABO: Interactive Journal for Women in the Arts, 1640–1830,* and *Christian Scholar's Review.*

Jessica Hooten Wilson (PhD, Baylor University) is the Louise Cowan Scholar in Residence at the University of Dallas in their Humanities and Classical Education graduate program. She is the author of three books, including *Giving the Devil His Due: Demonic Authority in the Fiction of Flannery O'Connor and Fyodor Dostoevsky,* and the coeditor of *Solzhenitsyn and American Culture: The Russian Soul in the West.*

Matthew D. Wright (PhD, University of Texas) is associate professor of government in the Torrey Honors College at Biola University. He is the author of *A Vindication of Politics: On the Common Good and Human Flourishing.*